An American Fighter Pilot in the R.A.F

An American Fighter Pilot in the R.A.F

Two Accounts by a Spitfire and Hurricane Pilot During the Battle of Britain & in the Far East During the Second War

Tally-Ho!

and

Last Flight from Singapore

Arthur Gerald Donahue

LEONAUR

An American Fighter Pilot in the R.A.F
Two Accounts by a Spitfire and Hurricane Pilot During the Battle of Britain & in the Far East During the Second War
Tally-Ho!
and
Last Flight from Singapore
By Arthur Gerald Donahue

FIRST EDITION

First published under the titles
Tally-Ho!
and
Last Flight from Singapore

Leonaur is an imprint
of Oakpast Ltd

Copyright in this form © 2014 Oakpast Ltd

ISBN: 978-1-78282-397-1 (hardcover)
ISBN: 978-1-78282-398-8 (softcover)

http://www.leonaur.com

Publisher's Notes

The views expressed in this book are not necessarily those of the publisher.

Contents

Tally-Ho! 7

Last Flight from Singapore 149

Tally-Ho!

Arthur Gerald Donahue
Pilot Officer, R.A.F.

Contents

A Farm Boy Goes Abroad	13
Apprenticeship in War!	22
Tally-Ho!	36
Victory—and Its Price	48
Defeat	59
Recovery	69
Back to Work	74
Impatience	81
Back to the Front Tally-Ho Again	89
Hun-Chasing	99
A Day at War	111
We Stage a Comeback	127
Interlude	135
The Watch over the Channel	140

TO A CERTAIN VERY GALLANT
OFFICER AND AVIATOR,
WITHOUT WHOSE KINDNESSES
THIS WOULD PROBABLY
NOT HAVE BEEN WRITTEN,
BUT WHOM I MUST
LEAVE UNNAMED
UNTIL BRIGHTER DAYS

CHAPTER 1

A Farm Boy Goes Abroad

I'm afraid that if this story is to be judged by the standards of the thousands of air stories that have been available to the American public in magazines the last few years, it will be classed as a failure. It is not very bloodcurdling, with fewer people taking part in the entire story than meet death in the first three pages of most air stories.

The hero is not tall and muscular and steely-eyed, with grim, wind-bitten, hawklike features; and his accomplishments in the story are few. Worse yet, he's anything but fearless; he scares as easily as you do, perhaps more easily, and in the whole story he never does anything particularly heroic. Worst of all is his identity, because actually he's only me.

But this story is true, and I hope that some of you may consider its shortcomings compensated for by the fact that the characters in this story really exist—or existed; that the occurrences in this story, though less spectacular, really occurred; and that the characters who meet death in it really did meet death, in the savage and desperate struggle that is being fought for the safety of the world, including you.

The most that can be said for myself is that I tried and tried hard, and fought hard, as I hope to be still trying and fighting when you read this; and I have probably accomplished as much against the enemy as the average of those who were in action at the same times as I. And I did have the privilege of being numbered among the few score pilots who met the first German mass onslaughts in the Air Blitzkrieg against England. Of these facts I shall always be proud, even if I fail to add more to them.

And in this tale of an ordinary American from a Midwest farm coming to a warring country, joining its fighting forces, mingling with its fighting men, and finally fighting and falling and fighting again, I hope that I can tell you enough of "what it's like" to keep your interest. If I fail it will be my fault as a writer, for I'm sure that what I've seen and experienced will interest average Americans if I describe it right. I'm an ordinary American myself, and it has been tremendously interesting to me!

I was born and raised on a farm at St. Charles, Minnesota, and at the age of eighteen I went into commercial flying. During the years of the depression this wasn't always too lucrative, and at various times I worked as garage mechanic, construction worker, and truck driver, in addition to working on my father's farm quite often. Always, however, I tried to work at some place where I could also keep my hand in flying part of the time—barnstorming, instructing, and the like, and working as aircraft mechanic. For the most part of the year and a half before I went to war I was engaged as an instructor at the International Flying School at Laredo, Texas.

As I remember, when I started flying there were about a hundred and twenty licensed pilots in Minnesota; and if you had lined us all up at that time and ranked us according to our possibilities of ever flying in a war, I'd have been in about the one hundred nineteenth place. The only one less likely than myself would have been my good friend Shorty Deponti of Minneapolis. Shorty would never fly in a war for two very good reasons: first, there wasn't enough money in it; and second, there wasn't enough money in it. My flying instructor, Max Conrad of Winona, would be more easily moved because he'd get higher pay out of allowances for his five daughters. I didn't have any of the qualifications of a soldier. I was neither big nor very strong; I was quite mild-tempered and absolutely afraid to fight, and I was more cautious in my flying than the average pilot then. Yet I believe I am the only one of them all to have gone to war. Tom Hennessy, whom I'd have ranked in those days as the most likely prospect, is now married and settled down sensibly on an airline.

When the war started I should have liked to volunteer at once for England. I felt that this was America's war as much as England's and France's, because America was part of the world, which Hitler and his minions were so plainly out to conquer. Consideration for my folks, whom I didn't want to saddle with a lot of worries, held me back. As the next best thing, I applied for a commission in the United States Army Air Corps Reserve, so that I could learn something about military flying anyway. This looked easy on paper, but I found myself frustrated for months by delays that were mostly hard to understand.

I paid a visit home in mid-June of 1940, and was cultivating corn on my dad's farm at the time of the collapse of France and the evacuation of Dunkirk. I had heard that American pilots were being hired for non-combatant jobs with the Royal Air Force, so when I left home I went to Canada to investigate. I was promptly hired, and about ten days later I boarded a boat for England.

It was a big passenger liner and should have been gayly painted and lighted, with flags flying and decks lined with tourists as it sailed—at least that's the way they were in all the pictures I'd seen. But instead it was painted in dull drab colours and there were only a handful of passengers. Nevertheless it was my first ocean trip, and I was plenty thrilled. Orders were posted about that we must keep our portholes closed at night and not show any lights on deck; and I realised that whether I fought or not I was in part of the war now.

I boarded the ship in late afternoon, and after I was settled and had had my supper I went out on deck. We were sailing down the St. Lawrence River and it was nearly dark. Not a light showed on the ship. At the stern I saw some men on a platform above the main deck swinging what looked like the boom of a big crane out so it hung over the water, and I wondered what they intended to lift with a crane out there. Then my eyes became accustomed to the darkness and I saw that it wasn't a crane at all, but a big cannon being prepared for use—more evidence of war! Remember, I was just an ordinary American, to whom war and battles and actual shooting at human targets were unreal things that only occurred in newspapers or movies or books. This was real, and it wasn't in a newspaper or movie or book, and I just stood there awhile gawping at it!

I enjoyed every moment of the trip across. I had a whole cabin to myself, and the excellence of the service and food gave me a feeling of luxury. Here on the smooth Atlantic life was so peaceful and relaxed that it was difficult to remember, except when I looked at the grim cannon at the stern of the ship, that within a few days I should be among a people fighting for existence, with their backs to the wall.

The prettiest sight of the trip was furnished by a number of icebergs one afternoon—something I didn't expect to see in July. The sun was shining brightly, making them appear crystal-white and gleaming. We were nearly always within sight of half a dozen, for several hours, and we sailed quite close to some. One which passed close had apparently shifted its position in the water, and a wide ring of blue marking its old water line was visible. It contrasted beautifully with the white of the rest of the iceberg, cutting across it diagonally. The blue band, I suppose, was clear pure ice, while the rest of the berg was ice and snow, very white. It was about a mile away and was at least one hundred fifty feet high. It was one of the most beautiful and striking pieces of scenery nature ever produced.

We arrived in an English port on a dreary, foggy Sunday morning after a final twenty-four hours of constant zigzagging by our ship to upset the aim of any lurking enemy submarines. The ship stood in midstream for hours while we passengers leaned on the deck railings and dodged the sea gulls that flapped overhead, squawking and bombing indiscriminately.

We left the ship in late afternoon and an R.A.F. officer took me in tow and escorted me from the dock to a green and tan camouflaged automobile which was parked near by. Instead of a license plate on the front of the car there was a plate with three big letters: "R.A.F."

My baggage having been loaded on, we set out for the railway station, and I got my first look at an English city. I had never realised that English cities were so different from American cities, with their winding irregular streets and their closely packed stone houses and business buildings of wholly different architecture from ours. Traffic is left-hand in England, and it seemed impossible for so many cars to be driving on the wrong side of the street with no accidents! I expected we'd crack up every minute. We didn't, though, and at the railway station the officer got me a ticket for London.

I found that my train didn't leave until midnight, so I set out to find a restaurant and eat supper. On the ship each passenger had received a gas mask in a little cardboard carrying case, and I now carried mine. However, after walking about a block I realised that it looked out of place. No one else carried any, and people were staring at mine. I went back to the station and put it away in my suitcase!

Then I sallied forth again and found a restaurant; but I still didn't get any supper. I understood but little of the menu on the wall and nothing of the prices, which were in English money of course, with its set of signs absolutely foreign to any American. Furthermore I realised that I didn't have any idea of how you ordered a meal here, and I just didn't have the nerve to try to bluff it. Retreating to the station once more, I got some chocolate bars from an automatic vender.

After a time an English girl came in whom I had met on the boat, and I found that she was waiting for the same train. At my suggestion we went out together for supper, and by that time it was dark.

And I *mean* dark. Not a street light showed, not a window or doorway gave a crack of light. It was my first experience in a blackout, of course. The few cars and busses on the street crawled along at five miles an hour, with nothing but dim little parking lights to see by. Many of the people walking had lighted cigarettes, and it helped them to keep from running into each other. That was once I wished that I was a smoker.

There was a sense of freedom about it, though, for we could walk in the middle of the street, as many did, because the cars moved so slowly we didn't have to worry about being run down. We just stepped out of their way! There were a few very dim stop and go lights, and here and there dim blue lights marking the entrances to air-raid shelters. These and the little lights of cars, the glowing cigarette tips, and an occasional dimmed flashlight were the only breaks in the darkness. Posts, stairways, building corners, and similar objects were all painted white so that people wouldn't walk into them.

That was a cloudy night. On clear nights it isn't so bad and the traffic moves faster, particularly if there is moonlight too. Houses and buildings, of course, have their windows and doorways curtained so that the lights can be used inside; and until I got used to it I always had a sensation of bewilderment when I stepped out of a brightly lighted restaurant or other building, absently expecting to be in a brightly lighted street, and then found nothing outside but total darkness.

The passenger car in which we rode to London was divided into little carriagelike compartments, each having room for four passengers riding forward and four facing backward. The lights in our compartment were very dim and shielded so they only lit up a little section of the middle of it, and even then we had to have curtains drawn all around. We rode "First Class." "Third Class" coaches are less comfortable, but are cheaper; there isn't any second class. I marvelled at the speed the train made through the blacked-out country. The locomotive used only the faintest headlights or none at all, and the engineers must have had cats' eyes to do it.

I'm still glad it was a beautiful fresh morning when we walked out of the station at the end of the journey, for my first glimpse of the world's greatest city.

I'll always try to keep my first impression of London, for it will never be like that again. The streets, houses, buildings, trees, and parks were all at their best in the bright sunlight. Far overhead the silvery barrage balloons hung silent and motionless, like sentinels. The raids

Messerschmitt 109 in flight

hadn't begun then, nor the devastation. But ever one knew they were coming; and London impressed me so much with its greatness and beauty as it stood that morning awaiting its trial, prepared and unafraid.

It's hard to give a specific reason why I became a combat pilot. Of course I'd always wanted to be one; and once I was in England the significance of the struggle seemed to carry me away. This was mid-July. France had fallen, and the invasion of England seemed imminent. Its success would open the whole world to a barbarian conquest. I had a growing admiration for the British people and a sincere desire to help them all I could. I couldn't help feeling that it would be fighting for my own country, too.

I felt drawn into the struggle like a moth to a candle. That's a pretty good comparison, too, for it developed that I was to get burned once and be drawn right back into it again!

Knowing that one of England's greatest problems was inferiority in numbers in the air, I felt it a duty as a follower of the civilized way of life to throw my lot in if they would take me. To fight side by side with these people against the enemies of civilization would be the greatest of all privileges. I had never done any military flying, but was confident of my ability to adapt myself.

Inquiries revealed that the way was wide open. I could be a fighter (pursuit) pilot if I wished, by first taking an advanced training course. Also I could probably get where the fighting was heaviest if I wished, because pilots as a rule were given preference in this regard. I shouldn't need to tell my folks I was fighting, because they wouldn't expect me to tell much about my work on account of censorship. The whole set-up had too much appeal for my resistance.

I knew I should be scared to death many times and should regret my decision often, for as I said before, I am not overendowed with courage; but I also knew that I'd never forgive myself if I rejected this opportunity. So in a fateful moment on the day after my arrival I held my pen poised while making one last reflection on what I was doing, and then signed on the dotted line. I thereby surrendered my independence for the duration of the war and became a proud member of the Royal Air Force. I also presumed that I was surrendering my citizenship, for I understood that the law was so interpreted at that time.

I was given a commission as pilot officer, which corresponds to the rank of second lieutenant in the army; and was allowed two days' leave to buy a uniform. I was impressed with the swiftness and lack of red tape with which I was accepted. I had simply shown them that I had the goods and they had said in effect: "All right. We'll buy. Sign here, and you can start delivering." It was a refreshing contrast to my experiences in my own country.

My uniform was soon made up, and on the evening of the fourth day after arrival in England I walked down the streets of London a full-fledged officer of His Majesty's Royal Air Force. That is, I walked a little way. I was with an American boy working in London whom I'd met the day before, and who was going to show me about. We walked about a block and then met a couple of airmen in uniform ("airmen" is the term for all non-commissioned ranks in the R.A.F.). They of course saluted me as an officer; and I of course was obliged to return their salute. Then the terrible realisation dawned on me—not having been inducted into the R.A.F. in the normal way, I hadn't learned how to salute!

It was do or die, though, and I "did"—in a terribly blundering fashion, it seemed to me; and I fancied them to be staring back at me, wondering what was wrong. There were plenty of soldiers and airmen on the streets, and by the time I'd walked a few more blocks and been saluted half a dozen times I had lost all interest in the sights.

I said to my companion: "This can't go on. Let's find a *café* or restaurant where we can stay inside until after dark."

He suggested a little place on Kingsway, where we could get American Coca-Cola, and I sighed thankfully as we entered this haven. There was a girl sitting at the table next to us, in the uniform of the Women's Auxiliary Air Force. This is the women's branch of the R.A.F. Its members work side by side with R.A.F. men at R.A.F. stations, doing work that they are capable of, and their status is exactly the same. They are usually called "Waffs" from the initials of their organisation, W.A.A.F. I appealed to her, and she instructed me in the proper way of saluting. I suppose that was one of the few times in history when a member of the ranks instructed an officer on how to salute!

Fortified with this instruction and a little practice I felt safe in sallying forth again, and we went for a long walk about the interesting parts of the town, looking at some of the sights I had often read about—Buckingham Palace, St. James's Palace, the buildings of Parliament, the great clock "Big Ben," the home of Scotland Yard, Trafalgar Square, and many other places that were a big thrill to me. Even bigger were the thrills I got walking past Buckingham and St. James's palaces when the guards there presented arms to me, and I began to realise what a weight of tradition I had taken on when I put on the king's uniform for my first time that evening.

One didn't have to walk far through London then to realise there was going to be no thought of declaring it an "open city," or of abandoning it except building by building and street by street if the barbarian Hun came; and I began to realise that the type of resistance that the Nazis would face here was very different from what confronted them in France.

London was a fortress. Anti-tank barriers and traps were located all about. Sandbag and concrete barricades and breastworks were erected everywhere, protected every building. Gun emplacements marred the beauty of the parks.

The prime minister had said, "We shall not falter." I got a feeling, realising the implication of all these preparations, that history would prove him right.

CHAPTER 2

Apprenticeship in War!

Next day I journeyed by train to the advanced training school to which I had been assigned. Travelling this time by day, I found the English landscape surprisingly like that of southern Wisconsin—rolling country, very green, with lots of small pastures and a great deal of woodland. The one big difference was that there were no red barns. Many of the barns in England, like other buildings, are of stone, and the rest all seem to be painted white or gray.

My school was one of many such that are known as "Operational Training Units." At these places newly trained pilots are given their final brushing up and actual experience in flying the latest fighter planes under the guidance of experienced fighter pilots who teach them the newest tactics. In addition, experienced pilots who have been doing other kinds of flying and want to become fighter pilots, as well as pilots from other air forces, receive the same training in order to learn British fighting tactics and the behaviour of fighting planes. There were many Polish pilots and a few Belgians at this place undergoing training.

It was my first visit to a wartime airdrome, and I found it an impressive contrast to airports I was familiar with. In the United States everything possible is done to make an airport conspicuous and easy to locate—bright markings on hangars, buildings, etc., conspicuous runways, big arrows pointing toward the airport on the tops of buildings near by, and so on, for the convenience of visiting pilots.

The visiting pilots who come here are not welcome, and everything is done to hide the airdrome from them. Hangars, shops, offices, and even driveways and roads are camouflaged, as well as vehicles themselves. All are painted in crazy wavy combinations of dull greens, grays, browns, and black, so designed that at great altitudes the airdrome merges in with the countryside and can scarcely be seen.

Most impressive of all to me was the grim dull colouring of the airplanes themselves. They were painted dull green and brown in the wavy pattern, except the undersides, which were gray. Concession is made even in the national markings, which for British planes consist of a red bull's-eye surrounded by concentric white and blue rings. On the top side of the wings this is altered by omitting the white ring, because that is too conspicuous from above, so there is just a larger red bull's-eye and a wider blue ring around it. The Spitfire fighting planes have a peculiarly shaped wing, very wide and tapered in such a way that it resembles the wings of some moths. The round red and blue marking near each tip enhances this resemblance so much that the planes themselves look like giant moths from above.

The entire airdrome bristled with sandbags, trenches, dugouts, and machine-gun and anti-aircraft emplacements.

A building known as the "officers' mess" is provided for officers at airdromes and other military stations in England. This usually contains a dining room, bar, billiard room, and a large comfortable lounge. Here the officers spend most of their leisure time, and the officers' mess is a large part of their life. The building may or may not contain quarters for the officers as well. At this station it did not, and we roomed in other buildings. Each officer has the services of a "batman," or valet, who takes care of his room, makes his bed, presses his uniform, polishes his buttons, wakens him in the morning, and in general makes himself useful. This was all quite strange to me, and I went to bed pondering on the many strange things I must get used to in fighting the Huns.

Next morning I was assigned to a "flight" of several pilots who arrived for training at the same time I did, and I reported to my flight commander's office. While waiting to see him I read a notice on the wall advising students to take their training here seriously. I still remember the closing words:

> ... for in all probability this is the last training you will receive before being committed to combat with the enemy.

It gave me a little thrill. I was getting close to realities.

An instructor took me up in an American-built military plane, a North American, which is a type widely used for advanced training here, and I did a couple of landings for him. He seemed satisfied and assigned me to a single-seat advanced trainer of English make and gave me some practice work to do in it.

I had never flown anything that cruised faster than one hundred ten miles per hour before I left the States. This machine cruised at one hundred eighty; and I thought it more wonderful than anything I'd ever imagined. I practiced in it for a few days and then was told I might go on to flying Spitfires.

This was the very height of my hopes. Of all England's superb fighting planes, the Supermarine Spitfires are generally considered masters of them all and the world's deadliest fighters. The pilots assigned to fly them consider themselves the luckiest of pilots. They are single-seat low-wing monoplanes. The engines are twelve-cylinder Rolls Royce of about ten hundred fifty horsepower with an "emergency boost" giving them nearly fourteen hundred horsepower for actual combat. Each has eight machine guns, mounted in the wings. All the guns point forward and are fired by a single button on the top of the pilot's control stick. The Spitfires, together with the Hawker "Hurricanes" which are contemporary fighters also carrying eight guns, are often called "flying machine-gun nests." The cruising speed of a Spitfire is nearly three hundred miles per hour and the top speed nearly four hundred.

To myself, who had been instructing for the last year and a half in trainers of forty horsepower that cruised at sixty miles per hour, this was such a change that there just didn't seem to be any connection with my former flying. The first time I took a Spitfire up, I felt more like a passenger than a pilot. However, I began to get used to the speed after a few hours. I practiced acrobatics mainly at first, to get familiar with the behaviour of the airplanes. In doing this I got my initiation to a new factor, which limits a pilot's ability to manoeuvre at high speeds. This factor is known as the "black-out"—no connection with the black-out of cities at night.

If you swing a pail of water over your head the water will stay in the pail even when it is upside down, because centrifugal force pushes it against the bottom of the pail. Similarly, if an airplane is turned or looped quickly the centrifugal force tends to push the blood in the pilot's body downward, toward the bottom of the plane and away from his head. In ordinary airplanes this doesn't matter because his heart keeps pumping the blood right back up to his head. But modern fighting (pursuit) planes are so fast that it is quite easy in a turn or loop for the centrifugal force to drain the blood from the pilot's head. When this happens his brain stops working. At three hundred

Spitfire in Flight
Top View

miles per hour only a few degrees of change in direction per second is enough to cause a pilot to "black out." A pilot's physical strength in resisting black-out is what determines the rate at which he can turn at high speeds, but it is impossible for any pilot to turn very quickly at three hundred miles an hour or more.

Strangely, when one starts to black out in a turn or loop his eyes fail before his brain. My first experience in blacking out occurred the first time I tried to loop in a Spitfire. I was cruising along at about two hundred eighty and drew the control stick back about an inch, rather abruptly, to start my loop. Instantly the airplane surged upward in response, so hard that I was jammed down in the seat, feeling terribly heavy, feeling my cheeks sag downward and my mouth sag open from the centrifugal force on my lower jaw, and a misty, yellowish gray curtain closed off my vision! I eased the stick forward again to stop the change in direction and my sight came back instantly. I saw that I had raised the nose of the plane only a few degrees.

This loss of vision is the warning a pilot receives. If he continues to turn or loop that hard he will lose consciousness in a few seconds. In looping I found that I had to ease the nose up ever so slowly at first until the speed had dropped to around two hundred, after which I could pull the plane around quite fast without blacking out.

It's an uncanny thing. In combat you may be circling to get your guns to bear on the enemy. He is circling, too, but you have almost caught up with him. He is just outside of your gun-sights; and if you could only pull your plane around a few extra degrees, all at once, you would have him in your sights and be able to open fire. But you can't do that. You can turn just so fast and that is all, for if you turn any faster your vision fades and you can't see either him or your sights!

A pilot can increase his resistance to "black-out" by practice in doing lots of tight turns at high speed. He learns to contract the muscles of his abdomen and take deep breaths and hold them while he's turning, because that leaves less room for the blood to drain to down in his body. In this way physical strength often enters modern air fighting. The pilot who can resist black-out best is the one who can manoeuvre fastest at speeds much above 200.

Leaning forward also helps, because then one's head isn't as high above his heart, and so his heart can pump the blood up to his head easier. I have some very vivid recollections of moments in combat when trying to throw an enemy "off my tail" (in other words from directly behind me which is the best position to shoot from) when I was leaning forward as far as my straps would permit, taking big gasps of air and holding them, and tensing my body muscles in the desperation one feels when his life is at stake, trying to fight off that damnable misty curtain from my eyes while fairly hauling my plane around in the most sickening turns. It invariably worked, too, and when I "came up for air" after a few seconds and looked around I usually found that my enemy had lost his advantage and it was my turn to take the offensive.

There was an English boy named Peter, a big dark-haired husky fellow, who started this training course the same time I did. We took to each other as soon as we met, and became very close pals. He had been in the Navy at sixteen, and at twenty he was bronzed and hardened and looked and acted several years older. We practiced nearly all our flying together and with a squadron leader who was also taking the course.

We did a lot of "dog fighting" practice. We would take off together, Peter and I, and climb to ten or fifteen thousand feet. Then we would separate and fly in opposite directions a few seconds, so that we could turn around and fly back toward each other. Then when we'd meet we'd engage in vicious mock combats—turning, twisting, rolling, climbing, and diving to get into firing position on each other. When one of us succeeded in getting the other in his gun sights he pressed with his thumb on the guard over the firing button on his machine, sending salvo after salvo of imaginary bullets after his pal. This guard over the firing button was just a temporary affair, to keep the pilot from accidentally pressing the button itself when he didn't want to use the guns; and across it were painted in red letters the words "Guns Loaded."

I became well acquainted with some of the Poles who were training here. They were a fine bunch of fellows. Most of them had fought the Hun over Poland and again in France. Now they were being prepared to fight with the Royal Air Force. They were cheerful, happy-go-lucky fellows—except when the subject of Nazis was brought up. Then you saw evidence of the terrible hatred for the dogs who had ravaged their homeland and their people.

On one occasion one of the English boys, joking, chided one of the Polish boys, saying that he was supposed to love his enemies. It didn't anger the other because he knew it was a jest; but he replied with a pitiful attempt to smile and keep his voice light, "Would you love your enemies when they kill *your* mother, and put your sister in a brothel for soldiers?"

I hope I never find myself in as perilous a position as that of a Nazi pilot being attacked by one of our Poles.

Days passed, and we began to develop a polish in our handling of the Spitfires. I had been at the training base about ten days when the papers carried the news that the State Department of the United States had announced that Americans fighting for Britain would not lose their citizenship. My friends congratulated me, and I felt pretty good. But I also felt proud that I hadn't waited to learn that before I volunteered.

In the lounge at the officers' mess I was often the centre of conversations about the United States and the war. I was continually asked if I thought the United States would join or at least give more help, and when. I answered their questions as well as I could, giving the American people's side as I had seen it but not necessarily taking that side. A mean of all such conversations would have run something like this:

"When's your country going to give us some help, America," ("America" is about the only nickname I have in England outside of the usual "Art.")

"I don't know," I reply. "They've sent me, haven't they?"

"Yes, but we're never sure whether that was helping us or Germany. Seriously, though, what do they think about it—don't they realise this is a world menace we're fighting?"

"Yes," I admit, "most of them seem to realise it now. They seem pretty well agreed that if Hitler wins here it will only be a matter of time before their turn will come. But they'd rather have it that way, it seems, than to take any chances of having their boys fight on foreign soil."

"What? You mean they'd rather wait and fight in their own country?"

"I guess so," I admit again.

"Do they know what that means?"

"They should."

"Sounds as if they don't like their women and children," says one.

"Or their homes and cities," from another.

"Besides," I add, "they say, 'What did we get out of helping England in the last war?'"

"They got rid of their menace, didn't they? Where do they think they'd be if the *Kaiser* controlled England and France and Canada?"

"They forget that they ever had a menace then, and all they remember is that it cost them money."

"Do they think England got rich on it?"

"If you ask me, they don't think, very deeply."

I wasn't standing up for my countrymen in these conversations because I didn't sympathise with their attitude. I'd fight the battles which were America's as well as England's in the air, but I wouldn't fight America's battles in the officers' mess.

I had just come out of the officers' mess from dinner one noon when the local air-raid sirens sounded. It was the first air-raid warning I had ever heard.

It was a cloudy day, there being a high dark overcast that covered the sky. Lower down there were a lot of scattered thick clouds; and looking between these I could see, very high up, a long curving trail of smoke across the sky. I asked some of the boys who were watching what it was, and one of them said, "It must have been a Jerry made that. See, there's some Spitfires going up after him."

I could see several Spitfires above the clouds, and as I knew that my flight commander was up on a training flight with some of the boys I wondered if theirs were the Spitfires I could see. I had never seen a German airplane, and I strained my eyes trying to see this one, but couldn't.

Suddenly above the sound of the several engines roaring up there we heard a distant *r-r~rat-a-tat-tat!* The engines kept on droning as the machines scurried about, and now the Spitfires were so high we couldn't see them either. They all seemed to be working north of the airdrome.

All activity at the airdrome had of course stopped when the air-raid warning sounded, but no one was in shelter. Every one was outside trying to see the show. Now little black puffs of smoke began appearing here and there far up in the sky north of us, and a few seconds later we heard a succession of little noises like a feather duster being shaken outside a window—anti-aircraft shells exploding, I realised—the first time I had ever seen an attempt to take a human life. Then came a succession of heavy distant *"booms"*—bombs exploding, the others said.

Now the planes seemed to be getting closer overhead again. Another and longer *r-r-rat-a-tat-tat!* reached our ears and every one grew tense and breathless watching the sky. A long minute elapsed, and then:

"There he *is!*" The voice of one of the overwrought boys who called out almost ended in a scream; and then we saw it too. First there was just an indistinct swirling in the bottom mists of one of the clouds, and then it came clear. It was an enormous strange-looking twin-engined airplane, and it was in a tailspin, nose down and gyrating 'round and' round as it fell. It was the first time I had ever seen a big airplane in a tailspin, and I was spellbound.

"It's a Jerry, all right!" said an awed voice.

A tiny figure parted from it, fell a way, and then the white canopy of a parachute blossomed above it. Then another and another came clear, and their parachutes blossomed out.

The great machine kept spinning down and down, seeming slow and majestic even in this, its death dive. As it got lower and lower I tried to realise that it wouldn't be recovering from the spin at the regulation 1500 feet minimum altitude, as exhibition or student planes that I watched always did. It wasn't going to pay any attention to the nearing ground. It was going to spin in! Almost unbelieving, I watched it make its last great corkscrewing revolution, just sweeping over the treetops of a near-by grove and disappearing behind them.

A moment later there was a heavy crash, and then every one was running in the direction of the grove and the victorious Spitfires were diving and zooming and rolling over the spot and some of them went to circling around the descending parachutes with their unhappy occupants, like Indians doing a dance around trussed-up captives. The Polish boys who were watching with us were very angry because none of the Spitfire pilots shot the Nazis in their parachutes—Nazi pilots had machine-gunned many Polish pilots in their parachutes in the Polish campaign!

We soon learned the whole story. The machine was a Junkers 88 bomber that had come to raid a nearby village. When the Spitfires took chase the pilot tried to get away, jettisoning his bombs in open country, but one of the Spitfires caught him anyway. It was the plane piloted by our flight commander; with his second burst of machine-gun fire he had dislodged one engine from the bomber so that it fell completely out of the airplane! The German pilot was then unable to control his unbalanced airplane and it went into the fatal tailspin. One other member of the crew bailed out in addition to the three we saw, but he wasn't as fortunate. They found his body in a woods. The rip-cord by which he could have opened his parachute was severed by a bullet.

Every day we wondered when the promised German invasion

would start. This was the last of July and Hitler had promised to take over London by August 15th. Peter and I hoped the invasion wouldn't start until we finished our training. The mass air raids had not yet begun on England, but there was a great deal of air fighting over the English Channel.

We had made our requests to be posted to a squadron near the Channel—the same squadron for both of us if possible. Those were the squadrons getting the action now, and if the invasion were launched it seemed likely that the Channel would be the hottest place then, too. We were spoiling for all the action we could get.

Peter and I reported as usual in our flight commander's office on the morning of the day before our training was scheduled to end.

"What shall we do this morning, sir?" I asked, meaning what flying should we do.

He looked at us a little oddly and then said: "Nothing. You boys have been a little ahead of your schedule, and you've covered everything I can give you. The rest you'll have to learn—other ways!"

We knew what he meant by that. Our next instruction would be from our enemies!

"You boys can take the day off," he added.

We saluted and went out. When we were outside, we turned to each other and shook hands, grinning. Peter said, "Congratulations, war pilot!" We had arrived.

That afternoon we were informed, to our delight, that we had been posted to one of the squadrons close to the English Channel. We asked how close it was to the Channel and were told, "From your advance base you can see the French coast on a clear day!"

We were given railway warrants and told to leave the next afternoon. I spent most of the rest of the day studying pictures of German fighting and bombing planes.

Next morning we packed. In the afternoon a large lorry left the airport for the railway station carrying a precious cargo. More than a score of newly trained fighter pilots rode in it, all bound for various squadrons. Over half were Poles and Belgians, eager for vengeance; and most of them were to exact their vengeance from the Nazis soon.

We all took a train to London, where we separated on various lines for our destinations. There was plenty of handshaking and goodbyes.

"Take care of yourself, and watch your tail, Pal!"

"Thanks, old man, same to you! Hope you get a hundred of them!"

Many well-wishes such as these, and then Peter and I were alone waiting for the train that would take us on a branch line to our squadron's home base, an airdrome near London.

Sitting and walking about in the gathering darkness, waiting for our train, we got to talking about America. It was Peter's ambition to go to America after the war, and to stay there if he could find a job with a future in it. I told him I thought it would be swell if we could go back to the States together after this was over, that I was sure he could find a job and get ahead. He said: "Let's plan on that. If we both come through this war in one piece I'll go back with you."

I thought of what a swell pal he'd be to have over in America, and was glad of the plan.

We arrived at our airdrome late in the evening, and were fixed up with rooms in the officers' mess and told to report to our squadron leader in the morning. We met some of our new mates, who hadn't gone to bed yet. Conversation was all about the news they had just received from one of the oldest members of the squadron. He had been missing since a battle over the Channel some time back, and had been counted as dead. Now they had received word that he was alive, a prisoner of war in a German hospital. They were jubilant over the news.

An elderly, thin-featured, dark-haired man in the uniform of a pilot officer introduced himself to us.

"My name's F——," he said, speaking slowly and with a solemn mien that was contradicted by a twinkle in his eye, "but every one calls me 'Number One.' You see, I am Number One stooge of your squadron. You know stooges are people who don't fly, don't you?

"There are three of us officer stooges in the squadron. We're really very nice people, too. I hardly count myself. I'm just the Intelligence officer, sort of a father-confessor to whom you are supposed to tell all the blows you've struck at your fellowmen, the Huns, each time after you come back from shooting holes in them. You'll meet the other stooges in the morning. 'Number Two' is the squadron's chief mechanic, and 'Number Three' is the adjutant."

We liked the man at once, and from the twinkle in his eye and the dry humour with which he spoke about himself and the rest we suspected that our squadron must be a good-natured bunch.

We were right. From commanding officer right down to the lowest ranks, they were all a cheerful, easy-natured, hard-working, happy-go-lucky group, an ideal bunch to work with or fight with or have fun with.

And as time went on I was to learn that the same was true of nearly all the boys and men in the R.A.F.—good-natured, fun-loving, informal chaps, laughing in the face of tragedy because it did no good to cry, and fighting because their country is forced to, not because it's their trade or because they want to. No professional soldiers, most of these: they are your brother who was working in a drugstore to earn money to go to college and study to be a lawyer, until his country had to rise to call a halt to world gangsterism; and young Joe who was doing well in the insurance office downtown; your neighbour's boy who had just graduated from high school and had his head full of changing ideas, all involving a secure future; the Smith boy who had just gotten married and settled down on his father's farm—his father is running the farm again now, after having planned to retire; and young Ray King, the spoiled, spendthrift, ne'er-do-well son of the local banker, who everyone had prophesied would come to no good, chastised and sobered now by his consecration to a high cause.

Certainly no "international bankers," these lads, in whose plans war had had no part—nor in the plans of their parents either. Their parents, too, are ordinary people, who had approved their government's course in giving beaten Germany a chance to rise again so that her people could live happily and normally, until an insane, hate-crazed spellbinder had wrested control of the nation and turned it into a great war machine and started it on a march of world conquest and murder.

Then and only then, completely educated on both sides of the question by a free press, and by a free radio from which they could listen daily to thousands of words of Nazi propaganda in the English language, these ordinary people had risen and demanded that their government call a halt and make a stand now, because they could see that there was no other way out. And so these boys had abandoned all their cherished plans and gone into training to learn how to kill, and were now making the best of their new task of defending the existence of their people and of civilization.

Next morning, August 4th, we reported to our squadron leader, whose rank in the R.A.F. corresponds to that of major in the Army. What follows will make him blush if he reads it, but I must describe him a little.

He is one of the most impressive personalities I have known. He is slender, with fine wavy hair and moustache, and piercing blue eyes. I seldom remember the colour of a person's eyes, but I couldn't forget his. He is very witty in his speech, has a personal magnetism that lends an almost feminine beauty to one's impression of him, and he fairly radiates strength of character and will power. We liked him at once and felt great confidence in him.

He outlined to us the work that his squadron was doing and the tactics they used; and gave us advice from his experiences with the Huns. This was all done in matter-of-fact tones that initiated us to the detached, impersonal, and unemotional attitude that fighter pilots quickly develop toward the taking—and losing—of human life.

He told us apologetically that it appeared to be a quiet time just now. There had been no fighting over the Channel for a week. We knew from the papers that, a week before, his squadron had played the main part in the biggest battle yet fought over the Channel.

"We gave them a good licking that time," he said, "and apparently they've been staying home licking their wounds ever since. We haven't seen a one all week, but perhaps it's the lull before a storm."

He explained that the squadron spent most of its time at this airdrome, its home base, and the pilots all lived here. But part of the time was also spent in shifts with other squadrons at the advance base, an airdrome close to the Channel, from which the enemy planes could be intercepted more quickly when they came across.

He told us the type of German fighting plane encountered most frequently was the single-seat Messerschmitt 109 Fighter, and he gave us some pointers on fighting them. There was another type fighter, the Heinkel 113, which was supposed to outperform the Messerschmitt, but none had been seen in this area yet. [1]

Then there was the twin-engined Messerschmitt 110 to watch out for. It could be used either as a fighter or as a light bomber, but was considered easy meat by our fighters. The only danger lay in a surprise attack by one of them, because this type carried very heavy armament including two cannons, and if one of them got a good shot at you it would be bad. They weren't to be feared otherwise, though. "You can shoot them down very easily," he said.

---

1. Heinkel 113 would, in fact, never be seen for it never existed. It was a German propoganda plot;—Leonaur Editors

There were three types of large bombers used by the Germans: the Dornier, the Heinkel in (made by the same company but otherwise unrelated to the little Heinkel 113 Fighter), and the Junkers 88. All these were twin-engined. And of course there was the Junkers 87 dive bomber, more familiarly known as the "*Stuka*." This was the type which terrorised the armies in France with mass attacks, dropping screaming bombs on them. This type was particularly easy meat for fighters and easiest of all to shoot down. It was an awkward-looking, slow, single-engined machine.

Our squadron leader said that up to this time the only raids had been on ship convoys in the Channel. "But we have every reason to expect," he added, "that they will be sending bigger raids over to bomb our coastal cities and perhaps even London itself, as soon as they get their bases organised in France."

How truly he spoke!

That afternoon we were taken on a short patrol to familiarize us with our new territory, because the next morning the squadron was scheduled to fly to its advance base at about eight o'clock. There we would put in a shift of several hours "at readiness"—staying close to our machines ready to take off at a moment's notice.

I might explain here that most patrolling by fighter squadrons is done under the direction of a controller on the ground who gives the squadron orders by radio. Each plane has a radio receiver and transmitter, and the pilot keeps his receiver turned on all the time. He has headphones in his helmet and a microphone in the oxygen mask that fits over his nose and mouth.

CHAPTER 3

Tally-Ho!

Our last instructions by our squadron leader before we left for our advance base next morning were in regard to staying in formation, any time the squadron was looking for the enemy.

"It's essential that the squadron stick together as a compact unit as long as possible, until the enemy is actually being engaged. So whenever we're on patrol, and especially when the scent is good and warm, stay in formation. Fly wide enough apart from your leader so that you won't be in danger of colliding with him, but don't lag behind if you can help it. If you see a Hun don't go after him until I give you the O.K. And if we sight a bunch of them, stay in formation until I call out the 'Tally-Ho!' Then you can break formation and pick your targets. And then," he added, patting us both on the back, "Heaven help your targets!"

We got our airplanes ready and put on our flying equipment. As it was warm, we didn't wear any flying suits over our uniforms, but we put on pneumatic life jackets that were issued to us. These are called "Mae Wests"—quite appropriately, too, as you would agree if you could see what they do to a pilot's contour.

We took off in sections of three and assumed squadron formation over the airdrome. An R.A.F. fighter squadron consists of twelve planes normally, and we flew in sections of three, the leader in front with his section.

It was a tremendous thrill for me to be aloft with a fighter squadron for the first time. We circled the airdrome majestically and then swept out eastward toward our advance base on the seacoast. I was enjoying this, even though it was only supposed to be a little cross-country jaunt.

I heard the whine of a radio transmitter in my headphones, and then our squadron leader's voice.

> Hello, Control! Hello, Control! Tiger Leader calling. Are you receiving me? Are you receiving me? Over.("Tiger" was the call name of our squadron.)

There was another transmitter whir, more distant, and a cheery voice sang out:

> Hallo-o, Tiger Leader, Tiger Leader! Control answering you. Control answering. Receiving you loud and clear, loud and clear. Are you receiving me, please? Are you receiving me? Control over to Tiger Leader.

Another whir and our leader's voice answering again:

> Hello, Control. Hello, Control. Tiger Leader answering. Yes, receiving you loud and clear also. Loud and clear. All Tiger aircraft are now air-borne. We are now air-borne. Tiger Leader over to control, listening out.

Control called once more to acknowledge this message, and then there was radio silence as we roared onward. We had to cover about seventy miles, which would take about fifteen minutes. It was a clear morning, and I idly wondered if we should be able to see the French coast that day. If so I should be seeing France for the first time. Also it would be my first view of enemy country, for that was German-occupied France.

Perhaps seven or eight minutes had elapsed when Control called us again. There was the transmitter's whine and a voice calling Tiger Leader and asking if he was receiving him. Then Tiger Leader's answer that he was "receiving you loud and clear."

Then the voice from Control again, this time slower, and with careful enunciation:

> All Tiger aircraft, patrol Dover at ten thousand feet; patrol Dover at ten thousand feet.

Our leader immediately opened his throttle and put his plane in a steep climb, at the same time altering his course in the direction of Dover. We of course did likewise to stay in formation with him.

I wondered what it meant. Had something been seen there, or were they expecting an attack? It still didn't seem possible that I actually might see an enemy. Planes with black crosses and swastikas still didn't seem to exist in reality to me, in spite of the one I had seen that spun in at our training base. Somehow that one, a great broken thing lying on the hillside after it crashed, didn't seem real to me in memory. It still didn't seem possible that I should actually see airplanes with black crosses in the air, whose pilots would be trying to kill me, and I them.

In less time than it takes to tell, our altimeters were registering ten thousand feet and we were racing level. The coast was visible now, not far ahead, with the waters of the English Channel beyond. I guessed that we were nearly over Dover.

Another command came through from Control. "Climb to fifteen thousand feet." And then the message that electrified me:

There are bandits (enemies) approaching from the north!

My pulses pounded, and my thoughts raced. This was it!

In quick response to this information, our leader sang out a command: "All Tiger aircraft, full throttle! Full throttle!"

That meant to use the emergency throttle that gave extra power to our engines.

I was flying in our leader's section, on his left. As he gave the command "Full throttle," his plane started to draw ahead, away from me. I pushed in my emergency throttle lever in response to the command, the first time I had ever used it, and my engine fairly screamed with new power. I felt my plane speeding up like a high-spirited horse that has been spurred.

Our leader now led us upward in a steeper climb than I had ever dreamed an airplane could perform. Trembling with excitement, trying to realise that this was actually happening and I wasn't dreaming, I pulled the guard off my firing button. For the first time in my life I was preparing to kill! The button was painted red, and it looked strangely grim now that it was uncovered. I turned its safety ring, which surrounded it, from the position which read "Safe" to the position which read "Fire."

Then I switched on the electric gun-sight. This projects an orange light in the image of a machine-gun sight upon a glass in the middle of the windshield. It's more accurate than mechanical sights.

We were going forward and upward at terrific speed, and reached fifteen thousand feet shortly. A new command came over our radio receivers:

Steer one-three-zero and climb to twenty thousand feet.

We obeyed, every pilot now watching above and below and on all sides, the sections of the squadron closing in more tightly and the rear-guard pilots wheeling in swift vertical banks one way, then the other, to watch against any surprise.

Our course led us out over the middle of the Channel, and the coast of France was plainly visible—answering one of my hopes. I was getting my first view of France, and enemy France at that.

I was using oxygen now, controlled by a little valve on my instrument panel that released it into a hose connected with the mask that covered my nose and mouth. Oxygen is necessary at high altitude to keep your mind working keenly and to keep you from getting tired and weak. Pilots who don't use it at high altitude tire out quickly, and their minds become sluggish. Also they are apt to faint without warning.

More orders followed. New courses to steer. New altitudes at which to fly.

Circle your present position.

Watch to the left.

Believe the enemy is now heading south and passing behind you.

Such orders as these interspersed the radio silences and kept us busy and on our toes while we hunted about for perhaps half an hour. I was in a sweat trying to look in every direction and still keep my place in formation. Our leader led us about like a group of charging cavalry.

As time went by, my hopes of seeing an enemy flagged.

We were at about twenty thousand feet altitude and a few miles north of Calais on the French coast, and doing a sweeping left turn. Looking in the rear vision mirror above my windshield I saw what looked like a little blazing torch falling in the sky behind me. For the instant I didn't realise that the first shots of battle had been fired, and I had to put my attention again on our leader's plane, to keep my place in formation with him.

I was flying on his left, and that meant I had to look to the right to see him; and out of the corner of my eye I noticed far below and beyond him the distant shape of another airplane heading for France. I hated to call out, in case it didn't mean anything, but it didn't seem reasonable that a British plane would be out here alone, heading in that direction. Also it seemed to be coloured blue-gray on top, and I was quite sure no British planes were coloured like that. It was too far away for me to make out its markings or even its design. Hesitating to call out, I looked at our squadron leader, to see if he had noticed it.

I saw that he hadn't, for he was looking the other way, to our left, where several distant black dots were visible in the air at about our level. And as I watched him I heard his transmitter whine and his voice sing out the Royal Air Force battle cry:

Ta-al-ly-ho-o!

As he sang it he swung his airplane over viciously into a wild vertical turn and laid out for the black dots on the left, which had now grown into airplanes; still little and distant but headed toward us. There weren't very many of them, and the entire squadron was breaking formation and wheeling toward them like a bunch of wild Indians.

I remembered the one I had seen heading the other way and our squadron leader's words that we might pick our own targets after the "Tally-ho" is given; and a second later I was peeling away from the squadron and down in pursuit of the lone machine which I had decided should be my target.

I went down in a screaming dive, pushing everything forward—throttle, emergency throttle, propeller control and all. The other had a good start, but I had the advantage of several thousand feet more altitude, and was gaining speed by diving. The wind shrieked against my windshield and the Rolls Royce engine bellowed, while the airspeed indicator needle moved steadily around its dial and on up past the four hundred miles an hour mark.

The Spitfire grew rigid in its course as if it were following a groove. The controls became terribly stiff, and I couldn't move the stick a quarter of an inch in any direction. It was hard to level out from the dive when I got down near the other's altitude. I had to pull out very gently to keep from blacking out too much. The misty curtain kept closing down in front of my eyes as I pulled the nose of my plane up, and I leaned forward and tensed my muscles to resist it. I was still a way behind the other when I got down to his level, but I was gaining on him fast, because of the extra speed I had from my dive.

I was holding my thumb over the firing button now and keeping my eyes glued to the little silhouette ahead, except for an occasional glance at the rear vision mirror to see that I wasn't being chased too. I imagine my heart was doing about fifteen hundred r.p.m., from the pounding I felt.

The other machine grew steadily larger in the circle of my gunsight as I drew closer. I could tell its distance by the amount of space it covered in the sight: six hundred yards, five hundred, four hundred—my speed was dying down a little, and I wasn't gaining quite as fast. He apparently was going wide open too.

Now I was only three hundred yards behind—close enough to open fire, but something made me hesitate. From directly behind, where I was now, it was hard to identify its type. Suppose it was a British machine after all?

To make sure I eased my machine upward just a little so I could look down on the other and see the upper side of it. The old feeling that airplanes with black crosses and swastikas on their wings and sides couldn't exist in reality still had hold of me; but it was banished forever by what I now saw.

For I could see that the other machine's wings were not curved, with nicely rounded tips, like a Spitfire's; and it was not camouflaged green and tan; and there were no red and blue circles near the tips. Instead, the wings were narrow, stiff-looking, with blunt, square-cut tips. They were pale blue-gray in colour, and near each tip, very vivid, was painted a simple black "plus" sign!

I knew from pictures that it must be a Messerschmitt 109, and I dropped back into firing position behind it. My sights centred on it, and I squeezed the firing button with my thumb. *B-r-r-rup-pup-u-pup!* The sound came to me muffled by my heavy helmet; but it was a venomous sound, and I could feel the Spitfire shudder and slow from the recoil as the eight Browning guns snarled and barked their terrific fast *staccato*. I held the button in for about a full one-second burst—about one hundred and sixty bullets.

Then my plane bounced sideways as it encountered the turbulent slipstream of the other, and I lost sight of him for a second. He must have gone into a diving turn just then, for when I spotted him again a few seconds later he was far below. Mentally cursing my carelessness or dumbness, I rolled over and went down after him again; and while I was overtaking him I reflected that for the first time I had tried to take the life of another man. It didn't bother my conscience.

I caught up with him just over Cape Gris Nez on the French coast, and that was how I entered France for the first time! As I drew close he abandoned flight and turned to face me like a cornered animal; but I was too close behind him now, and I simply followed him in the turn, cutting it shorter than he could and crowding in on him.

I knew I was outmanoeuvring him, and felt I had him now. He was almost in the circle of my gun-sights. This time I'd keep him there!

Powp!

It sounded exactly as if some one had blown up a big paper sack and burst it behind my ears; and it shook the plane and was followed by a noise like hail on a tin roof.

I realised that I had been hit somewhere behind me in my machine by a second Hun, and guessed that it was an exploding cannon shell that made the noise. Most German fighters are equipped with cannon as well as machine guns.

I put all the strength I could muster on my controls to whip my machine into a turn in the opposite direction, then saw that I'd wasted the effort. My new attacker had already flashed by below and ahead, and I now saw him wheeling to come back, his black crosses vivid on top of his wings as he appeared spread-eagled in a vertical turn. The square-cut wingtips of his Messerschmitt looked crude but grim.

He must have dived on me and fired a shot as he went down past. I reflected a little grimly that a new "first" had occurred for me—for the first time *another* man had tried to take *my* life!

It's hard to recall details of the ensuing combat, but I know it was pretty wild. I made lots of blunders. It was terribly hard for me in my inexperience to try to get an advantage on one of my enemies, so I could open fire, without the other popping up immediately in firing position behind me. The three of us scrambled about in a terrible melee, climbing, diving, rolling, and pirouetting in screaming vertical turns to get at each other. A combat such as this is well called a "dog fight." One moment I would be manoeuvring for my life to get away from one who was almost on my tail, and in the next moment I would have one of them in the same kind of spot and would be trying just as desperately to hold him long enough to get a shot.

And sometimes when I got separated from both of them a moment I would see bright flashes and puffs of white or black smoke in the air near me—shells from German anti-aircraft guns. The batteries on the coast below had joined the fight and were shooting at me whenever they got a chance to do so without hitting their own machines.

This went on for several minutes, before I finally managed to get one of them all by himself away from the other for a few seconds. I was in a beautiful firing position right on his tail.

Then I got a heart-breaking shock: my gun-sight wasn't working!

The precious image in orange light wasn't to be seen on the glass in front of me. Feverishly I fumbled and found the switch for it. Yes, it was on. I tried the rheostat which controls the intensity of the light for day or night use. It was on full bright.

It was hard to do this and keep behind the other's tail. He was dodging wildly, expecting my bullets every second, I suppose. I jiggled the rheostat and turned it back and forth, and hit the reflector sight base with my hand and shook it. Still no result. It took precious seconds to do this checking, and the loss of time was very nearly fatal.

A set of four long vibrating snaky white fingers reached across my right wing from behind and stretched far ahead. They were about an inch thick and made of white smoke and pulsated with bright molten-looking objects streaking through them. I knew they were tracers—the trails of smoke left by bullets to mark their course. Chemicals coated on the bullets do it. They show the pilot where his bullets are going. In this case they showed me too, and I knew I was being fired at by the other German pilot from behind. I panicked and rolled into a turn so violent that my machine shuddered terribly and slipped over into a tailspin—at more than two hundred miles an hour! It must have made me look like an amateur, but it shook off my attacker.

I felt that I was in a pretty bad spot without a gun-sight, but decided to bluff them a little bit rather than to turn tail right away and let them know something was wrong.

The melee continued. I was terribly hot and tired and sweaty, and was conscious of that more than of being scared. I wished I could rest. The bright sun beat down hotly through the transparent hatch over my cockpit. My clothes were heavy and I was hampered by my parachute straps and seat harness straps as I twisted about in the cockpit trying to see above, below, behind, and to the sides to keep track of my playmates.

During those next few minutes I think I must have blacked out at least twenty times in turns. I remember starting to spin at least once from turning too violently. I wanted to flee but couldn't get my directions straight because I was manoeuvring so fast. My compass couldn't help me unless I'd give it a chance to settle down. It was spinning like a top.

Finally I noticed across the water, in the distance, a ribbon of white lining the horizon, and I remembered reading years ago in my geography book about the *"white cliffs of Dover."* Just then that looked like the promised land.

One of my enemies was heading the other way. I made a pass at the second and he headed in the opposite direction from Dover, too, and I turned out across the sea and homeward. It was an ignominious way to end a fight which had begun with such promise, but I thought it was the wisest. My enemies took after me, but when they drew close I turned around as if to go after them and they turned back. They were apparently willing to call it a draw, and I didn't feel quite so badly after that.

When I went to land at our advance base I found that the trimming controls for my tail were out of order. The wheels actuating them spun loosely, so I knew the cables must be broken.

On landing I taxied to one end of the field, where I saw the rest of my squadron's planes, already down. I was flagged into place, and mechanics and armourers swarmed over my Spitfire. Some jerked off the removable metal covers above and below the machine guns in the wings while others ran up with belts of ammunition and began to refill the guns. A gasoline truck roared up and stopped in front of the plane, and they began refilling the tanks. In a few minutes my machine would be completely checked, refuelled, and refilled with ammunition.

My squadron mates crowded around to hear my story. All but one of them were down now, and they had already heard one another's stories. I told them mine as well as I could remember, and had to admit regretfully that I had come away without bringing down either of my enemies.

We examined my plane, and it was easy to see that it had been struck by an exploding cannon shell, as I had thought. The shell had blown a fairly large hole in one side of the fuselage just behind the cockpit, in the lower part of the red, white, and blue insignia. It would have been a bull's-eye if it had been a foot higher.

The control cables which ran close by where the shell had hit, were in bad shape. In addition to the trimming control cables being broken, the main elevator and rudder cables were also nearly severed by the blast. A battery connection was broken by the explosion, and that explained the failure of my electric gun-sight. The bottom of the plane was littered with bits of light shrapnel from the shell and there were a myriad small holes in the other side of the fuselage from the shell hole, where pieces of shrapnel had gone out. The shrapnel must have made the noise "like hail on a tin roof" that I had heard after the explosion. My machine truly carried an "after the battle" appearance.

Rearming and refuelling a Spitfire

It would have to have a new fuselage installed.

I heard the story of the rest of the squadron. They had charged into the formation of Messerschmitts that they were heading for when I left them, and had shot down two for sure. There were also two other "probables" which they had seen going down but which they couldn't claim definitely because they weren't seen to hit the sea. One of the boys had damaged still another—had seen pieces fly off it when he fired.

In addition a Henschel 126 German reconnaissance machine had come steaming along right into the centre of the *mêlée*, a terrible mistake for its pilot to make, for these machines only have two or three machine guns and can't travel much over two hundred miles an hour, so that they are cold meat for fighters. He must have been going on some business of his own and blundered into the middle of the show somehow, before he realised it. Two of our boys spotted this machine and went to work on it, but they were nearly out of ammunition by that time and they emptied all the bullets they had left into it without bringing it down. It just kept sailing right on, but they thought they killed the rear gunner at least because he quit shooting back at them. It was credited to the squadron as being "damaged."

This is one of three categories into which R.A.F. successes are divided. The other two are "probably destroyed" and "confirmed victories" (definitely destroyed). Only the number of confirmed victories is given out in the report of enemy aircraft destroyed.

The score for the squadron that morning was two confirmed, two probables, and two damaged.

None of our planes that were back was even hit except mine; but one had not returned yet and the outlook grew bad. Two of the boys remembered seeing what looked like a Spitfire going down in flames in the distance behind the squadron at the start of the battle. This boy who was missing was one of the "rear guard" pilots, protecting the rear of the squadron. I also remembered the glimpse I had in my mirror at that time, of something that looked like a torch falling in the distance behind us. When no trace could be found of him and it was learned that no other British planes were missing, we knew he must have been the pilot. There were a lot of Messerschmitts about that morning, and it was pretty evident what had happened.

He must have seen some Messerschmitts coming up to attack the squadron from behind, had turned back and engaged them, and thus, fighting alone to protect his mates, he had gone out in a blaze of glory.

Our squadron leader paid him a simple but meaningful tribute that we wished he could have heard.

"I noticed," he said, "that we *weren't* attacked from the rear."

I sought out Peter, and we lay on the grass near our machines and basked in the warm sunshine. There were a lot of scratches on my flying boots from shrapnel, and we found a little piece imbedded in one of them.

I felt strangely tired and lazy, not realising that this was my initiation to a strange feeling of exhaustion with which I was to get better acquainted in the following days. I didn't want to sleep, but I didn't want to move, or talk, or fly, or anything else either, just relax. It's a feeling that's always pervaded me after a fight or a nerve-racking patrol. As nearly as I can describe it, it is a sensation of being drained completely, in every part of your body, though I don't know what of. But you seem to want to just surrender to relaxation, sitting or lying inert and absorbing whatever it is back into your system. I've heard many other pilots say they get the same feeling.

Peter asked, "Will you do me a favour, Chum?"

"Sure. What is it?"

"Let me have your notebook for a minute and I'll tell you."

I gave him the little memorandum book which I always carry, opening it to a blank page. He wrote a girl's name and telephone number in it.

"If anything happens to me," he said, "will you telephone this number and tell her the story? And then—" He paused, and indicated the silver identification wristlet which he wore on his left wrist. It had a little name plate, and also little charms of some sort strung on it. "If it's possible," he finished, "I'd like to have you see that she gets this."

"O.K.," I said lightly, "and let's hope that I never have to do that for you."

Looking at the notebook, I tried to realise that I had bought it only three months before, in a drugstore in Manitowoc, Wisconsin.

I still have that notebook, Peter, and the page you wrote on that day is still in it; though, of course, I don't need it any more because I've telephoned the number and told *her* the story, long since.

Chapter 4

Victory—and Its Price

It was hard to realise that this had all actually happened and wasn't a dream. This was August 5th, scarcely six weeks from the time I had been at home in Minnesota, cultivating corn! That corn wouldn't be big enough to cut yet!

In England the letters "U-S" have a different meaning than they do in America. Here they mean "unserviceable."

My machine was U-S now, because the fuselage was ruined, so I couldn't fly back to our home airdrome with the rest of the squadron when our shift was over at noon. However, the squadron had a little two-seat training plane for the use of the pilots, and after the boys flew home one of them came back in this machine and picked me up, and I had a nice ride home.

In the afternoon I visited "Number One," our intelligence officer, in his office and made out my first combat report. After I finished I spent some time in his office, studying models of various types of German bombers which showed their gun positions and the arcs of fire of the guns.

Next morning when we were collected in our pilots' hut, Number One visited us and passed around some mimeographed papers to us, saying, "Here's the latest intelligence dope for you boys to look over when you have time."

I found that one set of papers was full of information about the enemy's activity during the past two or three days and nights, what units of their air force were operating and where, changes in the status or position of enemy *staffels* (squadrons) and *gruppes* (wings), and developments in design and armament of enemy aircraft.

Another set gave summaries of recent activities of the three divisions of the R.A.F.: Bomber Command, Coastal Command, and

Fighter Command. A third set proved most interesting to me. This gave accounts of activities of the front-line fighter squadrons during the past two days.

Each squadron that was called up on patrol during this period was listed, and its activities detailed. In the case of engagements the name of each pilot who made contact with the enemy was given, together with a summary from his combat report; and if he was credited with destroying, probably destroying, or damaging any of the enemy this was also given. Our own casualties were listed, with names, and details where known.

These summaries are published every two or three days and given to the pilots of all the squadrons to read, so that each of us is able to know just what our losses and successes are. I have never seen them omit any losses by my squadron or other squadrons whose activities I knew of, nor have they exaggerated our successes; and they never fail to check with the information concerning R.A.F. successes and losses that is given in public *communiqués*.

You can see that we pilots are in a position to know if the information in R.A.F. *communiqués* is true, and any fighter pilot will tell you that it is. It was quite interesting and edifying for us to read the papers Tuesday, the day after our combat, containing the German report of our encounter, taken from a German High Command *communiqué* that was relayed from New York. This stated that we lost eight machines in the fight and all the German planes "returned safely"!

Tuesday and Wednesday were quiet. Apparently the Boche aviators were staying home and "licking their wounds" again.

We had plenty of leisure; and Peter and I visited the "Operations" room from which our orders came by radio while we were on the chase. It was an intriguing and interesting place. In the middle of a large room was a table several feet wide and long, on which was an enormous map of southern England, the English Channel, and northern France. Little wooden blocks were placed on it to represent planes and their positions, as well as ship convoys. As reports came in of new positions for planes or ships, girls standing around the table moved the blocks to the new positions. Enemy planes and ships were "plotted" on this board in the same way as our own.

There was a gallery around the room, in which the control officers sat so that they could see the complete picture of the positions of their own and enemy planes and ships. All the time we were looking for the Nazis that morning our moves and those of the enemy were plotted about on this map. Our controller was able to see our relative positions on it at a glance; and on the basis of what he saw in that room he ordered us about in the air far out over the Channel until we found the enemy!

Daily he played a deadly game of chess on that map, using the pilots as chessmen, with unseen controllers on the other side of the Channel who directed the movements of our enemies.

Wednesday morning some of our squadron cooperated in giving the ground defences at our home airdrome some practice. The station commander had arranged to have a mock attack on the airdrome by combined air and ground forces. We were to furnish six airplanes to play the part of defending fighters, while a Hurricane squadron which was also based here was to furnish six airplanes to play the part of "enemy" bombers. The six Hurricanes were to fly over as if they were bombing the airdrome, and our six Spitfires would attack and pretend to shoot them down.

There was only one flaw in the station commander's plans: he forgot to take into consideration the friendly but intense rivalry between the pilots of Hurricane and Spitfire airplanes. Pilots of these two types of fighters argue by the hour on which is the better, and the pilots of either type never pass up an opportunity to demonstrate the superiority of their type over the other.

Everything went according to plan when the mock attack began. The six Hurricanes which were to take the part of the bombers had left earlier in the morning and gone to another airdrome from which to start on their "raid." Our six Spitfires went up and began patrolling the airdrome, waiting for the bombers. I wasn't included in the six pilots used, so I watched the show from the ground, standing in front of our pilots' hut. Soon the Hurricanes appeared, flying in good bomber formation, right over the airdrome. The Spitfires went in to "attack"—and that was where the plans went wrong.

Now bombers, when attacked, endeavour to stay close together in formation so that the gunners of all of them can fire on each enemy that gets close, all at the same time. These six Hurricane pilots probably intended to stay in formation originally, until the Spitfires attacked and the full import dawned on them: six Spitfires were going to get on their tails and pretend to shoot them down.

Never!!

As the Spitfires closed in, the formation of Hurricanes literally exploded, in all directions, in the most unorthodox manner for bombers as their pilots broke away to do combat with their rivals, our Spitfire pilots. It was absolutely earnest combat in everything except that they didn't use their guns, and for the next few moments the air above the airdrome was full of milling, wheeling, twisting, diving, zooming, rolling, and gyrating Spitfires and Hurricanes, as the rival pilots strove their mightiest and cleverest to prove the superiority of their respective machines.

It seemed impossible that they could avoid collisions. The din of Rolls Royce engines racing at full throttle nearly made our ears ring. Number One, who was standing beside us watching the show, remarked in his slow, sage manner, "I'm awfully glad that all our boys are crazy. No sane pilot could possibly fly in that melee up there for a minute without colliding with someone!" I agreed with him.

After a few minutes the boys had all had enough, for dog-fighting even in fun is a terrific strain, and the machines of both types came stringing back in, one by one, and landing. Little was proved by it all, because it was such a *mêlée* that no one knew whom he was fighting— in fact at times Spitfire pilots had found themselves engaging other Spitfires, and Hurricane pilots other Hurricanes! It merely started another endless chain of arguments in the mess.

It was very illustrative of the high spirit of all the boys. Our squadron leader, remarking about the spirit in his squadron, had said the day before: "It's like holding in a team of wild horses when I keep them in formation when there are Huns near. I'm almost afraid to give the 'Tally-ho' because I know I'll be alone about two seconds later! They just peel off like banana skins when they get the word to go after the Huns!"

Thursday of that week, August 8th, was the beginning of the German mass air raids on this country—the date commonly referred to as the start of the great Battle over Britain. Of course we didn't know it that morning.

We had to fly to our advance base at dawn, and it was an unforgettably beautiful flight for me. It was just getting light when we took off, and the countryside was dim below us. Wicked blue flames flared back from the exhausts of all the engines as I looked at the planes in formation about me.

We seemed to hover motionless except for the slight upward or downward drift of one machine or another in relation to the rest, which seemed to lend a sort of pulsating life to the whole formation; and the dark carpet of the earth below steadily slid backward beneath us. The sun, just rising and very red and big and beautiful, made weird lights over the tops of our camouflaged wings. We were like a herd of giant beasts in some strange new kind of world. It reminded me of a motion picture named "Dawn Patrol" which I had seen in some other life in another world far away.

We landed at our advance base, and saw our airplanes refuelled and ready to take off. It was a chilly morning, and most of us turned in under blankets on cots provided for us and hoped that the Huns slept late and wouldn't bother us until we had completed our night's sleep. We had gotten up at about three a.m.

It seemed like it would be another quiet day. Nothing happened until about eleven a.m. Then the telephone rang, and the call was for our squadron leader. When he finished speaking he turned to us with a little smile and said: "Operations just called to tell us to be on our toes. There's a lot of activity on the other side, and they have a 'fifty plus' raid plotted, coming across farther down the coast. It may turn and head our way though."

A "fifty plus" raid meant a group of fifty or more enemy airplanes!

In a few minutes the telephone rang again. The telephone orderly listened a moment and then turned to us and said, "Squadron into your aircraft, and patrol base at ten thousand feet!"

Instantly we were on our feet and racing pell-mell out to our airplanes. An airman helped me on with my parachute. I climbed into the cockpit of my machine and, trembling with excitement, adjusted my straps and put on my helmet. Down the line of planes starters whined, and first one engine then another coughed to life. I pressed my own starter button and my engine joined the chorus. There was no "warming up," no taxiing across the field to take off into the wind. Upwind, downwind, or crosswind, we took off straight ahead. Better a difficult take-off than to give a deadly enemy a minute's extra advantage!

We roared off like a stampeding herd of buffalo, climbing steeply and wide open. Two thousand feet, four thousand—there were thick fluffy clouds at five thousand, and we flashed up through their misty chasms, caverns, hills and valleys; and then they were dropping away below us and forming a snowy carpet for us to look down on. The sun shone brilliantly above. New orders came over the radio from our controller, much as on the previous chase. Sometimes we were over coastal cities, sometimes over the Channel, circling here, patrolling there, watching for the elusive enemy. I recalled the scene in the operations room and wondered if the girls plotting our positions were any less nonchalant now when there was a real chase on.

Nearly an hour passed without our seeing anything. One flight (six of our twelve planes) was ordered to land, and I guessed that the trail was getting cold. Peter and I were in the flight remaining on patrol.

We were about eight thousand feet up, the six of us patrolling over the Channel, and for a couple of minutes we had received no new orders. The sun was very hot, and I wished I hadn't worn my tunic.

Our only warning was the sudden whine of a transmitter and a voice shouting "Bandits astern!!"

It was blood-chilling. Our squadron leader was quick on the trigger and led us in a violent turn, just in time. A myriad gray Messerschmitts were swarming down out of the sun, diving from above and behind and shooting as they came.

"Tal-l-ly— ho-o!"

Our leader's voice was steady and strong and reassuring and in that moment filled with all his personal magnetism and strength of character. It was reassuring in its calm call to battle, and caught up shattered nerves and self-control in each of us. He led us together down into the middle of the swarm of Huns, whose speed had carried them far down ahead of us and who were now wheeling back towards us as they came up out of their dives.

There seemed to be about thirty; it was probably a "*gruppe*" of twenty-seven, and they simply absorbed the six of us. We picked targets and went after them and were soon completely lost from each other. One Messerschmitt was coming up in a climbing turn ahead of me, and allowing for its speed I aimed a burst of fire just ahead of its nose. I had no time to see if I hit it.

My guns gave me a feeling of power. They sounded terribly capable and completed the steadying effect of our leader's voice on my nerves.

Another Messerschmitt coming head-on spat his four white tracers at me but they arched over my head. We seemed to be milling about like a swarm of great gnats in this giant eerie amphitheatre above the clouds. Sets of long white tracers crisscrossed the air and hung all about, like Christmas decorations! They stay visible for several seconds after they're fired.

Something about the shape of the Messerschmitts reminded me of rats sailing about on their little narrow, stiff-looking, square-tipped

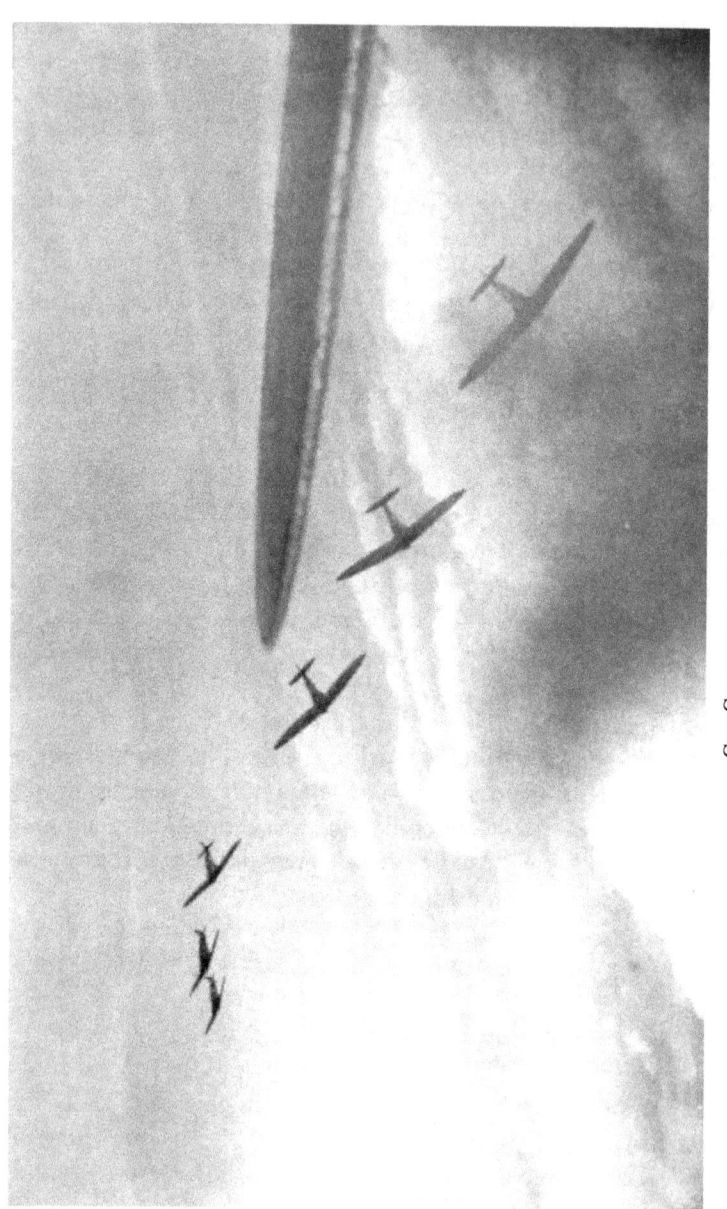

Six Spitfires attacking

wings. I think it's because of the shape of their noses, and the way their radiators are carried tucked up under their noses like the forefeet of a rat when he's running close to the floor.

One came at me from the side, his guns blazing out their tracers and his cannon firing through a hole in the centre of his propeller, puffing blue smoke for all the world like a John Deere tractor! It wasn't a pretty sight. Two of the tracers erupted from guns on either side of its nose, at the top, and two from the wings. It looked like a hideous rat-shaped fountain spurting jets of water from its nostrils and mouth corners!

We *mêléed* about for several minutes, the fight quickly spreading out over wide territory. I got short shots at several of our playmates, just firing whenever I saw something with black crosses in front of me and not having time to see the result.

Then one got on my tail and gave me a burst just as I saw him, and I laid over into a vertical turn; and as he did likewise, following me, I hauled my Spitfire around as tight as I could. We were going fast and I had to lean forward and hold my breath and fight to keep from blacking out, and I turned this way for several seconds. Then I eased my turn so that I could straighten up and look out of my cockpit, and I spotted the other in front of me. I had turned so much shorter than he could that I was almost around and on *his* tail now. He apparently became aware of it at the same time, for he abandoned his turn and took to flight; but he was a little late now.

He went into a dive, twisting about wildly to upset my aim as I opened fire. I pressed my firing button three or four times for bursts of about a second each, and then he quit twisting. I was able to hold the sight dead on him while I held the firing button in for a good three-second burst, and let it go at that.

I didn't think he needed any more, for I knew of only one reason for him to stop twisting. He disappeared into the clouds below, diving straight down, and although he might have gotten home he certainly wasn't headed right then.

Two more were following me down closely, and in pulling out of my dive I plunged momentarily through the clouds and then up out of them, turning to meet these two. The powder smoke from my guns smelled strong, and I felt good. This was battle royal!

But my newest opponents failed me. As I zoomed up out of the clouds I saw them just disappearing into the clouds and heading homeward. Another diving out of nowhere took a snap shot at me as he went by and down into the clouds, also heading for home.

Recovering from the shock that gave me, I looked around and found no more planes of either nationality in view. I appeared to be in sole possession of this part of the battlefield. This was well out over the Channel and I knew I must be nearly out of ammunition, so I headed for shore and our advance base.

All but one of our planes were already down safely when I taxied into line on the ground. Peter was "still adrift," I learned, and it gave me a little shock. There was still plenty of time for him to show up, though.

We compared notes. Others of the squadron had sent two Messerschmitts down in flames. I couldn't claim mine as a confirmed victory unless some one saw it hit the sea, because it wasn't in flames. We can claim a victory if the enemy is seen in flames or if the pilot jumps out in his parachute; but otherwise it must be seen by someone to hit the sea or ground. Mine went down quite a way out over the Channel (if it went down) and there wasn't much likelihood of its being seen.

We began to worry about Peter when he didn't show up after a reasonable time. One of our boys remembered seeing a parachute floating down during the fight, but didn't know whether or not it was a German. Our squadron leader got on the telephone to try to get news of him. Our shift at the advance base was over now and another squadron had arrived to relieve us. Our squadron leader sent us home and remained himself to try to locate Peter.

We were late for dinner when we got home, and it was warmed over and I suppose that was partly why I couldn't eat. But the main reason was Peter. The chances of good news were growing smaller each minute; but it finally came! Peter had been picked up, wounded but alive, and was already in a hospital. Later we got more details. He had several bullet wounds but none of them was serious in itself, and his only danger was shock and loss of blood. He was "in wonderful spirits, cursing the Huns and spoiling for another go at them!" They thought that if he pulled through the first night he would be out of danger.

The world seemed brighter after that. I thought a lot of this big tough good-natured pal of mine.

It developed that our fight was only one of a series of battles all along the Channel. The mass raids had started, and the aerial "Battle for Britain" was on!

The next day, Friday, we were scheduled to take the readiness shift at our advance base for the afternoon, from one p.m. until dark. In the morning we were just a reserve squadron. There was some activity in the morning but we weren't called out, and it quieted down about noon; looked as if it would be a quiet afternoon for us.

Our squadron leader decided not to go with us and had one of the flight commanders take over the squadron for the afternoon. He couldn't fly with us always, as the commanding officer of a squadron has lots of office work to do, and he wanted to get caught up with his that day. He reassured us though: "I'll keep in close touch with Operations and have a machine ready, and if anything big starts turning up I'll be blazing down there at 'four pounds boost and twenty-six hundred r.p.m.' to join you!"

There was some activity about mid-afternoon, and we were sent up on two patrols; but our squadron failed to make contact with the enemy. However, toward the end of the second patrol two of our boys were detached and sent to intercept two Messerschmitt 109's that were attacking the balloon barrage at Dover. They found the 109's and had a short, sharp dog fight among the balloons and low clouds and bursting anti-aircraft shells over the city. The Messerschmitts ran for it and got away in the clouds, but the boys thought they had damaged both of them.

Mann got a cannon shell in the wing of the Spitfire he was flying and was very worried about it because it was our squadron leader's regular machine. By that time the C.O., as we usually called him, had arrived, carrying out his promise to come down if anything started to happen, and he forgave Mann for it, good-naturedly.

Then while we were getting refuelled the main battle of the afternoon was fought near us over the Channel, between other British squadrons and a large mass of Huns. We all stood on top of a bomb shelter trying to watch it. We could hear the roaring of engines and machine guns, but it was too high and far away for us to see anything of it.

By the time we were refuelled and ready to go it was over, and there was nothing more for us to do until about eight o'clock in the evening, when we were given permission to take off and return to our home base.

The first thing I did when we got home was to telephone the hospital for news of Peter. It was encouraging. He was still holding his own and doing fine, and they thought he was practically out of danger. I wrote him a letter, cussing him out for lying around in bed when we had lots of work to do. The C.O. told me I could have the following Tuesday off to go and visit him. His hospital was quite a distance away.

We weren't scheduled to do readiness the next day, although we were supposed to be available on the airdrome in case something big came up and the squadrons that were on duty needed help. I got up rather late and learned from the station commander, who had already been in touch with the hospital, that Peter was still holding his own.

Breakfast tasted good. I took stock of the events of the week in relation to myself, and decided it hadn't been bad. I certainly wasn't sorry I had come here. Although I was still pretty scared while on patrol I felt that, given a little more time to get used to it, I'd be all right. I'd been through two good engagements and felt quite sure that I'd already accomplished a little for the flag I was fighting under. Moreover I'd learned a lot and thought I'd be able to accomplish a lot more in time to come.

I was in our squadron office about midmorning when an orderly brought in a telegram for the adjutant. The adjutant looked at it and then handed it to me, and as I read it my mouth went dry and part of my world went crumbling.

It was from the hospital. Peter had had a relapse that morning and passed away.

Chapter 5

Defeat

I kept trying to tell myself, in the dazed moments that followed, that this was good for me, that it would give me the hardening that I needed; and somehow that seemed to help me keep control of my pounding heart and wild emotions. When I was alone I murmured aloud: "I'll make it up for you, Pal. I'll get the ones you won't be getting now. Wait and see if I don't!"

Gradually the waves of feeling grew less intense, and I felt cleaned and chastened, and toughened a little too, perhaps; and by keeping my mind away from the tragedy of it I managed to eat my meals and act normally.

The next day was Sunday, but I didn't get to go to Mass. There were some other blood sacrifices being made, to the ambitions of a hate-crazed, power-maddened little man who wanted to take the place of God.

We had the morning shift at the advance base again, from dawn until one o'clock, and there was quite a lot going on. We did one patrol without managing to intercept the enemy, and on that patrol my oxygen apparatus broke down. It would take a while to repair it, so the C.O. told me I might fly without oxygen if I wished, and if we got ordered above fifteen thousand feet I should break away and come back down.

We had hardly been refuelled before we were off again, and as the mechanics hadn't had time to fix my oxygen apparatus yet I went along anyway without oxygen, as the C.O. suggested. We patrolled around awhile at ten thousand feet, then were ordered to fifteen thousand, and after a few minutes twenty thousand. Control said there were a large number of bandits which had gone inland and were coming back out, climbing; and our squadron was to try to intercept them on their way out.

I broke away from the squadron after they got above fifteen thousand feet, but I hated to go back and land with so much going on. I thought that if a fight started it would probably work down lower, and I might get in on the last of it if I stayed around. By listening to the orders the squadron was given over the R/T (radio telephone) I could keep track of where the squadron was and where the enemy must be expected.

I went back down to ten thousand feet, as I didn't feel too comfortable at fifteen thousand without oxygen; and then cruised around listening to the R/T messages and watching for Huns on my own. Suddenly I heard the distant voice of one of the boys in the squadron calling over the R/T, "Many bandits approaching from the starboard!"

There was a moment's radio silence and then another voice: "Look out! There's more of them behind and above!"

Then our leader's voice, "All right! Tally-ho!"

Then there was absolute radio silence and I knew that the battle must be on. I watched all around and above me, but couldn't see any airplanes and couldn't tell where this was occurring, though I knew it must be close by. I wished I could find some enemies at my altitude somewhere.

All at once I saw some puffs from anti-aircraft shells a few miles away and not very high. I reasoned that where there were anti-aircraft shells exploding there must be enemy aircraft, and I headed in that direction, toward Dover. As I got near I saw what it was all about. Enemy airplanes must be attacking the balloon barrage, for one of the balloons was burning beautifully. Great scarlet flames and clouds of pitch-black smoke were rolling upward from it. A furious barrage of anti-aircraft fire was going up on the opposite side of Dover over the harbour, and I headed wide open for it.

The fire ceased just before I got there, and I swung out over the harbour looking in all directions but couldn't see any enemy. Then I saw the smoke puffs of more anti-aircraft going up on the other side of town again and I wheeled and made a bee-line toward them. When I got there the shells were bursting all around me and some of them close enough to be uncomfortable, but still I could see no Hun. I got away from there, and the firing ceased.

As I neared the airdrome I saw a Spitfire coming straight down in a vertical dive, from very high. It looked as if it was hit, and my heart sank and I prayed that it wasn't another of our squadron's boys. Then I sighed with relief as it began pulling out of the dive at about five thousand feet and headed for the airdrome.

I was at about seven thousand feet now and losing altitude toward the airdrome and relaxing a little. There were some nice fluffy clouds below me and I would be dropping through them in a minute. A dot on my rear vision mirror attracted my attention, and looking back I saw what appeared to be another Spitfire quite a distance behind and above me but overtaking me rapidly. I guessed that both of these Spitfires were boys of the squadron returning from the fight.

I watched it idly as it got closer behind me. The pilot was doing something which is considered bad taste in following directly behind me. This is bad for a fighter pilot to do because the pilot of the plane being overtaken may not notice him until he is close behind, with the result that he gets an awful scare when he does see him, thinking it's an enemy on his tail. So normally, fighter pilots never approach a friendly plane from directly behind, but always from well to one side.

This Spitfire pilot kept on overtaking me from directly behind, and it irked me a little, like seeing someone go through a "Stop" sign in front of you. Then when he kept getting closer I began to wonder if perhaps the pilot mistook me for a Messerschmitt or something. Airplanes aren't too easy to recognise in profile, and he was certainly acting like he was going to attack me. He was only five or six hundred yards behind me and gaining fast, so I decided to give him a better chance to see my identity before he got close enough for accurate shooting.

I tipped my plane over in a vertical turn so that he could see the shape of my wings, and the next instant I realised that it wasn't that pilot, but myself, who had made a mistake in identity. He knew I was a Spitfire all right, and that's why he was attacking—his "Spitfire" wasn't a Spitfire at all, but a Messerschmitt 109, and his tracers were reaching out across the space between us! It was too far for accurate shooting though, and I got out of his way and he continued his dive and disappeared into the clouds.

It taught me a lesson, and since then I have never allowed another airplane to get anywhere near behind me until I have scrutinized it and made positive identification.

I didn't think any of his bullets had hit my machine until I went to check my air speed, then I found that my air speed indicator wasn't working. On landing I found that a bullet had gone through my wing, cutting the air speed indicator pressure tube, and causing the instrument to fail.

I had reason to be disappointed because I wasn't able to be with the squadron that time. They had a terrific show, having found far more enemies than they could take care of.

They had first intercepted a bunch of 109's (Messerschmitts) and had got all split up fighting them and chasing them. Our C.O. had shot down one and then chased another most of the way across the Channel, but ran out of ammunition before he got it down. It was losing height when he left it, though, with white clouds of steam and glycol (radiator fluid) streaming behind, and the pilot had jettisoned the hood of his cockpit preparatory to bailing out.

"Orange" had got a 109 and then chased a formation of forty 110's (the twin-engined type of Messerschmitt fighter and light bomber) most of the way across the Channel. On catching them he "sort of nibbled at one at the rear of the formation," as he termed it, exhausting all the ammunition he had left and getting some small pieces to fly off it; but it stayed in formation and he assumed that it probably got home—"though not in very good condition," he added.

Others had also had good results, and the final outcome, after checking with reports of machines that crashed in the vicinity, was four confirmed for the squadron.

The only casualty was Bud. He was ruefully inspecting his rather battle-scarred Spitfire. A good proportion of one side of his tail was shot away by cannon fire, one wing damaged, and one tire flat! A 109 had surprised him from behind as he was returning from the fight, and had scored a couple of pretty good hits. When Bud heard and felt the explosion of a cannon shell on his machine he had rolled over quickly and dived straight down and got away, not knowing how badly he was crippled.

We had one more patrol, which proved uneventful, and then our shift was over and we returned to our home airdrome. Our C.O. went to visit Peter's parents that afternoon, so before he left I told him the request Peter had made me about his wristlet and he said he would have it taken care of. The funeral was to be Tuesday morning, and I planned to attend.

Monday, August 12th, was a pretty busy day.

We had one patrol in the latter part of the afternoon without making any interception; and while we were on the ground getting refuelled Operations telephoned and said there was a "450 plus" raid

Heinkel 113 fighter

forming up over the French coast. I guess we were all feeling a little subdued when we got scrambled again a few minutes later. We knew that if we intercepted it we'd be fortunate if there was more than one other squadron at the most with us in the fight.

However, we were up only a short time when we intercepted a comparatively small formation of enemy fighters, perhaps twenty or thirty. The "Tally-ho" went up and we got all split up. I saw a formation of three that were flying by themselves a short distance away from the rest, and they started going in a circle as I went in to attack, just following each other round and round.

Their wings were different and more graceful-looking than those of Messerschmitts, and I recognised the machines as the new Heinkel 113 Fighters. They were good-looking airplanes, and I remember that they were painted all white. We *mêléed* about a little, and I ended up by getting chased down into the clouds below us, and I lost track of them for the moment.

I was cruising along in a rift between the clouds when I saw above me and to the southeast more airplanes than I had ever seen at one time in my life. It was the "450 plus" raid coming across. It takes those big mass formations a long time to get organized. They have to circle around over one spot for a long time while the various groups of planes get into their places in the formation.

This raid was now organised and was halfway across the Channel.

I wasn't very high, perhaps seven thousand feet, and above me and to the southeast at very high altitude the sky seemed to be filled with fighters. I could see their wings flashing high above, almost everywhere I looked. Farther southeast, not far off the French coast yet, the bombers were coming. I mistook, them at first for an enormous black cloud.

I decided I had better get back to the advance base to rejoin the others, who would be collecting there after the fight we'd just had.

I had gone just a little way in the direction of our advance base, cruising along among the clouds, when right across in front of me flashed a Heinkel 113 again, just skimming the tops of the clouds. I opened up throttle and emergency throttle and turned after it. I didn't think the pilot had seen me, because he was higher than I. I guessed that it was one of the three I had just engaged, and looked back carefully but couldn't see the other two. Then I was getting close enough to open fire, and didn't look back for a moment.

Powp! Powp!!

The familiar sound of exploding cannon shells wracked my eardrums and my plane shook. Shrapnel banged and rattled and white tracers streamed by. For all my care, I had been surprised from behind by a second Hun!

I tried desperately to make a quick turn to evade him, but for some reason I didn't seem able to turn, and my plane was just going up in a gentle climb, straight ahead. The firing lasted only a second, but I expected it would start again. I was above the clouds just a little now, and I *must* get down into them for concealment!

I pushed ahead on the stick—that's how you make an airplane dive—but this time the stick just flopped limply all the way forward to the instrument panel, with no result. Elevator cables gone, I realised. Then I saw why I couldn't turn. My feet were pumping wildly back and forth on the rudder pedals and they were entirely loose too, and produced no response—rudder cables gone too!

This was bad. I could smell powder smoke, hot and strong, but it didn't make me feel tough this time. It was from the cannon shells and incendiary bullets that had hit my machine. Smoke from an incendiary bullet was curling up beside me. It was lodged in the frame of the machine and smouldering there.

My heart pounded and my mouth tasted salty, and I wondered if this was the end of the line. This was very bad.

I could still pull back on the stick and get response, but that didn't help because it made me go up and I wanted to go down, to get back to the safety of the clouds. If I could just get rolled over, I thought, my controls would work opposite and I should then be able to dive. The aileron controls on my wings seemed all right, and perhaps I could get rolled over. My attacker was off to one side of me, out of firing position, but I knew he would be back on my tail again in a moment. He had just overshot me and swung off to the side and would come back as soon as he could get behind me again. There might be a chance to get rolled over first, I thought, then down into the safety of the clouds below, and maybe I could land somehow.

First I jerked open the hatch over my cockpit, so that I could get away in a hurry if things didn't work out.

I had just done that when I was suddenly receiving a salvo from a third plane behind me—no doubt the other Heinkel. The din and confusion were awful inside the cockpit. I remember seeing some of the instrument panel breaking up, and holes dotting the gas tank in front of me.

Smoke trails of tracer bullets appeared right inside the cockpit. Bullets were going by between my legs, and I remember seeing the bright flash of an incendiary bullet going past my leg and into the gas tank.

I remember being surprised that I wasn't scared any more. I suppose I was too dazed. There was a finality about the salvo, and it lasted at least two or three seconds. Then there was a kind of silence.

I wondered if one of them was going to open up on me again.

A light glowed in the bottom of the fuselage, somewhere up in front. Then a little red tongue of flame licked out inquiringly from under the gas tank in front of my feet and curled up the side of it and became a hot little bonfire in one corner of the cockpit. I remembered my parachute, and jerked the locking pin that secured my seat straps, and started to climb out just as the whole cockpit became a furnace.

There was a fraction of a second of searing heat just as I was getting my head and shoulders out, then I was jerked and dragged the rest of the way out with terrible roughness and flung down the side of the fuselage and away all in a fraction of a second by the force of the two hundred-mile-an-hour wind that caught me. Then I was falling and reaching for my rip-cord and pulling it. A moment of suspense, and then a heavy pull that stopped my fall and there I hung, quite safe if not sound.

I was surprised at how nice and substantial the parachute felt. Everything was calm and quiet, and it was hard to realise that I was only a few seconds out of a battle.

Looking myself over I found that I was even less to look at than usual. I was aching all over, but it appeared to be mostly from bruises that I received from being dragged out of the cockpit so quickly. One of my trouser legs was torn and burned completely off, and my bare leg, which couldn't be called attractive at best, was anything but pretty now. It was bruised and skinned in a dozen places, and there was a sizable burned area around my ankle where the skin hung loosely.

But I could find no bullet wounds. Bruises and burns only—my right hand and the right side of my face were burned too. But it felt so good to be alive after what my prospects were a few moments before that I didn't mind the aches and pains.

I sighed and said aloud, feeling that the occasion demanded some recognition, "Well, Art, this is what you asked for. How do you like it?"

But I was still in for one of the worst scares of my young life.

It was perhaps a minute or more after I bailed out. I was down under the clouds now. The sound of an airplane gliding came to me and I wondered what its nationality was. I couldn't look up, because of the way my parachute harness held me, and I couldn't see it. I knew that in the Polish campaign some Nazi pilots often machine-gunned Polish pilots who were coming down in parachutes, and I had a little moment of anxiety. Then my anxiety was changed to panic.

A *staccato* burst of shots sounded, and *my parachute canopy quivered with each shot!* It lasted for perhaps a second. I could think of nothing but that a Hun was firing at me and hitting my parachute canopy. I knew that if I pulled the shroud lines on one side it would partly collapse the canopy and I would fall faster, so I just went hand over hand up the shroud lines on one side until the canopy was two-thirds collapsed—I wasn't taking any halfway measures!

That changed my position so I was looking up and could see the canopy, and I was surprised that there didn't seem to be any bullet holes in it. Then another volley sounded and the canopy quivered in the same way, and still no bullet holes appeared in it.

Then I looked downward and discovered where the shots came from. Smoke was drifting away from an anti-aircraft battery on the ground beneath me! They must have been firing at an airplane somewhere overhead, and the concussions made my canopy quiver. I can laugh at it now, but it was really one of the worst moments of panic I've ever had.

I landed in a little oat field near a group of soldiers, who held their rifles ready as they approached, until I stood up and they could see the remnants of my R.A.F. uniform. They started to escort me to their quarters; when I was halfway there my left knee began to give out, and they carried me the rest of the way. That was the last I walked for three weeks.

They gave me first aid in their quarters, and the boy who worked on me gave me a shock. "You'll get about a six weeks lay-up out of this, sir," he speculated.

"Don't be silly!" I said. "This won't keep me laid up more than two or three days, will it?"

"Well, you've got a couple pretty nasty burns there on your leg and your hand. The one on your face isn't so bad, but the other two ought to take a month to heal. Then you'll get a spot of 'sick leave' of course—yes, I'd make it all of six weeks before you're all fit again."

This was something, I realised. I had expected they'd bandage up my hand and leg and give me forty-eight hours off and tell me to be careful for a day or two—that is, if they were worth bandaging at all!

Several Tommies were in the room watching the proceedings and talking and joking with me. One of them left and came back after a couple minutes with a flask of whisky.

"You want to appreciate this, sir," he counselled. "It isn't every day that a Scotsman will give you good Scotch whisky!"

After a time an ambulance came. I climbed off the cot I was lying on, onto a stretcher that they laid beside it, and they put me aboard. I was taken to a near-by village where they parked me awhile, and then put me into another ambulance that drove for a long time before we got to a little hospital where I was unloaded and put to bed.

The head doctor, an Army captain, looked me over and said that he would have to cut away the skin from the burned areas; and so a cot on wheels was brought in by my bed and I climbed onto it and was taken into the operating room. A nurse pricked a needle into my arm, and then the lights faded. When I awoke I was back in my bed again.

The official British Air Ministry Communiqué issued early on the morning of August 13, 1940, stated:

> It is now established that sixty-one enemy aircraft were destroyed in yesterday's air fight over our coasts. Thirteen of our fighters were lost, but the pilot of one of them was saved.

Chapter 6

Recovery

I found that all my burned spots were covered with some black dope, and the nurses told me that it was a new type of treatment that didn't leave any permanent scars.

There were three German pilots in another wing of the hospital who had been taken prisoner that evening, who all had burns also. When they found themselves painted with this stuff they raised an awful row, and the nurses and doctor had quite a time reassuring them that it was to heal them, and not to mark them for life! They kept putting more of it on my burns as fast as it would dry, until finally a sort of tough black scab was formed by it over each burn.

My hand and wrist gave me the most trouble, as my forearm, hand, and fingers swelled way up after a day or so and became terribly tender. Even the blood circulation made them throb, and the only way I could keep the pain under control was to have my hand propped way up high and hold it perfectly still. If I allowed my arm to rest down level, the increased blood pressure made it unbearable. The slightest quick movement caused an agony of aching, as did any quickening of the pulse—caused, for instance, by the sight of a good-looking nurse.

There was nothing for me to do but let nature take its course, so I lay as still as I could, counting the hours that went to make up each day. They treated me so well that I actually felt spoiled, though. This was a newly established hospital, readied for the expected invasion of England, and I was the first British casualty they had received. All the previous patients they'd had were captured German airmen.

This hospital was near Canterbury, not far back from the southeast coast, and the big mass air raids which the Nazis were launching usually passed overhead or somewhere near. On the average there were one or two every day that we could hear.

At first the sound would be like a distant storm approaching—just a heavy, distant murmuring and rumbling that gradually grew louder. It still sounded like a great wind approaching until finally as it was getting quite distinct little individual sounds would separate themselves from the rest. The smooth high-pitched moan of a Messerschmitt in a power dive would rise above the rest of the sound momentarily, echoed by the sound of another doing likewise a few seconds later.

About that time we would begin to hear the barking of distant anti-aircraft guns and the sound of their shells exploding. Then as the great storm came closer the guns near by would take up the chorus, barking fast and savagely. Then the raiders would be passing overhead with a tremendous convulsion of sound.

Sometimes they were being intercepted by our fighters already, and then we would hear vicious, cascading staccato roars from the guns of Spitfires and Hurricanes, interspersed with the banging of the cannons on Messerschmitt and Heinkel fighters—terrific outbursts of agonised whining from enemy Daimler-Benz engines in power dives mingled with the throaty *rhoom-rhoom-rhoom* of the Rolls Royces on our own fighters as they milled about; and sometimes the noise of one would rise to an ear-splitting pitch as a stricken machine came diving down to destruction.

The nurses would stand by the windows watching and telling what they saw, and whenever they saw a machine come down they would tell me whether it looked like a bomber or a fighter and whether they thought it was "one of ours" or "one of theirs."

For the next half-hour after a raid had passed over going inland there would usually be intermittent activity overhead—individual planes passing over that got separated from their formations, scattered planes from broken formations, damaged Nazis making for home, etc. Sometimes there was a quick burst of machine-gun fire as a fighter surprised an enemy.

More than once I heard a Messerschmitt being surprised overhead. Their Daimler-Benz engines make a low humming sound when they're cruising, but when the pilots open them up quickly or dive them they make an unearthly moaning whine, about the pitch of an angry hornet.

I would be listening to the humming of a Daimler-Benz cruising, and the *rhoom-rhoom* of a Rolls Royce turning pretty fast: and all at once there would be the roar of guns from a Spitfire or Hurricane. That would be answered instantly by the quick crescendo of the Daimler-Benz changing from its normal cruising right up the scale to its most agonised whine, over the space of about a second, as the surprised Nazi pilot "pushed everything forward" and opened up with every ounce of his engine's power to get away. The response was similar to that you get from stepping on the tail of a cat.

Perhaps fifteen minutes or half an hour after passing inland the main body of the raid would come back on its way home. Usually the enemy were pretty badly disorganized by this time, and somewhat reduced in number. Most often there wouldn't be one big formation any more, just lots of scattered smaller ones, the pilots scared and shaken and flying with their engines wide open, and being harried by our fighters all the way.

After things had quieted down the nurses often picked up a few empty cartridge cases on the lawn outside—ejected from the machine guns of fighters overhead.

Thursday of that week was August 15th, one of the days when the air fighting reached its peak. There was almost constant activity overhead all day. I hadn't slept well the night before and dozed a good share of the afternoon. I wasn't bothered much by pain now. My arm and hand were just as swollen and tender, but I'd learned to keep from moving them and had them propped up high. I was sleeping lightly, and I suppose the constant sound of airplanes passing overhead caused me to dream that I was flying again and on patrol. I seemed to be separated from my formation and cruising along looking for them.

Just then a Messerschmitt opened fire somewhere over the hospital—at a British plane, I suppose—with his cannon and machine guns. In my dream I suddenly saw a Messerschmitt behind me, and the firing was coming from him. Tracers were converging on my cockpit, and cannon shells exploding in my fuselage, and I grabbed wildly for the controls trying to throw my Spitfire into an evasive turn.

The dream came to an abrupt end, and I found myself half out of bed, grabbing at empty air, and conscious of about the most intense agony in my outraged hand and arm and fingers that I have ever experienced! It made me dizzy, and I cried out a little; and the pain continued quite intense even after I got settled back and had my arm where it belonged again, because my heart kept pounding for a while. It was so ridiculous that I had to laugh even while it was still paining; and Nurse Green, who heard me cry out, came in and found me half laughing and half sobbing from pain and weakness—I was very weak from shock at this time. The pain quieted down finally, and I dropped off to sleep again only to have the same thing happen again about half an hour later. After that I was afraid to let myself sleep during an air raid until my hand was better.

After about ten days I was moved to a beautiful mansion near Maidstone that had been turned into a convalescent station for officers. More pilots kept coming in here, one every day or two, so we got fresh news on how the fight actually was going. They all said the same thing: that the pilots were tired and the squadrons at times decimated, but that the morale of the pilots was good and they were shooting down a terrific number of German machines. The Nazi pilots in the mass raids seemed to be very poorly trained for the most part, and scared to death. They all said that they thought the R.A.F. would be able to hold out if the raids didn't get a lot heavier.

My leg finally got well enough for me to walk outside and watch the air fighting from the lawns of the mansion. Most of the actual fighting was too high to see, but we often saw stricken machines coming down.

Sometimes a machine would dive straight all the way in and we could hear it before it was within sight, coming with an unearthly scream just like that of a big shell, caused by the wind from its terrific speed. A fighter will reach nearly seven hundred miles per hour in a vertical dive. It seems that the Messerschmitts, when the pilot is hit, usually roll over and drop off into a vertical dive which they maintain all the way down. I saw at least three or four go in that way while I was at this place.

They came down in other ways, too. Sometimes they would tailspin down, spinning terribly fast, almost like a top. Sometimes they came down in flames, turning and twisting as they dropped, their bodies wrapped in bright flames and black smoke billowing out and leaving a long ominous trail behind. Often, too, they just came in for a forced landing, with wrecked engines or punctured radiators or both, usually leaving a long white trail of steam and glycol behind them.

Although the fighters were usually too high to see when they came over, the bombers often were low enough, and we would cheer or boo the local antiaircraft guns as they succeeded or failed in getting close to the enemy, as indicated by the puffs of smoke from their exploding shells.

One day some of us rode out to a farm where a Messerschmitt had dived in the day before. It was in a stubble field. There was a hole about six feet across and fifteen feet deep, but the only signs of the airplane were some fragments of the wings on the ground outside the hole. The fuselage, or body, of the machine was farther down, the guards told us, and dirt from the sides of the hole had filled in above it. They estimated that the engine was down about thirty feet! The pilot had bailed out of the machine, so they probably wouldn't bother to dig it up.

Looking down into the hole, and speculating on the violence that would cause it to be made in a split second, I thought, "It's a vicious war, all right!"

I hadn't heard from my squadron in all this time since I was shot down. I knew that the boys would come to see me if they could, but under the strain of the terrific fighting they wouldn't have time. Our squadron had had little rest even before this blitzkrieg began. They had had hard fighting all summer, having taken part in the Dunkirk battles and in the frequent clashes over ship convoys in the Channel.

I finally received a letter from our C.O. The first lines gratified me, for they related that the squadron had been moved out of the fighting zone for a rest.

He touched just a little on what they had been through after I was out of it. "They came over by the hundred, and we fought them as long as hearts and nerves could stand it!"

I wondered which of the brave lads I knew in the squadron had fought their last battles. He didn't say in the letter; and I felt rotten because I had had to desert them in their toughest trial.

I felt proud, though, because a man who had daily gone up to do deeds more heroic than any ocean flight had remembered to write and wish me well.

I was finally released from the hospital in mid-September and was given two weeks "sick leave" to rest up before rejoining the squadron.

CHAPTER 7

Back to Work

The first thing I did was to visit the airdrome where the squadron was stationed when I was with them before, to get my belongings. I had some misgivings because I knew the place had been bombed; but I found that the officers' mess was only slightly damaged and my belongings were all right. My batman had kept them put away for me.

The station commander and other station personnel greeted me warmly, and it was almost like being home again. I met two pilots whom I had trained with, and who were in another squadron which was now based here. They were having lots of fighting, always against tremendous odds, but were cheerful and happy-go-lucky as ever. (One of them was killed just a few days later.)

There had been a big battle right over this airdrome the day before, and I talked to a Spitfire pilot who had collided with a Hurricane in the melee and had been thrown clear of the wreckage and got down by parachute, unhurt. The wreckage of the two machines collided with a Dornier bomber on the way down and the Dornier had crashed with all its crew, all three machines ending up close together right near the airdrome. He was the only survivor of the three machines, the Hurricane pilot having been killed too.

What a battle *that* must have been!

I wanted to do some shopping and see some sights, so I went to London and took a room in a lodging house, planning to spend most of my leave there. This was a mistake, and I didn't stay long. This was when London was "getting it" at the worst. In the daytime it was all right. Although the mass day raids were being launched frequently, they seldom got over London in any numbers, and when the warning siren blew people just kept watch on the sky, ready to take shelter if enemy planes came overhead—which was very infrequent.

But at night! Well, the first night was far from over before I was convinced that a change in my schedule was in order, as regarded staying in London.

I got along fine for the first few hours of darkness. The sirens sounded shortly after dusk, announcing that the first of the night raiders were approaching; and most of the other lodgers went down cellar to sleep on temporary cots. I displayed my courage (?) by joining the minority who slept in their rooms upstairs, but first I took a walk outside to watch the show. I could hear German planes droning overhead, and there was continuous barking from the anti-aircraft guns scattered about the city, echoed by the distant, eerie *whoompf* of the shells exploding high above. Far up among the stars the exploding shells appeared as little silent red flashes winking about first one point then another in space, where enemy planes were located. No searchlights were on.

No bombs appeared to be dropping anywhere. From the sound there seemed to be at least a dozen Huns over the city, scattered about, but they just seemed to be droning around aimlessly. There were few people on the darkened streets and very few cars about. What people I met were mostly wearing helmets, and I began to feel a little self-conscious without mine. Once in a while I'd hear a little humming noise followed by the noise of something small and metallic dropping near by. These were the little pieces of shrapnel falling, from shells that had exploded overhead. I knew the shrapnel wasn't likely to injure me, as the pieces are small and don't fall very fast; but one of them could give me a good bump if it hit me on the head when I didn't have a helmet, so I soon went back to my room and retired. Few noises bother me, and I got to sleep all right in spite of the gunfire.

About midnight I was suddenly awakened by a distant sound like steam escaping from a radiator. It was a ghostly sort of noise, like something slipping through the air in the distance at great speed, and it was rising in intensity. In perhaps four or five seconds it rose to a noise like that of a locomotive letting off steam close by, and then to a fiendish shriek, ending in a heavy explosion not far away, that shook the building.

I had heard a big bomb falling for my first time! In the last second it had seemed to be coming straight for the house, and after it was over I found my heart pounding and my courage taking flight.

That was the start. It kept up for about an hour, during which I alternately tried burying my head under the covers so that I couldn't hear the bombs so plainly, and then straightening out and calling myself a coward and trying to ignore them, so that I could sleep. Neither method worked.

There was a bomb every two or three minutes on the average. They made various sounds. Sometimes they fell with a long wailing sound, like an American fire siren. Sometimes it was a whistle building to a crescendo; but when they were close it usually sounded like a locomotive passing overhead and letting off steam. Sometimes there would be a "stick" of four or five in a row—the entire load from one machine being dropped at once. None landed really close, but each sounded, before it hit, as if it were aimed for a point midway between the washbowl in one corner of my room and the suitcase under my bed.

Occasionally there was the *ding-dong-ding-dong* of a fire engine as it rushed through the empty streets to some place that had been hit. The anti-aircraft fire was almost continuous, and there were terrific outbursts of barking from the guns near by whenever a Hun got close overhead—which was pretty often. I got to listening to the droning and feeling comforted whenever it got distant; only to be that much more alarmed and tensed when it grew close again.

I tried the old saying on myself that "cowards die a thousand times and brave men die but once"; but it didn't do any good—I was too willing to admit I was a coward! I tried figuring out how tiny was the chance of being hit by a bomb, and that would quiet my fears a little for a minute or so—and then I'd hear another bomb coming down!

I'd have been exhausted if the bombing hadn't ceased after about an hour. Then I went back to sleep only to be awakened again at about four a.m. and kept on nerves' edge for another half-hour or so by some more of the performance.

The "all clear" sounded with the first light of dawn, and it was a heavenly sound. I sank gratefully into a long sound sleep.

I had some shopping and business that I had to take care of, so I stayed one more day. Going downtown I found that several big stores on Oxford Street, the shopping centre, had been hit during the night. I think there were some pictures published in America of the bomb damage there. I saw dozens of salesgirls and clerks out on the sidewalks and street, sweeping up broken glass and splinters while firemen were playing streams of water on partially burned buildings that were still smouldering.

That night I didn't get much sleep either and the next day I bought a railway ticket to Plymouth, on the southwest coast of England. That is a famous resort country, and I had the addresses of some friends there; so I went out to spend a quiet week end and see a little of England. There had been practically no bombing there, and Saturday afternoon when there was an air-raid warning I was astonished to see everyone take to shelters. They weren't used to it like the Londoners—yet. I had an enjoyable week end there and then visited another friend who lived near Southampton and that way I got to see quite a bit of southern England.

I had left most of my belongings in my rooming house in London, so when I arrived back from my tour early one morning I went directly there. It wasn't far from the railway station, and I walked. About two blocks from the place I found the street roped off, and farther down, across the street from my destination, parts of the buildings were in ruins. Wrecking crews were already at work, and there was the familiar tinkling sound of broken glass being swept up. A "stick" of four bombs had landed in a row on the buildings right across the street from my room, just before daylight that morning! When I went up to my room I found a workman replacing broken windows.

That was enough for me. I decided to spend the rest of my leave with my squadron at their station.

There was a joke going the rounds about that time that applied quite nicely. In England if not in America, would-be slackers in time of war sometimes got a white feather pinned on them as a sign of cowardice. The joke then was about a London boy who left London to join the army, and had a white feather pinned on him. I was in his class; I was returning to my squadron rather than stay in London, which was the real danger zone at that time. I had learned not to mind being shot at, very much, but I couldn't get used to bombing!

Often during my leave I met other R.A.F. officers who turned out to be fighter pilots—riding on the train, walking about London, or in restaurants; and we naturally would fall into a conversation in which each asked the other what squadron he belonged to. When I mentioned the name of my squadron the other would often reply with recognition, "Oh, ——— Squadron? Oh, yes! They were down at ——— all summer, weren't they? Got knocked about pretty badly too, didn't they?"

And I would reply: "Yes, that's right. Yes, they lost most of their original pilots—about half of them over Dunkirk alone. They're up north resting now, and training in some new pilots."

I found that my squadron had built up a high reputation, though at a heartbreaking price.

I rejoined my squadron several days before my leave expired, feeling like a prodigal son and wondering if I'd be remembered; and was so warmly received I almost wanted to cry. There were many new faces, and I found the new boys to be a fine bunch, easy to get along with.

I learned that the heroism of some of the boys hadn't gone unrecognized. Three Distinguished Flying Crosses and one Distinguished Flying Medal had gone to the squadron. Our C.O. had been awarded the Distinguished Flying Cross and there was talk that he might get a bar added to it. He had ten confirmed victories as well as several probables. "Orange," who had six confirmed victories, and Willie, who had four confirmed, also had received the D.F.C. Andy, who had four confirmed, received the Distinguished Flying Medal instead of the Cross, because he was a flight sergeant and not a commissioned officer at the time, and the D.F.C. is awarded only to commissioned officers. He had worked up from the ranks to become an exceptional fighter pilot. He had just been awarded a commission as pilot officer but wasn't living in the officers' mess yet because he hadn't yet purchased his uniform.

The squadron was resting at this airdrome in the east central part of England, too far north for enemy fighters to come. There was very little to do, just an occasional chase after some lone bomber sneaking over in the clouds in bad weather.

There is little danger in attacking German bombers, because they only have two or three machine guns to protect themselves from any one quarter at the most, as compared to our eight. And there is no nerve strain in hunting for them in country where enemy fighters can't operate, because you don't have to be alert against being attacked yourself. The enemy's twin-engined long-range Messerschmitt fighters, the 110's, could probably come this far, but we consider them next to harmless as they are very easy to shoot down. The little Messerschmitt 109's, which are Germany's standard fighter, seldom came beyond the centre of London, when they came that far.

The boys ate enormous meals, did practice flights occasionally, and rested up for the day when they would be sent back into the blitz which was still raging almost daily over London and southeast England.

I wasn't supposed to fly until the two weeks of my sick leave expired, so I got in a lot of good conscientious loafing. Finally my time was up, and after being checked out and O.K.'d by the squadron's doctor I went out on the field one morning and made my first flight in over six weeks. It was a grand thrill.

That night Andy appeared in the officers' mess for the first time, wearing his new uniform as an officer, with the pretty, striped purple and white silk ribbon of his Distinguished Flying Medal looking very neat under his wings on the left side of his chest. If any one deserved a commission and the right to wear the King's uniform, he did. He had been a mainstay of the squadron all through from the time of Dunkirk, acting as leader of the squadron's rear-guard section most of the time, often with pilots of higher rank following him in his section; and he had certainly "served his King and Country well."

We were all glad afterward that he got to spend that evening in the mess, and I'm glad that I spent a pleasant hour with him in his room before we went to bed, chatting with him about America, in which he was very interested, and lending him some American magazines. We arranged that the next morning Percy, a new pilot, and I would fly with him in a section of three machines to a target range where we would do some aerial target practice.

Next morning Andy had to give a group of new pilots some practice flying before we went to the target range; so as I was badly in need of some practice too I went for a little cross-country jaunt in my machine, familiarising myself with our present sector of operations.

While I was up I could hear distant voices over the R/T which I knew were those of Andy and the pilots he was flying with. When I heard them plainly I could tell it was usually Andy giving one of the others some order, or coaching them on their flying. I didn't pay much attention to what was being said, but I noticed that when I was returning to the airdrome Control seemed to be calling "Yellow One" and having difficulty in getting a reply. Each section has a colour designating it for convenience, and each member of the section has a number, depending on his position in it. "Yellow One" would be the leader of Yellow section; but as there were one or two other sections flying also and I hadn't paid attention to what colours they were calling themselves today, I didn't know who Yellow One was. I assumed that whoever was leading Yellow section was having trouble with his R/T.

The leader of Yellow section was Andy, and he wasn't having trouble with his R/T. Percy ran out to meet me as I taxied in, and with agonized face told me, "Andy and Nels have collided and Andy's 'gone in,' and it looks like there isn't much hope!"

There wasn't. After half an hour's dumb sad waiting around the telephone in our pilots' hut we heard the story. His tail had been sheared off and his machine had gone all the way down, tumbling over and over, and for some reason he hadn't bailed out. Nels had managed to land safely at another airdrome, as his machine wasn't badly damaged.

Just another little sacrifice among the many thousands to curb one man's savage desire for power, of course; but I think for most of us in the squadron the loss of Andy was one of the most painful we'd had to bear.

CHAPTER 8

Impatience

The day we were waiting for, when we could go back to front-line fighting, was a long time coming. Occasionally an order would come through posting one of our new pilots to one of the squadrons that were in the blitz and replacing him with a new pilot for us to train up. Then there would be a lot of good-byes and well-wishes to the boy who was off for the front, including the oft-repeated counsel to "watch your tail and keep your rear vision mirror polished."

But though we grew more and more impatient to get back into the fray no orders came for the squadron to move. I was particularly anxious to get back and even things up for my own defeat. I had no confirmed victories before being shot down myself, and as I told my friends I hated to go about with a score of minus one to my credit

The great squadron of all Polish pilots and ground personnel joined us, having been sent up here to rest also. They had gotten 126 confirmed victories in less than six weeks, which I believe is a record for any R.A.F. squadron in that length of time. They fought savagely, for their pilots had nothing to lose. Most of them had seen so much of murder and terror and tragedy among their people before they escaped from Poland that they didn't care to live. One night I traded one of my uniform buttons with one of their ace pilots, for one of his, and I still wear it and am very proud of it.

Gilly told me a great deal of how the squadron fared after I was shot down in August, for the rest of the time that they remained in the blitz. The day after I was downed had been pretty bad. He was leading the squadron's rear-guard section on a patrol when they were sent to break up a raid that was forming up over Cape Gris Nez on the French coast. The squadron had sighted sixty Messerschmitts and turned to sail into them, and Gilly's section happened to be on the outside of the turn because of their rear-guard manoeuvres, with the result that they got left quite a way behind.

And then the three of them were attacked from behind by nearly fifty Messerschmitts. Gilly alone of the three in his section got back. He shot down one Messerschmitt off Bud's tail, but Bud was already going down in flames, and then his own machine was being riddled from behind, by another Messerschmitt. Steam blinded him so he couldn't see, and he had to open his hatch, unfasten his straps, and stand up to see out; and that way he flew all the way back across the Channel with this Messerschmitt following him and shooting at him, so that he had to keep twisting violently one way then the other, all the time.

Somehow his wrecked engine managed to keep going until just before he reached the coast, when it seized up, out of oil and with radiator dry of course, and he made a forced landing on the belly of his machine with the wheels retracted. The Messerschmitt pilot had exhausted his ammunition by the time Gilly's engine stopped, and he gave up the chase. Gilly's machine was riddled with bullets and completely ruined.

A day or two later Mann got a bullet in his hip and his machine badly damaged, but he managed to fly back to the airdrome. He was still in the hospital and was expected to be laid up for several months. The C.O. had his machine shot down in flames on one of those days, and he bailed out unhurt, although when he landed in his parachute in a small village he had a hard time convincing the residents that he wasn't a German spy who should be shot.

The climax of the week's events was the raid on the squadron's own airdrome. They were on patrol right over the airdrome, trying to intercept a German formation at twenty-five thousand feet, when another big formation of bombers attacked the airdrome from low altitude. The squadron dived straight down at more than six hundred miles per hour and sailed into the bombers. Altogether they shot down ten bombers with no casualties to themselves.

Gilly got one of them, a Heinkel. He got it away from its formation and the pilot must have been pretty good, for when Gilly attacked he did all sorts of acrobatics with the big machine to evade him. Gilly followed, shooting whenever he got a chance, and finally caught him in a stalled turn and gave him a good long burst that finished him, and the Heinkel turned over and dived straight down in from about five thousand feet, bursting into flames when it hit.

Other squadrons that joined the fight shot down eighteen German planes and the ground defences got two, which with the ten our squadron got made a total of thirty machines and crews that the raid cost the *Luftwaffe*.

Considering that only a small amount of damage was done by the bombing it was quite a victory for the R.A.F. However, it very nearly finished the frazzled nerves of some of the boys of our squadron, and that night the grateful news came that they were to pack up and move to this place in the north next day.

Early in October we were ordered to move to a base farther south, which though not yet in the blitz area was nevertheless quite close to it, and there was a lot more activity by hit-and-run bombers. An outside factor unfortunately interfered just then and kept me out of the squadron and in idleness for the first two weeks, but I finally got back with them again and started doing my share of the work. The bombers were coming over individually and trying all sorts of tricks to get us sidetracked long enough to get through and bomb a city or harbour in our area. Often they came over very high, carrying only small bomb loads. The whole squadron was seldom sent up at once, but there were many patrols by sections of three.

Have you ever made clouds? I have. It was on these patrols that I first made them and became acquainted with the strangest, weirdest, and most beautiful phenomenon that I have encountered in flying. They are generally called "vapour trails" by pilots, and the phenomenon usually occurs only in the thin cold air at high altitudes, although I have seen it as low as eight thousand feet in the winter. I had seen these trails a few times in the summer, when fighters were flying at thirty or thirty-five thousand feet overhead, appearing as thin white lines curving about the sky overhead. Now in the fall the air was cold enough for trails to be made sometimes as low as twenty thousand feet.

I understand that the wings and propeller of a high-speed airplane rushing through the air cause sudden changes in the air pressure in its path, so that moisture in the air condenses into cloud and the condensed droplets then freeze instantly, before they have time to evaporate again.

Whatever be the cause, the effect is the weirdest thing imaginable. As a formation of planes enters the altitude at which vaporization begins to take place, each pilot begins to notice what seem like wisps of white smoke streaming back from the tails of the other machines.

When they have climbed a little bit higher these become good-sized clouds billowing back, about the size of the cloud of dust that a car rolls up when moving fast on a dusty road, though of course streaming back several times as fast. Indeed, the pilot's view in the rear vision mirror of his machine while he is "vaporising" is just like what you get looking in the rear vision mirror of your car when billowing clouds of dust behind you obscure everything else in your mirror.

As a rule these trails stay put for an hour or so, recording in the sky the tracks of the planes that have been there and gone, until they gradually widen out and diffuse themselves in the atmosphere. From the ground the machines, when they are vaporising, look like invisible paintbrushes drawing silvery white lines across the blue dome of the sky, slowly and majestically; for the planes are too high to be seen themselves usually, and because of the distance the movement seems to be very slow.

To sit on the ground watching the trails made by, say, a section of three planes of your own squadron on patrol, and try to realise that at the head of each silver line curving across the sky five or six miles overhead is a pal who was sitting beside you in the pilots' hut a half-hour before, is in my belief to stretch the imagination beyond its capacity. It's certainly beyond mine! And it's interesting too, to land after having flown high overhead, and to look up and see your own track inscribed up there in the sky.

One bright sunny morning three of us were up on patrol, trying to find a bandit which was reported approaching the coast at a point in our area, and we headed out over the sea. We were at about twenty thousand feet, which is not in the stratosphere, but is so high that the sky is a more intense blue and the sun brighter and everything more frigid and wintry-looking. I had been engrossed for a moment checking my instruments and closing my radiator shutter, because it was very cold up there and my engine was beginning to run too cold. Glancing up, I noticed, emblazoned in the sky far above and ahead of us, something that I could only imagine at first as being a comet. It was a little patch of brilliant silver against the blue, in the exact shape of a comet, awe-inspiring in the weird stratosphere, and it nearly scared me out of my wits.

Then reason came back, and after making a quick estimate of its height and position I called over the R/T to our formation leader, "Bandit ahead and to starboard! He's about thirty thousand feet and making a very short vapour trail!"

We opened throttle and gave chase, but after a minute the trail disappeared, and as we were too far away to see the airplane itself we of course lost it. Its pilot had apparently observed that he was making this trail and had dived to a lower altitude where it quit forming. Apparently the atmospheric conditions at his altitude were such that the cloud formation made by his machine evaporated and became invisible again after a split second, so that his visible trail remained only a few hundred feet long and took on the appearance of a comet. That was the first *short* vapour trail I had seen, although I've seen many since.

While at this place we got a good demonstration of the intelligence and initiative of Nazi bombing pilots one morning. This was a big airdrome and should have been an ideal bombing target, for there were dozens of big military buildings built close together—enormous hangars, shops, office buildings, big permanent barracks and messes, and dozens of houses for "married quarters." On an airdrome of this kind nearly two thousand men are required. It wasn't much over a hundred miles from the nearest German air base in Holland, yet not a single building had been hit by bombing so far, though I understand that the Nazi news dispatches had had it completely wiped out twice and badly damaged several times in addition.

One morning three of us who were on "dawn readiness" had just finished our early breakfast and were walking out of the officers' mess toward the car we would drive to the dispersal hut when we heard the droning of strange engines near by that resembled the sound of Daimler-Benz engines too much for comfort. It was in the quarter-light before dawn, and the stars were beginning to disappear.

Out of the east and not over two thousand feet up we saw the majestic outlines of a big Heinkel bomber coming directly overhead. If the pilot had released his bombs just then he couldn't have helped scoring hits on our hangars or other buildings, or on us. We waited expectantly, ready to throw ourselves on the ground, but no bombs came, and we gazed almost thunderstruck as the big machine sailed serenely on over. The crew couldn't possibly have helped seeing the buildings of the airdrome as they passed over.

Cosmer, our flight commander, shouted: "Come on! He's going to turn around and make his 'bombing run' coming back! Let's get down to our machines as quick as we can!"

Stan, who was driving, kept one hand on the horn button, and the guards threw aside barbed wire and other barricades in advance of us as we raced through the camp and out across the field. Cosmer was raging and calling the Hun names. The thought of having our airdrome bombed maddened all of us.

"The lousy ———!" he kept repeating. "He's going to bomb us for sure! Oh, why weren't we up five minutes earlier and down by our machines now?" He was on his knees on the back seat of the careening car, looking out the back window.

All at once he shouted: "Look! He's dropping 'em now!" Then, in a puzzled tone, "I wonder where that is?"

Great terrifying yellow splashes of light were flickering against the dim blue sky just above the horizon, seemingly four or five miles west of us, several of them in succession; and after they ceased a lurid yellow glow remained.

"Oh, he's started a fire too!" Cosmer was almost crying with rage. "Come on, let's get in our machines and get off as quick as we can!"

We were at the pilots' hut now, and we dashed in and grabbed our helmets and parachutes. There was no time to bother with flying suits. Mechanics seeing our car racing across the field had already started up three machines for us, and we were air-borne in no time; but we found no trace of the Hun, who had apparently headed out to sea and homeward as soon as he dropped his load. Neither could we find the spot which he had bombed, though after we gave up the chase we circled the area where the flashes had seemed to come from. There wasn't any fire to be seen either. There was a little village, but we could see no signs of damage in it.

An hour later we learned that the bombs had been aimed at the little village, though for what possible reason the pilot preferred a harmless little country village to a big military airdrome I don't know. Fortunately his aim was terrible considering how low he was, and all the bombs landed in an open field near by. The yellow glow we had seen after the bombs had finished exploding, and which we thought was a fire that had been started, was merely from a bunch of incendiary bombs he had dropped along with the big ones. They were burning away harmlessly in the field.

The only explanation that we could imagine for it all was that the pilot didn't notice our airdrome until he was too far over it to drop his bombs, and then he didn't have nerve enough to come back again and take a crack at us. So he just dumped his bombs in the direction of the village and beat it, probably returning home to tell his superiors about "direct hits on hangars, fuel depots, and ammunition dumps."

That seems to be a popular rhyme in Nazi war *communiqués*.

Just after we got back from that chase another section was sent off to hunt two bandits that were reported over the sea near the coast. One of the pilots of this section had trouble getting his machine started and didn't take off until the others were out of sight. He was a Free French pilot, whom we called "Chin."

The other two machines returned after about half an hour, having had no luck; but there was no sign of Chin. We began to worry. He hadn't joined up with the other two at all, and hadn't been heard from after he took off. Soon, however, we saw another Spitfire coming in and began to relax a little.

It was Chin's machine all right, and when he landed he seemed to have some trouble taxiing. Then we saw that one of his tires was flat. When he got closer to us we could also see that his guns had been fired, because the fabric covers over the holes in the wings in front of the guns were shot away. He was grinning from ear to ear as he climbed out of his machine, and in his halting English told us the story of the squadron's first action in several weeks.

He had gone out to sea in the direction that the other two planes had taken, hoping to find them and join up with them. Instead, after searching around for about twenty minutes he found two twin-engined Heinkel 115 German seaplanes flying low over the water together. He attacked, and in the running fight which followed he shot one of them down and got a few bullets in his own machine, one of them puncturing his tire.

This sort of life was of course occasionally exciting, but it seemed dull to us, with our hearts set on getting back into the front-line fighting. We began to get quite well settled, learned our way to and from all the local pubs in the black-out, got acquainted with the local townspeople, and so on.

One day I received a registered letter in the mail, containing a little jewel case. In it was a little solid gold badge in the shape of a caterpillar about an inch long, with an inscription engraved in very tiny letters on the back—a souvenir of my "party" on August 12. It is the emblem of the Caterpillar Club, to which anyone is eligible who has saved his life by a parachute. The idea is that caterpillars make the silk from which the parachutes are made. It came from the Irving Company, makers of parachutes.

October ended and the great "Battle for Britain" seemed to be abating considerably according to the news, and still we were not moved into the front-line fighting. And then one day early in November it came! Forty-eight hours' notice for the squadron to move to ———, a famous airdrome on the outskirts of London! Jubilantly always, if occasionally a bit grimly, we bade goodbye to our friends and to our comparatively secure life here, and prepared to move back to the battle zone!

CHAPTER 9

Back to the Front Tally-Ho Again

The two days we were given were busy ones. It's always a big event when a squadron moves. While twelve pilots are all that fly in a squadron at one time, it also has its own personnel of mechanics and helpers who move with the squadron; its own office and staff, a hundred *per cent* reserve of pilots and a fifty *per cent* reserve of airplanes, as well as all sorts of equipment and spares. The total personnel is well over two hundred.

There was a lot of packing to do and there were lots of arrangements to make, particularly in regard to transportation. The order came on Friday. Saturday night some of us had a little farewell party with some friends in a nearby village, and Percy got tight for the first time in his life and was murmuring all the way home about wanting to get four Huns down before Christmas.

Next day we moved. That was the 10th of November. Three of our reserve airplanes were ready to go (there were six in reserve but the other three were undergoing maintenance) so we flew down as a squadron of fifteen instead of the regular twelve.

The station personnel at our new airdrome greeted us warmly. We were replacing a squadron which had been there through most of the blitz and were being moved up north to rest just as we had been in August.

With wisdom born of previous moves I made a bee line for the officers' mess as soon as I was free, and "signed in." The best rooms are first come first served, and I got a very nice double room for myself and Jonah, with whom I'd arranged to room. Jonah was going on leave shortly and was to get married, so he'd be living out most of the time; but he would want a place in the mess to keep his flying equipment and some of his clothes, and to sleep nights when he had to be on duty early in the morning.

I was particularly delighted because our room had a fireplace, for fireplaces are the English institution that I love most of all. (This was a very old station that had been established in the First World War, and in the entry to the mess there were on display pieces of Zeppelins that had been shot down by planes operating from here in 1915 and 1916.) There were also a couple of the most beautiful, coloured photos of Spitfires in flight, framed and hanging on the wall.

A second Spitfire squadron was stationed at this airdrome, and I found that their C.O. had been a roommate of mine in the hospital in August. In peacetime he had been a world-famous athlete.

Our first shift at readiness was to be from dawn to one o'clock the next day, which was Armistice Day—of all days to be going back into action!

I went to bed that night with mingled feelings of tenseness and fear, of course, and a kind of a fierce joy. From now on it would be playing for keeps again. Instead of hunting in threes after timid bombers and reconnaissance machines without having to guard against being attacked ourselves, we should now fly nearly always as a full squadron, hunting an enemy far superior in numbers who would also be hunting us and watching for a chance to attack us by surprise under circumstances favourable to hit-and-run tactics.

Because the only type of attack which the Nazi fighter pilots ever carry out against British fighters is by surprise, we had to fly in a type of formation that could guard itself well from surprises and be effective for attacking also. We were shown the newest type of formation used by the front-line squadrons, which while not spectacular was simple and very flexible.

Getting my machine ready next morning, I practically made a ceremony of changing the setting of my gun-sight—in my efforts to be nonchalant and unceremonious about it. These sights can be adjusted for the wing span of the type of plane you expect to be shooting at. As you move the adjustment, a gap in a line across the middle of the sight narrows or widens; and the wing span of whatever machine it's set for will just fill the gap when you are at the proper distance behind it to open fire.

Up north, where the enemy's fighters never came, I'd had it set for machines of seventy-foot wing span, for that's about the average span of the Heinkel, Junkers, and Dornier bombers that we hunted. Now I changed it to thirty-two and one-half feet, which is the span of the

HURDLING SQUADRON LEADER

The Squadron Leader who has represented Great Britain as a hurdler in the Olympics, with four of his pilots.

Messerschmitt 109 fighters.

I also gave my rear vision mirror an extra going over with my handkerchief. The memory of the month I'd spent in hospitals for not watching my mirror was still quite fresh in my mind.

This airdrome was equipped with a loud-speaker system, with speakers on all the buildings; and about nine o'clock a voice boomed over them: "—— Squadron take off. Patrol base at ten thousand feet!"

Three minutes later we were in the air and climbing in squadron formation to the altitude ordered. Further orders followed over the R/T; Control was trying to bring us into contact with some enemy planes that were approaching London. Finally in the distance south of and above us we saw, among some puffs of anti-aircraft smoke, several enemy fighters scurrying about, very tiny in the distance. We climbed after them and they turned back. We weren't able to catch them because they had the advantage in height and we lost speed in climbing; and after following them out to the east coast and part way across the Channel we were ordered back to land. It was a nice little exercise, giving the new members of the squadron a chance to see what the new area of operations looked like and giving the rest of us a chance to refresh our memories of it.

We had only been on the ground a short time when we were off again under orders to join another squadron and fly with them, the two squadrons together making a wing, with ourselves leading.

It sounded as if something big might be up. We picked up the other squadron at about ten thousand feet over the airdrome, and after they were in line behind us we started climbing. Then our controller's voice sounded in our headphones: "Steer towards Ramsgate and climb to twenty-five thousand feet."

Ramsgate is a town on the southeast coast, a few miles northeast of Dover. We climbed steeply and nearly wide open. It was a dark morning, with the sky covered by a high overcast. We entered the overcast at about eighteen thousand feet, and it proved to be sort of heavy haze, from which we emerged at about twenty-three thousand. About that time Control's voice came again with another order.

"In a couple of minutes I will give you a new course to steer that will lead you toward an objective. There are Junkers 87 and Messerschmitt 109 aircraft approaching this objective."

My heart began to pound as I switched on my gun-sight, removed the cover from my firing button, and turned the safety ring on the button to the position which read "Fire." The news that there were Junkers 87's involved filled me with anticipation. Those are the "*Stuka*" dive-bombers that were so terrible in their attacks on the armies in France. They hold no terrors for British fighter pilots, for they are the most vulnerable of all the standard German machines. Pilots who have been fortunate enough to engage them usually report that a two- or three-second burst of fire is all that's necessary to bring them down, and they are so slow and big that they are easy to hit. I'd never engaged anything but enemy fighters before, and the prospect of finding something easy was inviting.

Putting two and two together I guessed that our "objective" must be a ship convoy, and the Junkers 87's would be coming to dive-bomb it. The 87's got treated so badly whenever they came over England that the Nazis hardly ever used them now except against shipping. The Messerschmitts would be accompanying the Junkers 87's as an escort to protect them from our fighters.

A moment later we were ordered to steer a course of 45 degrees and lost height quickly to five thousand feet. We headed northeast and began diving at about a thirty-degree angle, back into the haze, and just then someone in the squadron called over the R/T, "Bandits ahead and above us!"

Sure enough, the queer little figures of about twenty Messerschmitt 109's were streaking towards us from in front, passing right over us and so close that we could easily make out details of their markings. It was almost like seeing old friends again. They were painted very dark gray, with their black crosses outlined in white so they could be seen against the gray, and their noses, clear back to their cockpits, were a dull yellow. In the summer they had all been almost white, or light blue-gray.

"Keep formation! Keep formation!" Our C.O.'s voice warned us. "Stay in formation and let them alone!"

I caught on. This was a Hun trick to keep us diverted up here while the raid was going on down below. As these Huns were above us we should be at a disadvantage in attacking them anyway. We kept going downward, and they turned around after they were behind us and followed us down very half-heartedly, not getting close enough to attack.

We broke through the haze and saw we were out over the sea. Far below and ahead were the dim outlines of a long line of ships, and we began to dive very steeply. Our speed was terrific, and my controls were becoming rigid from it. Tiny gnatlike figures were milling about over the sea near the distant convoy, and the air around there was peppered with black puffs of smoke from anti-aircraft guns. A good-sized battle must be in progress.

Our C.O. led us in a gentle diving turn at the last, curving around toward where most of the airplanes seemed to be. It was dull and murky out here, and hard to make out at any distance what kind of machines they were. There were no formations now, just dozens of airplanes scurrying about in ones, twos, and threes.

I strained my eyes to identify the nearest ones, and finally discerned the square-cut wing tips of Messerschmitts. Then we were closing down into a swarm of them and we could see they were all Messerschmitts, and our C.O.'s voice seemed calm and almost nonchalant in all the confusion of speed and noise and emotions as we heard him call out the battle cry once more.

TAL-L-LY—HO-O!

We overshot the first enemy machines because we had too much speed left from our dives, and turned back toward them, breaking formation as we did so in order not to hamper one another. Trying to remember to be careful, I kept close watch on my tail as I swung around toward the Huns. In the distance I saw one coming straight toward me, head on. Under such circumstances it's best to keep heading directly at the approaching machine, not giving way until the last instant. If you turn ahead of time while the other is still heading toward you, he gets a good shot at your exposed flank while you cannot shoot at him at all because you've pointed your airplane away from him and your guns point with your airplane.

This Nazi must have panicked when he recognized my machine as an enemy, and that was probably fatal for him. For he started turning away from me when we were still about five hundred yards apart. I could hardly believe my eyes as I saw myself presented with the easiest shot I'd ever had—at his unprotected side. The pilot is protected from the front by his engine and from the rear by his armour; but there is no protection from bullets from the side.

When we were about four hundred yards apart and he had turned about fifteen degrees I opened up on him, allowing for his speed and aiming just ahead of his machine. Once more I was sensing the terrific thrill and sense of power that come from the sound and feel and smell of one's guns in combat.

He kept turning and exposing himself even more to me as we closed together, and at the last I was just firing point-blank at him and had to jerk back on the stick to avoid ramming his machine, and passed over his tail. Just then I saw two other Huns on my right and went on the defensive again, trying to be careful. They turned away from me, and I swung back to see what became of my victim; I couldn't find him and as we were so low over the water I thought I knew where he had gone.

Then I turned back toward the other two, but they were heading homeward and were too far away for me to overtake. I climbed up a little and headed toward the convoy, hoping to find some more trouble. On the way I met three 109's in formation, heading homeward. They ignored me and I let them alone too, remembering that the last time I had attacked three enemy fighters singly I got shot down myself. Besides, I still had Junkers 87's in my head. That's why I was heading toward the convoy, as I thought they would be trying to bomb it.

I had been four or five miles from the convoy when I attacked the Messerschmitt. Going to the convoy and circling it, I investigated and was investigated by various aircraft that I saw; but they always turned out to be Spitfires or Hurricanes when we got close enough for identification. I just couldn't find any more Huns at all.

There's something amusing about the way fighter pilots investigate each other under such circumstances. It reminds me of the way two strange dogs approach each other—very much alert against any hostile moves, circling sideways around each other until they decide whether or not they're going to be friends. Two fighters will approach and start circling each other while they get closer, neither one giving the other any advantage and each ready to change the gentle turn he's making into a vicious pirouette to get on the other's tail if he proves hostile; until finally they are close enough to identify each other's machines. At times of poor visibility like this we are especially careful.

I flew up and down the length of the convoy for several minutes, hoping to find some more enemies, but all I found were other Spitfires and a few Hurricanes, all doing what I was. The enemy had apparently fled completely.

I watched the ships to see if any of them had been damaged in the raid, but could only see one that looked as if it had been hit; and it was sailing right along in its place.

Next day, incidentally, we were all edified to learn from the German High Command *communiqué*, relayed from New York, that eleven ships were sunk in the raid! I imagine Great Britain would be in a more favourable position in this war if she had ever had as many ships as Herr Goebbels has already sunk.

Finally, satisfied that there weren't any more enemies about, I headed homeward, joining on the way three or four other boys of the squadron who were drifting toward the airdrome too.

Taxiing my Spitfire to its position on the edge of the field I saw mechanics grinning as they observed the tattered bits of yellow cloth fluttering from the leading edges of my wings around the gun holes. This was all that remained of the cover patches over these holes, the rest having been shot away, as occurs each time the guns are fired. The mechanics always watch for this on each machine as it taxis in from a patrol, to see if these covers have been shot away indicating a fight. They are fully as interested as we are in the accomplishments of the squadron, in which they play such a highly important part. Armourers made haste to remove the plates above and below the guns, in my wings, as soon as I stopped taxiing, so that they could check the guns and install fresh ammunition belts. The kid who helped me out of the cockpit asked, "Did you get anything, sir?"

"I think I got a 109, but I doubt if I'll get it confirmed."

Excitement filled the air, as always after a fight. When pilots return from a "show" they are in a hurry to get out of their machines and meet the other pilots and find out what each knows about what happened as a whole, and how each made out.

Each individual pilot usually knows little of the whole of what happened after the leader's cry of "Tally-ho." He careens about, cramped in his little tight cockpit with limited visibility, seeing little of what goes on except in his immediate vicinity, watching his tail against surprises, evading Huns that get behind him and attacking others when he is in a favourable position to do so (and other times too, if he chooses); but like one bee in the middle of a swarm he doesn't get much idea of what has happened as a whole. The fights usually spread out over too big an area. When he can't find any more enemies or runs out of ammunition or low on fuel, or when his machine is damaged, he returns home.

Naturally then he is anxious to find out as much as he can from the other boys. How many Huns were there? Why were they there, and what were they up to? Was there more than one formation? Could he have found more trouble in a different area or higher up or lower down? What other squadrons took part? How many did we get?

Most important question of all is, "Is everybody all right?"—meaning the other pilots. Often that question can't be answered for a while. It is common after a good scrap for one or two or even more planes of a squadron not to show up at the airdrome; but there can be a number of reasons for that. The pilot of one may have had to land at another airdrome, having run short of fuel or lost his bearings in the fight. Maybe he had to make a forced landing somewhere, with his radiator punctured or his engine damaged by bullets or cannon shells. He may have had to "bail out" with his machine on fire or out of control. In any of these cases the news is likely to be slow in coming through. And of course sometimes the heartbreaking word finally comes through that one of the familiar faces in the mess is now but a memory to us and his loved ones; in which case tonight when we have time one or two of us who knew him well can spend an hour or so going through his belongings and personal effects, packing them and sending them home.

That way his room will be empty for some one else to occupy without delay. We try to keep sentiment to a minimum; we're all in the same boat more or less, and he'll find plenty of friends where he's going, who got there ahead of him.

This time there were no casualties of any kind in our squadron, and every one got back to the home airdrome without mishap. Jack and Chaddy had had some shots at a 109, and Jack was very proud of a bullet hole the mechanics found in his rudder. Our C.O. had damaged another 109, and one or two of the other boys had had shots. We hadn't accomplished much, all told, but several new pilots had been brought through their first fight safely, which was important. The whole story of the fight revealed that we were a little late in arriving, which explained why we didn't have more to do.

A large formation of these Junkers 87 "*Stukas*," escorted by Messerschmitt 109 Fighters, had approached the convoy, and two squadrons of British Hurricanes had intercepted them first before they got to the convoy. The Hurricanes shot down seven of the 87's and most of the rest fled. Only a few got through to drop their bombs. The Messerschmitts then staged a sort of hit-and-run attack on the Hurricanes, and we got there just when they were running.

The Hurricanes shot down three or four of the Messerschmitts too, but they lost two of their own machines and pilots in the last part of the scrap. Jonah saw one of them go down. He first saw it making for shore with steam and glycol streaming back from the radiator, but it appeared to be under good control and he thought the pilot was trying to make a forced landing on the beach. Then just as it reached shore and was about a hundred feet up it nosed straight down and dived into the ground and went up in flames.

That was the morning the Italians made their first and last raid on England. It was going on at the same time that our fight occurred but farther south. We had learned some time previously that Italian bomber and fighter squadrons were being based in northern France, but they hadn't made an appearance over the Channel or England.

On this morning, however, a good-sized formation of old Caproni bombers and Fiat biplane fighters were intercepted by a Hurricane squadron. After the Hurricane pilots recovered from the shock of seeing such ancient aircraft in modern war skies they waded in and shot down thirteen of them without getting a single bullet in any of their own machines. The Hurricane pilots who did it said it was like shooting tame ducks.

After that some of the Italian fighters used to fly out over mid-Channel once in a while, stooging around and trying to look fierce apparently, until one day near the end of the month the other squadron that was stationed at our airdrome found them and shot down another eight. That apparently was enough, and a few days later the remaining Italians moved back to Italy. They hadn't shot down a single British airplane in all the time they had been based across the Channel from us, "daily ranging far and wide over England, side by side with the German Air Force, seeking out and destroying the remnants of the Royal Air Force," or something like that, according to the silly Italian dictator.

It was cold-blooded murder to send their pilots up in their little slow, unarmoured biplanes with only two or four machine guns against our powerful eight-gun Spitfires and Hurricanes, and they must have been sent for political reasons, like some pilots that were killed in the United States in 1934. I hope the era of dictators is drawing to a close. Lust for power makes even good men turn to doing ruthless deeds.

CHAPTER 10

Hun-Chasing

In the afternoon after our combat I saw a mechanic doping new fabric covers over the holes in the wings in front of the guns on my airplane, to replace those that were shot away. "You're wasting your time doing that!" I told him cheerfully.

He replied, "I hope you're right, sir."

I expected to be using my guns often now, but in this I was mistaken. The *Luftwaffe* was in the process of abandoning the mass day raids, and what raiding they did now was cautious, and on a small scale. The great air offensive which they had boasted would destroy the Royal Air Force and pave the way for the scheduled German invasion of England was entering its final and ignominious stages.

I have often heard doubts expressed that the R.A.F.'s accounts of our own and enemy losses could be correct. The abandoning by the Nazis of these mass raids should be proof that R.A.F. accounts of casualties, which showed that the Nazis lost at least four times as many airplanes as we did, could not have been exaggerations.

At the beginning of their air onslaught the Luftwaffe outnumbered us several times over. England admitted it, and Germany boasted of it. They deliberately announced their intention to wipe us out, as a first step to bombing freely and preparing for and supporting the invasion of England which they promised, and which is necessary for them ever to win this war.

The Royal Air Force had to maintain an overwhelming ratio of victories to losses in order to continue to exist!—and in order for England to continue to exist, too, for that matter. If the Huns could have destroyed even half as many British machines as they lost themselves, it would have paid them to continue the mass raids until the R.A.F. was wiped out, for they (the Huns) would still have plenty of airplanes left. The fact that we still existed after the mass raids were abandoned proves that we must have maintained at least a four-to-one ratio of victories to losses; and the fact that the Nazis abandoned the mass raiding was an admission that, in spite of their tremendous numerical superiority, they were losing a bigger percentage of their air force than we were losing of ours. In other words, their big air force was being worn down faster than our little one!

They were starting now a new type of raiding which, while it didn't accomplish much, was far less costly to them. Because their big bombers, slow and unwieldy, were such cold meat for our fighters and were shot down in such a wholesale manner during the day raids, they fixed up some of their little Messerschmitt fighters to carry bombs. They of course couldn't aim the bombs; there was no room for an extra person or a bomb aimer in the machines, and they didn't even have a bomb sight in them.

But that was immaterial in their program of terrorising the civilians of London, for London is so big and thickly populated that they didn't have to aim the bombs—if they just flew anywhere over the city and dropped them, there was a good chance of killing some people. Each plane so equipped usually carried a 550-pound bomb under its belly. The weight and wind resistance of the bomb of course impaired the performance of the Messerschmitts, but they were still much faster than any regular bombers, and being small they weren't as easy for us to spot when we were hunting for them. Also, once they had released their bombs, they had all their original performance back again and had just as much chance to race or fight their way home as any other fighter. They carried their regular machine guns and cannon just the same when they were carrying bombs as otherwise. In case they were intercepted before they reached their objective they jettisoned their bombs wherever they were, so that they'd have a better chance to get away without fighting, or could fight better if they had to fight.

So now we were often sent up to chase "Messerschmitt 109 bombers." Chasing them was easier than catching them, for they were very careful about it, coming over only when conditions were favourable for them to get through to London without having to fight. They flew at twenty-two or twenty-three thousand feet, usually, which seemed to be as high as they could get when carrying bombs; and they were often escorted by others without bombs, flying above them at any altitude up to thirty-five thousand feet. Both the British and the Germans have listening devices on their respective sides of the Channel, by which each side can tell when an enemy formation is flying on the opposite side, if it's anywhere near the coast; and they can keep track of its position and height. As soon as a formation of Messerschmitts would take off on the other side (all the fighter airdromes are near the coast) one or more of our squadrons would be sent up on patrol to be ready to intercept them if they came across. The Nazis of course kept track of the positions of our squadrons; and if our machines seemed to be in a good position to intercept their planes the Nazi controllers would order their pilots (by radio) not to start across.

Then they'd just fly up and down the French coast, and we'd fly up and down the English coast, "figuratively glaring at each other across the Channel," as I said in one of my letters home at about that time. They'd be hoping that we'd get sidetracked long enough for them to make a dash across and get by us; and we would sit up there hoping they'd try it. They got to using all sorts of tricks, sending over several small formations at a time at different points to draw us off guard, playing hide and seek in the clouds, and leading us all sorts of merry chases.

For example, one afternoon we were scrambled and ordered to patrol over Canterbury at fifteen thousand feet. Canterbury is a fairly large place a few miles from the coast, and is a handy point to stay around because it is easy to see and keep track of when pilots are busier watching the sky above than the ground below. After we'd hung around over there a few minutes Control called and said:

> Steer a course of 150 degrees and climb to twenty-three thousand feet. There are several bandits approaching Dungeness from Boulogne at about that altitude.

Our leader acknowledged the message and we went roaring out toward Dungeness, our gun-sights switched on, firing buttons off safety, and blood in our eyes, I suppose.

We steamed out over Dungeness, our C.O. anxiously calling Control. "Can you tell me where the bandits are now? We are circling Dungeness but can't see anything."

Control's voice answered:

> Sorry, they must have smelled you. They've turned back again. Steer three six zero. There is another formation of about fifteen bandits now approaching Manston from Cape Gris Nez at about your altitude.

We turned northward as ordered, and as we approached Manston Control called out: "Be careful. Keep a sharp lookout above! There may be more bandits very high above them!"

This was the warning for all of us to watch the sky above for vapour trails. We weren't "vaporising" at our present altitude, but airplanes very much above us probably would be.

A moment later one of our boys called out, "Vapour trails above and starboard!"

I looked carefully, and then I saw them, about twenty eerie little silver lines crawling across the sky above from the southeast, close together. They were undoubtedly the trails of Messerschmitts without bombs, flying at thirty or thirty-five thousand feet in the stratosphere, supposedly to protect those lower down which we were searching for and which would be carrying bombs.

We couldn't bother about those high ones now. If they wanted to come down to our level and fight, O.K., but we weren't going to climb up after them when there were others at our own altitude. Our rear guard would keep close watch on them so they couldn't pull a surprise attack from above. We kept going straight and level towards Manston, and when we got there Control called and said: "Sorry again! They are getting very careful. The bandits which were at your altitude have turned back. You may use your discretion about the ones above you."

The vapour trails were almost directly over us now.

Our C.O. answered Control: "Thank you. I think we'll climb up and try to have a go at them."

And heading southwest to get us out from under them he led us upward in a steep climb to try to reach their altitude. Soon it grew very cold in our cockpits, as our altimeter needles approached the thirty-thousand-foot mark on their dials. I could see the fluffy cloud trails streaming back from each of the other planes in the formation, for of course we were making vapor trails ourselves now. The Huns above, after making a big circle, had turned north now, and we did likewise, following them and climbing. They were still some distance above us. As we got farther up in the stratosphere the sky grew a more intense blue, and the sun was weirdly bright and wintry. We climbed on above thirty thousand.

The air at that altitude is so thin that even these high-powered machines lose most of their beautiful flying qualities. Controls work very easily and the airplane responds to them only sluggishly, as a car responds to the steering wheel on ice, instead of with the rigid alertness one gets accustomed to in these machines at normal altitudes. The powerful engine becomes lazy too. Somehow the air one is riding on feels terribly unsubstantial, and until one gets used to it he gets a feeling of insecurity, a feeling that he and his machine are on the verge of losing what little support the air gives up there, and just falling off into the eerie, seemingly limitless space below. The ground seems as far away as a distant continent, and he wonders if he will ever find his way back.

Visibility is unbelievable in the thin air up there. If there are no clouds below it isn't uncommon to see the whole of southeast England, northeast France, and Belgium, as well as the sea in between, just like looking at a map.

We could watch our enemies by their vapour trails, and they likewise could watch us; and as we drew near their altitude they turned southeast and headed homeward. We tried to head them off, but they had too much of a start. It is very hard to fight with an unwilling enemy.

These German attacks by bomb-carrying fighters began about mid-October, I believe, and were more or less abandoned by the first of December. They had become less and less successful and more and more expensive to themselves as our controllers and squadron leaders became experienced in combating them. Our squadron intercepted one of the last ones they attempted.

We were on patrol one morning at about twenty-two or twenty-three thousand feet, having chased around quite a bit after raids that started across the Channel and then turned back. We were right over Dungeness, heading about straight east, our only recent information being that "there are several bandits somewhere in your vicinity."

Suddenly one of our new pilots who hadn't had a fight yet called out on the R/T, in a very subdued voice that we all laughed about afterwards, "Bandits coming up on the starboard!"

And there they were, little ratlike 109's streaking across so that they passed just under us, going at right angles to our course. If they had been two hundred feet higher we'd have collided with them! They had simply blundered into us, and we into them.

Our C.O. shouted a quick "Tally-ho!" and the squadron exploded in all directions. So did the Hun formation. I didn't get to see it, but the boys who were closest to the 109's saw them let their bombs go—a dozen or so big bombs jettisoned to fall harmlessly on the beaches of Dungeness.

The Messerschmitts were scattering and diving, and it was more or less of a hide-and-seek proposition to find them. I didn't get a single shot. After hunting around for two or three minutes I gave up trying to find any of them as they had quite obviously taken the shortest route home.

However, I could see three or four pairs of vapour trails scattered about the sky higher up, all coming inland, and I decided to try to stalk one pair of them, climbing to a higher level and getting "up sun" of them. I was getting along pretty well, when looking above me in the other direction I saw the vapour trails of two others that were stalking *me*, and were just getting to a good position to attack. I panicked a little then and dived away from them, making the excuse to myself that I couldn't do anything but get hurt if I stayed up there with these two getting ready to take a crack at me.

Returning to our base, I found that once again the squadron had had no casualties and a little had been accomplished. Our C.O. had shot one Messerschmitt down into the sea for his eleventh confirmed victory, and one other pilot had damaged another 109. Our C.O. had also gone back up, the same as I did, to stalk one of the pairs that came over higher, and he got "jumped" by two Heinkel 113 fighters and had the sliding hatch over his cockpit shot away!

I took forty-eight hours' leave shortly after that, and spent it shopping in London. There was little bombing in London now, and the city had recovered quite well from the bombings it had undergone in the fall. I had a very pleasant and interesting time walking about and shopping and seeing the thousands of historical sights. I got some genuine English plum puddings, or Christmas puddings, and sent them to my folks for Christmas presents.

When I got back to the squadron I found that I had missed a spot of action with them, in which they hadn't fared so well. They had chased after some Messerschmitts among cloud and fog over the Channel and some of them got separated from the squadron. Chaddy found a 109 and damaged it and got shot up by another and had to make a forced landing with his engine wrecked by cannon shells.

"Hop" didn't come back. The last they saw of him he was diving in among some scattered clouds after some 109's that he had spotted, shouting "Tally-ho" over his R/T. No one ever found out what became of him; but we felt pretty sure that, however they got him, they knew they had a job on their hands before he went down.

With the end of November I had had three more weeks of "front-line" service since we moved to this airdrome, and as yet I had only used my guns the one time. I wasn't very proud of that record, but it was as much as most of the rest had done. Of course the weather interfered a lot, keeping both sides on the ground a good share of the time. But the Huns just weren't fighting anyway. They liked to come over our territory whenever they got a chance, but they avoided combat when they did so.

We had had only two fights so far, and for the amount of patrolling we did we could have had a dozen if the Nazis had shown the slightest desire to really tangle with us. We were still on the defensive, to be true. We never went over France, just waited for the Huns to come over our side, because we weren't big enough for offensive fighting yet. The patrolling we did, hunting for them, was often enjoyable though, because of the magnificent scenery where we flew, high among the beautiful and ever different cloud formations. Then there were the striking and unforgettable views we often got of British or German formations making their beautiful vapour trails in the cold blue stratosphere.

Because their bomb-carrying fighters were having so little success the Huns practically abandoned their use about the first of December, and after that they just sent over formations of ordinary fighters on what we term "offensive patrols."

Most of the time they kept one or more formations on patrol high up over their own side. It didn't pay us to keep a patrol in the air to guard against them all the time, so sometimes when none of our squadrons were aloft one of these high-flying patrols would come over our side, usually at from thirty to thirty-five thousand feet, making what's called an "offensive sweep." One or more of our squadrons would then be sent aloft in an effort to intercept them, or to at least drive them home.

The German strategy was to try to get around above us while we were climbing up to intercept them, and then to dive on the rear of our formation. Because we were climbing we wouldn't be going ahead very fast, while the Huns, by diving, could gain terrific speed by the time they reached us, take a shot as they went past, and scuttle for home without our being able to stop them. It was a tip-and-run method that involved little danger for them, although it couldn't accomplish much either. It didn't work very often, just once in a while at first, until the squadrons learned how to guard against it. Our squadron was never jumped that way, although we came close to it on two or three occasions.

Guarding against this tactic was mainly up to the top "weaver" of each of our formations. He had to be alert and watching the sky above and behind all the time. As a rule the job of rear guard was rotated among us, a different pair of pilots doing the job each day. I liked it myself, and I always got a thrill, knowing that they were depending on me to warn them against danger from above and behind. Only once did I come close to getting into trouble at it.

We were up quite high that morning, and my own altimeter was showing thirty-four thousand feet where I was, about a thousand feet above the rest of the squadron. We were hunting for some Huns that were reported to be at about thirty thousand feet, but we were flying a little higher than that so as to have the jump on them if we found them. The squadron was heading north, about over the Thames Estuary, and all the boys were of course making beautiful vapour trails below me.

It was strange trying to realise that each of those weird moth-shaped, beautifully camouflaged creatures plummeting along and spurning back its vapour trail below me in this eerie frigid stratosphere was piloted by a pal of mine. Up in front was our C.O., who had visited the Air Ministry a day or so previously and afterwards told me that he thought he could arrange for me to get back to America on leave soon. Just behind him and to the side was Percy, who would be practicing with me on our accordions in my room in the mess in the afternoon.

Jonah, who kept some of his things in my room and often slept there, was number three in the formation below. Ewan, who had had me home with him at his parents' magnificent old place in Buckinghamshire a few days before, was number eight. I could think of something intimate about each of the boys, yet now they looked like characters from some book about the distant future when I swooped low enough over their machines to make out their weirdly helmeted and goggled and masked heads beneath the transparent hoods over their cockpits; and I suppose I looked just as weird and distant to them, back over them and leaving my own vapor trail.

I was disturbed from these reflections by the sight of four vapour trails coming from the west and about a thousand feet above me. I called a warning to the squadron and then continued keeping the vapour trails under careful watch as they came closer. I had been on the right-hand leg of my course across the squadron and was just swinging toward the vapour trails when they got right overhead; and rather than lose sight of them by turning back I just continued my left turn until I had circled clear around and was headed south, in the opposite direction from the squadron. I could see the planes making the trails above, plainly, and recognized them as Messerschmitt 109's; and I was pretty scared for a minute because I was getting far away behind the squadron and giving these Huns just what they were looking for—a chance to drop on a straggler, the straggler being me.

Accordingly I kept turning directly toward them as they passed over, so that when they came down at me they would have to meet me head on, which would give them the poorest possible shot and would give me a chance to shoot back at them. To my surprise they didn't come down at me, and I never did know why. Probably they felt that as long as I obviously saw them and was facing them they wouldn't have a very good chance of getting me. They kept going straight on, and for a few seconds I was afraid to turn back toward the squadron, thinking this was a trick and they would come after me as soon as I turned tail.

When I did turn I tried to rush it too quickly and threw my plane into a tailspin, losing a thousand feet or so and looking like a complete amateur. The squadron was out of sight by this time, but I was able to track it down by the vapour trails and rejoined the rest after two or three minutes!

One morning about the 10th of December a beautiful piece of combined controlling and squadron leading enabled the other Spitfire squadron which was stationed at our airdrome (the same squadron which shot down the eight Italians) to carry out a perfect interception on a formation of these high-flying Messerschmitts. They got above and up sun of them, dropped on them, and shot down eight without a single casualty among themselves.

A few days later one of their pilots received a present of an Iron Cross, forwarded to him from a German prisoner. It developed that this German was one of the eight who had been shot down that morning, and had force-landed his machine in Kent. When police came to take him prisoner they found him grinding something into the ground with his heel. It was his Iron Cross. He explained to interrogators that he thought the British would shoot any German they captured who had such a decoration. When he was told that he was mistaken, that the British respect bravery among their foes as well as their own men, he was so relieved and impressed that he asked that they give his Iron Cross to the pilot who had shot him down—as a token of respect. They checked up, determined which pilot had shot the boy down, and sent it to him.

That is only one of many examples of the illusions which especially the younger Nazi pilots have. Frequently these boys, on being captured in England, insisted on being taken to the nearest German Army headquarters—it was useless for their captors to lie to them, they *knew* that all of England except London and a few other isolated areas was in German hands!

Our squadron had a good chase one day when I was off duty about this time. They were up hunting for some Messerschmitt 109's, and one of the boys sighted one of the twin-engined long-range 110's flying high above them. It was apparently over on reconnaissance work, the crew hoping to get through to take some pictures and get back safely by flying as high as possible. The squadron was at about thirty thousand feet and this machine was about thirty-five thousand. It turned and started to flee homeward at sight of our squadron.

Our C.O., sizing up the situation, called over the R/T:

"All right, boys! It's a free-for-all. Break formation and go get him!"

The result, according to the boys, was a perfect aerial fox-hunt. It developed that Trevor had the most powerful machine and was soon leading the pack. He gained on the Hun fast, and when they were out to sea a ways he finally got within shooting range. The rest of the squadron machines were keeping up as far as distance was concerned, but they weren't high enough yet. They were mostly right below Trevor.

Trevor opened up with a good burst from his guns, and the 110 immediately went into an evasive dive. That was fatal, for then the rest of the boys were able to pounce on him. Nearly everyone had a shot as the Hun was going down, and they practically shot him to pieces by the time he hit the sea. The victory was finally divided among the three pilots who had shot the most ammunition, each being credited with one-third of a victory!

The high-flying "offensive patrols" by the enemy also petered out about mid-December, and for the next three weeks there was almost nothing for us to do, the only daylight enemy activity being lone "snooping" bombers which came over occasionally in clouds or fog. Usually two or three planes took off when one of them came over;

but as the work was divided among the nearly two dozen front-line squadrons the average of us weren't up more than once or twice a week. All through from mid-November on, in fact, the weather was so often bad that we had lots of time off.

As a rule we were scheduled to be "at readiness" about half the time—either from dawn until lunch or from lunch until dark, each day. But when the weather was bad our readiness state would be changed so that we could stay in the mess, provided we were dressed and ready to go quickly and had a car waiting for us outside; or at times we would be "available at call," in which case we could be anywhere on the camp, or could stay in bed if we liked.

Toward the end of December things were so quiet that we were often released for the day. Then if it was early enough to make it worth while I usually walked over to the railway station and went downtown. The electric line was just a few minutes' walk from the mess, and the trains ran every twenty minutes.

I never got tired of walking about London and exploring. After dark I usually took in a movie before going home. It was often strange to be all engrossed in an American movie and completely lost in the American atmosphere, and then be reminded of where I was by the muffled booming of anti-aircraft guns opening up at the first night raider of the evening; and I'd wonder absently if it was going to be "blitzy going home" tonight.

This was altogether one of the easiest periods of my life. There was practically no work, and the flying we did was just enough to put a tang into the existence, like hunting on Sunday afternoon.

There was seldom any bombing in the vicinity of our airdrome, although the Huns passed over at night frequently; and some evenings there was a pretty continuous racket from the anti-aircraft guns around. There was one battery of three very heavy guns only a short distance from the mess, which we referred to as "Alfy." As a rule Alfy didn't waste shots, his shots being expensive, and he only fired at high-flying aircraft and then not very often at night. We were glad of that. We didn't mind the other guns around, which weren't as big and were farther away so that their noise didn't bother us.

But when Alfy spoke everyone in the mess jumped. It was a terrific *blam!!* repeated three times in quick succession, and the windows and doors would rattle and slam shut, and after our ears stopped ringing we'd hear a sighing sound as the three shells rocketed skyward. Then, seemingly a long time afterward, would come the distant, heavy *whoompf! . . . whoompf-whoompf!* of the shells exploding far above.

I have seen Alfy, in daylight, put a shell up right beside a German reconnaissance machine that was over thirty thousand feet high. I know it was that high; I was up there chasing it.

CHAPTER 11

A Day at War

I'll try to take you through just an average sort of day such as I passed during this quiet period of the war, to give you a little more insight into the kind of life we lead over here.

The day begins with my elderly batman waking me up by coming into my room at about six-thirty to get my uniform, shoes, and flying boots. I hear him moving about, and when he sees that I'm awake he asks, "What time do ye want calling, sir?"

The squadron is scheduled for morning readiness today, but if the weather is bad we shall probably get changed to available at call, so I ask in return, "What's the weather like?"

"Well, I cahn't tell very good, sir: 't's pretty dark yet. I wouldn't think it's so bad though. 'Tain't mistin' or anything."

"O.K.," I say. "Make it about seven-thirty, will you?"

And I drowse off, scarcely hearing his "Very good, sir."

I rouse slightly when he brings my uniform, shoes, and boots back in after polishing the buttons on the former and shining the latter; then I sink back to sleep again, to be wakened by his voice saying: "It's seven-thirty now, sir. Weather seems to be all right outside."

I rouse, wash, shave, and dress.

During the day pilots are allowed to depart a little from specified dress. We don't wear collars or ties ordinarily, because they hamper us in looking around in the air; and we usually wear roll-neck sweaters except in warm weather. We wear our heavy fur-lined flying boots instead of shoes, with the bottoms of our trousers tucked into them and perhaps a map or two stuck in there also. That's the handiest place to carry our maps.

Dressed, I walk down the hallway to the large dining hall, where other pilots of the squadron are drifting in, clomping with their big boots and rubbing their eyes sleepily. To make sure of the weather a few of us take a look outside. It's still dark, for England is much farther north than the United States and the nights are very long in winter. We see some stars shining, so we know the weather is probably going to be all right and we shan't get out of doing our readiness.

Copies of all the morning London papers are laid out on a table in one corner of the dining hall, and as we come into the hall some of us pick up copies to read while we're eating breakfast. We bid one another sleepy good mornings, and read, chat, and trade papers while we're eating. Breakfast consists as usual of cereal, bacon and eggs, toast, marmalade, and tea.

Just we pilots and the cooks and waiters are up. The ground personnel don't get up this early ordinarily, and the pilots of the other squadron, who don't go on readiness until this afternoon, will sleep later yet.

Breakfast over, it is time to get going, and we get our jackets and caps from the hallway and troop outside to the big old lorry waiting for us. Among the assortment of flying suits issued to each of us is a very heavy two-piece fur-lined leather affair, consisting of jacket and trousers, called an "Irving suit." While few of us ever use the trousers, most boys like to wear the jackets about the camp on cold days as well as in the air sometimes; so most of us are wearing these heavy brown Irving jackets.

We pile into the waiting lorry, laughing and joking and helping each other up; and after we're all in Pip remembers that he left his goggles in his room where he was repairing the strap on them last night, and has to go back after them.

Finally we get going and drive through between the darkened buildings on the airdrome, across the parade ground, and to the sergeants' mess. After a wait of a minute or so half a dozen sergeant pilots come trooping out, munching pieces of toast and pulling on their Irving jackets as they come. About a third of the pilots in the R.A.F. are sergeants.

The gray of approaching dawn is showing in the east as we drive past the great looming dark hangars and skirt the edge of the field going around to our flight headquarters. A squadron is divided into two flights, A Flight and B Flight, and while in some places both flights share the same headquarters we had separate headquarters here, located at some distance from each other along the edge of the field.

We can hear the bellowing of a Spitfire's Rolls Royce engine at full throttle, getting its morning "run-up" as we near B Flight's headquarters. We pass in front of the airplane, a big ghostly shape dimly visible in its parking space, its propeller forming a filmy gray disk and bright blue and yellow flames ripping back from its exhausts. Other engines are warming up as we drive by, and while the B Flight pilots are getting out of the lorry another one gets its run-up nearby and the very earth seems to shake from the terrific power that is being unleashed.

The C.O. is in charge of A Flight (to which I belong) today, as our regular flight commander has gone on leave. He has arrived at our headquarters ahead of us and already has his flying suit on. He starts making up the schedule for our flight and writing it with chalk on the bulletin board, while we are donning our flying suits and Mae Wests (life jackets).

In addition to its squadron markings, each airplane in a squadron has a letter painted on its side which simply designates which of the squadron's machines it is. The C.O.'s favourite machine is "D." He flies at the head of the flight, the number one machine of "Red" Section. So he writes at the top of the board:

"Red 1—C.O.—D."

Then he looks around and says, "Percy, you like to fly 'K,' don't you?"

"Yes, sir, that's right," Percy responds.

"All right." And the C.O. writes next underneath: "Red 2—Percy—K."

Then he turns to me. "Donny, is your machine serviceable?" He sometimes calls me "Donny" instead of my regular nickname of "Art."

"No, sir," I reply. "It's over in Maintenance today for its thirty-hour inspection. If you don't mind, I'd like to have Trevor's machine. He's off on leave. That's 'E.'"

"All right, Donny. 'E' it is, then. You can be Red 3 and Pip will be your second man, Red 4.

"If there's a squadron patrol you and Pip can do the rear guard. O.K.? That will leave the inseparables Chaddy and Jack to be Yellow One and Two. Does that sound all right to everybody?"

There are no objections. So the remaining three get their airplanes assigned, and taking our parachutes, helmets, and mittens we go out to our respective machines and get them in readiness. It's nearly eight-thirty now, and beginning to get light.

Readying the Spitfire I am using, I first put my parachute on the tail-plane, after making sure that there is no mist or frost where I lay it, for moisture is bad for a parachute; and I arrange its straps so that I can pick it up on the run and put it on in the shortest time. Then I hop upon the dull camouflaged wing behind the engine and climb down into the deep cockpit. There are no floor boards or upholstery or carpet, just the framework of the bottom of the fuselage to step on.

Inside the cockpit I first hang my helmet over the top of the control stick and plug in my radio cord and oxygen tube, in their places beside the seat, and make sure that the wires and oxygen tube hanging from the helmet are not twisted or tangled in any way that would interfere with my putting the helmet on quickly. I open the oxygen valves and make sure by the gauge that I have a full supply, and listen for any leaks in the connections and in the hose leading to my helmet, for a leak might cause me to run short on a long patrol.

I arrange the four seat and shoulder straps conveniently so that I can reach them and put them on quickly.

Now the all-important electric gun-sight. I switch it on to make sure it's working, and check its adjustments for the range I like and the size target for which I want it adjusted. I like to have mine adjusted for Messerschmitts, thirty-two-and-one-half-foot wing span, and for a certain range. Trevor, who ordinarily uses this machine, has the sight adjusted for seventy-foot wing span, which would be a bomber, and for a longer range. I change the adjustments to suit myself and then switch it off.

Then I turn on the gasoline valves, set the throttle to the correct position for starting, set the propeller control in fully "fine" position, which will allow the engine to turn over at maximum speed for taking off, and even put the ignition switches on. I unlock the engine primer pump on the instrument panel, and flip open the cover over the starter button. Next the radiator flaps. Noting the temperature this morning, I decide that three notches closed should be about right for them, and I move the lever controlling them to that position. After I get in the air I'll readjust them to get the engine temperature right. It's bad to run the engine too hot, but worse still to run it too cold, because the guns are heated from the radiator and if the engine is running too cold they won't get enough heat and won't work!

I make sure that the pressure is up in the air system. This operates the brakes and the landing flaps on the airplane, and most important of all it is used to fire the guns. Finally I adjust the seat to its best position for me (which is the highest position, incidentally) and place my mittens in a handy place beside the throttle.

That finishes the preparations, and I climb out and return to our flight building.

These careful preparations make it possible to be off the ground in three minutes from the time we get an order to go up. Engineers and scientists and designers spend fortunes on research and strive their utmost to incorporate features in our airplanes to give us more and more speed and power with which to climb up and overtake the enemy; and each minute we can save in getting off the ground on a scramble is worth a hundred extra horsepower in trying to intercept the enemy!

In the office at our flight building I leaf through the log sheets for the various airplanes of the flight, until I find the one for the machine I'm using. In this is maintained a record of inspections, refuellings, and flights. I check to see that mechanics and armourers have signed it in the columns required, indicating that the necessary inspections have been made on airplane, engine, instruments, radio, and guns, and that it has been filled with gas and oil and cooling liquid; and then I initial it in the column headed "Pilot."

Now I can relax.

The building is divided into two parts: one for pilots and the other for mechanics and other ground personnel, who are all termed "troops." Through the partition between we can hear the troops laughing and chatting and playing cards and darts and "Shove Ha'penny." Their work was begun early in the morning, and most of it finished by the time we came to readiness; so now most of them have nothing to do but stand by until the machines are used.

A number of comfortable chairs are provided for us pilots to sit in around the stove, and there are also a few cots to lie on. Chaddy and Jack make for the latter, because they were on a party last night. The lights are still on, since it has just been getting daylight; but now that it's light enough two of us go around taking down the black-out blinds from the windows; and then we turn off the lights.

Percy engages Pip in a darts game, while the C.O. and I prop our feet on the stove and read the latest "Intelligence Dope" which "Number One," our intelligence officer, left with us yesterday.

After a time, their darts game finished, Percy and Pip pull up chairs and join us around the stove where we talk fighting tactics and politics, and swap stories of our experiences. As the conversation gets interesting Chaddy and Jack get up from their cots and pull up chairs around the stove also. The C.O. tells us about his visit to the operations room at our old base last summer, just before the big blitz began, when some Spitfires of another squadron caught a German "Red Cross" plane doing reconnaissance along the English coast.

"As you know," he explains, "airplanes which carry on rescue or ambulance work have red crosses painted on them; and according to an international agreement they are not to be attacked. Of course they aren't supposed to carry out anything but rescue or ambulance work under this agreement; but you know how those Nazis are—they only recognise the parts of an agreement that work in their favour.

"They have quite a lot of ambulance planes, usually old out-of-date transport machines. Last summer it became pretty evident that they were using them for other purposes than rescue and ambulance work. They were actually flying over our own territory, getting by on our respect for this agreement not to attack them.

"However, it became so obvious that the Nazis were actually doing photography and reconnaissance work over our territory with these Red Cross machines that finally the British Government informed the German Government, through a neutral country, that if any more of them were found flying over our territory, under circumstances where they couldn't possibly be doing rescue work, they would be shot down.

"Well, on this morning that I was in the operations room, there was a section of three Spitfires of —— Squadron on patrol and I was sitting beside their controller, listening to their radio conversations and watching their position and that of the Hun they were looking for, as the positions were plotted about on the big map in the middle of the room. They were looking for a single enemy machine which was reported to be about, and their controller was watching their position and that of the Hun on the map, and giving them courses to steer to try to bring them together with it. We could see that they were very close to the Hun, and all at once the 'Tally-ho' went up as the boys sighted him. Then there was an intermittent conversation something like this:

"'Say, what kind of airplane is this, anyway?'

"'I don't know. Come on, let's knock it apart and see.'

"'Hold on! Wait! We can't shoot this thing, it's a rescue plane. See, it's got red crosses on it!'

"'What of it? We don't need anyone rescued over here. It's got black crosses on it too. Let's blow its head off!'"

The C.O. continues. "To make a long story short, they shot a few holes in the machine and forced it to land.

"It was a big old seaplane and landed in the water near shore and our patrol boats went out and captured it and its crew. Just as was suspected, there was no doctor on it nor even a stretcher or any kind of medical equipment. Instead, they had all sorts of cameras and photographic equipment on it. They were doing reconnaissance work and photographing our territory under the guise of rescue and ambulance work!

"It was right after that happened that the order came around to all squadrons that in the future we should shoot down any German red-cross planes found over or along our coast."

The telephone orderly comes in as our C.O. finishes the story. "Pardon, sir," he says to the C.O. "Operations are on the telephone and say there may be a 'section show' for three airplanes shortly, and they want to know which section it will be."

"Tell them it will be Red Section," our C.O. replies. Then to me: "Art, you come in with Percy and me and make the third man in the section if we go, will you? Then Pip can go into Chaddy's section and be Yellow Three if they want another section. O.K.?"

"O.K.," sir," we reply.

Nothing further happens for an hour or so. I am engrossed in a newspaper story, and most of the rest are drowsing. Blond, lanky Pip is sprawled on one of the cots as only Pip knows how to sprawl, and reading a magazine.

"Red Section take off!"

I come alive with a start. The telephone orderly has called it from the office, and an efficient excitement reigns. The C.O. and Percy and I bolt for the door. Pip and Chaddy and Jack start to get up, then realise it doesn't concern them and relax again. Sergeant M is shouting to the mechanics, "Start up! Start up! Red Section only—D, K, and E!"

We pause going out the door just long enough to get the rest of the message from the telephone orderly.

"Patrol Chatham at ten thousand feet and watch for one bandit approaching from the southeast!" He has to shout the last, because we are already on our way to our machines. My machine is farthest away, and when I reach it I am nearly winded from running in my heavy flying clothes and boots.

Mechanics are already there, and one is in the cockpit working the primer. I grab my parachute on the run, by its top straps, swing it onto my back and snap the straps into place around me while the mechanic in the cockpit works the starter and the engine comes to life.

He climbs out, and I swing up onto the wing and squeeze into the cockpit, and with his help I fasten my seat and shoulder straps. Then on with my helmet, and I snap the oxygen mask into place across my face, fasten the chin strap, and pull up the adjusting strap at the back. Then on with my mittens, release the parking brake, and I'm taxiing out onto the field. The other two machines are taxiing out too, and I swing my machine into place to the left and rear of where the C.O. has paused with his.

I see his helmeted head turned towards Percy's machine on the other side and his mittened thumb come up. Percy's thumb comes up in reply. I already have my thumb up when he looks my way, and he turns and looks ahead and a faint puff of smoke streaks back from the exhaust of his engine; and though I can scarcely hear his engine opening up because of my padded helmet, I see his idling propeller become invisible and his machine begin to move. I open my throttle part way and feel the tremendous surge of power as my own machine begins to move. At the same time I punch a button that starts my radio receiver and another that starts a time recording attachment on the clock in my instrument panel.

The acceleration from our mighty engines is terrific, and in a few seconds our machines are skimming the ground lightly at eighty miles an hour, and now we are off and roaring up over the edge of the field. I reach down for the lever controlling the landing gear motor, disengage it from the "down" position and move it to the "up" position. The others have done likewise, and on the C.O.'s machine (which I have to watch to keep my place in formation) I can see the two landing gear "legs" to which the wheels are attached rising upward and outward, awkwardly, and disappearing into his wings. I feel two little thumps as my own wheels come up into their retracted position in the wings, where they are folded during flight to decrease wind resistance. Now I pull back my propeller pitch control lever so that the engine can run slower, and of course I keep opening and closing the throttle as needed to keep my position in relation to the C.O.

We fly in a "V" type formation. The C.O. is leading us in a steep climbing turn around the airdrome, absently turning to the left—a holdover from the days when there were air traffic rules.

I reach up with one hand and pull the transparent sliding hatch closed over my head, being careful not to get my arm out in the wind—for we are nearing two hundred miles an hour already, and at that speed the wind would throw my arm back hard enough to give it a painful jerk.

With my hatch closed it is much quieter inside. A crackling in my ears tells me that my radio has warmed up and is now working. Only a few seconds have elapsed since we left the ground, and the airdrome is already over a thousand feet below.

I hear the C.O.'s voice in my headphones, calling Control.

"Hello, Control. Hello, Control. Tiger Red One calling. Are you receiving me, please? Are you receiving me? Over."

A distant voice answers:

Hello, Tiger Red One, Tiger Red One. Control answering. Yes, receiving you loud and clear, loud and clear. Are you receiving me, please? Over.

Our C.O. replies: "Hello, Control. Tiger Red One answering. Receiving you loud and clear also. Understand you have one bandit for us, approaching Chatham from the southeast at ten thousand feet. One bandit approaching Chatham from the southeast. Have you any other information? Over."

Hello, Tiger Red One. Yes, that is correct. No, I haven't anything new on it. Over.

"O.K., Control. Listening out."

We continue our upward climb, and during the next few minutes I check my oil pressure and radiator temperature, regulating the latter by means of my radiator flap control; adjust trimming controls so that my machine flies properly and doesn't tend to turn one way or the other or climb faster or slower than we are doing, and turn on the valve from my oxygen tank. This releases the oxygen to a regulator on my instrument panel so that, when I want to use oxygen, all I'll have to do is open another valve on the regulator. Up to ten thousand feet I won't use oxygen, saving it until we're ordered higher or are going into combat.

I turn my oxygen full on if I'm going into combat, even though that gives me a lot more than I need, because I'm sure then that there'll be no deficiency that would slow my thinking, and a surplus of it is supposed to help prevent fainting if one is wounded. This bandit we are after now must be a bomber, because enemy fighters never come over singly, and we don't consider attacking enemy bombers as "combat." It is unusual for anyone to get hurt attacking a German bomber.

In almost no time we are circling the city of Chatham, on the south side of the Thames, where the great naval dockyards are. At ten thousand feet we level off and throttle back our engines so that we are loafing at about two hundred miles an hour—which is way below the normal cruising speed of our machines, but saves gas. To the south and east is a heavy bank of clouds at about our altitude. Control calls us again:

> Hello, Tiger Red One, Tiger Red One Steer zero-five-five and lose height to seven thousand feet. The bandit has turned and is now heading towards Southend.

We do as we are told, swinging northeast and diving slightly. We see a lot of broken clouds in that direction a little below our altitude, and guess that the bandit is taking cover in them.

Control calls again, as we are nearly over Southend: "Keep a sharp lookout. The bandit is very close to you now."

I switch on my gun-sight and uncover my firing button and take it off safety. I do it absently, without the tremendous conflict of emotions that I had the first times last summer; and that is one of the very few evidences that I can see of any change that the war has made in me. I don't feel that it's hardened or toughened or aged me, but it does seem to have seasoned me to the point of nonchalance towards its savagery.

We circle about, watching for the enemy, but fail to see it. The pilot is clever, keeping himself well covered in cloud. Finally Control tells us that the bandit has turned and is heading southeast, towards Folkestone on the coast. We head in that direction, but the cloud cover in which the enemy appears to be hiding is very good, and we can't find him; though at the last we patrol well out to sea, nearly to the French coast. The bandit has apparently given up trying to bomb, and gone home.

Now we are ordered north a little way, and there, near the coast of Dover, we can see a small convoy of ships through rifts in the clouds under us. Control orders us to patrol over the convoy now, so we cruise back and forth over it at about ten thousand feet. There are broken clouds below us, and we keep track of the convoy by watching through the breaks in the clouds. Above, where we are, the sun is shining brightly. I alternately study the beautiful cloud formations as we pass over them, and watch the sky above for enemy fighters.

Our C.O. is inquisitive. "Hello, Control," he calls. "Have you any more bandits for us?"

Hello, Tiger Red One. No, I'm sorry, there doesn't seem to be anything about at present. Business is very bad today. I will try my best to dig something up for you, though.

I switch off my gun-sight and put the cover back over my firing button. We patrol our beat in the sky above the convoy for nearly an hour, during which no more bandits are reported about; and then Control orders us to land: "Sorry to have kept you up so long. I tried to find some work for you, but the Huns won't cooperate today."

We head back westward, losing height and descending through the clouds as we go, and in a few minutes have covered the sixty or seventy miles back to our airdrome and are circling preparatory to landing. Our engines are throttled well back now; and watching the C.O.'s machine I see his wheels drop from the wings and start to swing down into position for landing. I move my own landing gear control lever from the "up" position to "down"; and a few seconds later I feel thumps, and a green light comes on in my instrument panel, indicating that the wheels are down in position for landing.

I pull the sliding hatch open over my cockpit, and a rush of wind and sound greets me. I move my propeller pitch control into fully fine position, and now we are making our final gliding turn to come in to land, still in our "V" formation. I drop back and swing over to the right of the other two and take up position behind and to the right of Percy, so that we are all three in a straight line, each behind and to the right of the one in front of him, the C.O. leading. This is called "echelon" formation.

I see the C.O.'s wing flaps come down and then Percy's, and I switch the flap control on my instrument panel to the "down" position and hear a hiss of air and feel my machine surge up a little as my own landing flaps go down. These flaps cause the airplane to lose speed more quickly and to land more slowly.

We glide in over the obstructions at less than a hundred miles per hour, using our engines part of the time to help keep the machines under control at this comparatively slow speed until they are safely on the ground.

After I've taxied into place and shut off my engine I once more arrange everything "in readiness" in the cockpit, climb out and put my parachute back on the tail, and stroll back to the pilots' room with the C.O. and Percy. It was just another uneventful patrol, but we agree that it has been a pleasant ride.

When we open the door of the pilots' room Chaddy asks, "Did you see anything, sir?"

"Nope," our C.O. replies as he pulls up his chair and picks up the magazine he was reading. "We tried to find a bandit, but he couldn't make up his mind where he was going. First he approached Chatham, then Southend, then Folkestone, and he finally came to a decision on home apparently. At least we chased him nearly to France without seeing him, and he didn't come back. He was in cloud all the time, and we sort of escorted him around on his tour, it seems, without ever getting to see him. The rest of the time we spent sitting around over a convoy that's going through the Straits."

Once more we relax, but it's getting near one o'clock now, and soon the telephone orderly sticks his head out of the office door with the awaited message: "Operations says the squadron may now go to 'Available at call,' sir."

Our shift is over, and unless something very big starts we are off for the afternoon.

Entering the mess, I glance at the letter rack in the hall, see a letter in my box, take it out. It's from home, mailed a month ago, and I rush to my room and read it before washing up.

Having read my letter and washed, I join the rest of the boys in the dining hall. The pilots of the other squadron have had their dinner earlier because they relieved us, and most of the airdrome and Operations officers have finished eating and are in the lounge; so once again we have the dining room mainly to ourselves. Waiters bring us soup, and then we get our main course cafeteria style. There is choice of "curry and rice" or Yorkshire pudding for the main dish. Big, good-natured Sam, filling our plates, checks me. "You don't need to tell me—I know what you want when there's curry. You don't have to tell *me!*" And he heaps a generous helping of curry and rice on my plate. It's an English dish that I especially like, as Sam has learned long ago.

I help myself to potatoes and greens. Then we have a choice of tapioca pudding or rhubarb pie for dessert. The pie is made in a dish about the size of a dishpan, and you dip in to get what you want of it.

After lunch we may help ourselves to coffee in an urn in the hallway, in tiny cups about half the size of ordinary cups. It's atrocious compared with American coffee, though, and I seldom drink it. The only place where I've been able to get good coffee in England is the American Eagle Club on Charing Cross Road in London. (Note to Mr. Hutchinson of the Club: I expect two free cups of coffee for this plug, the next time I'm in town.)

In the lounge after lunch airdrome and Operations officers join in the conversation. Genial Squadron Leader A——, who was our controller this morning while we were on patrol, comes up to speak to our C.O. He has a pilot's wings on his uniform and three or four ribbons earned in the last war. "I'm awfully sorry I had to keep you boys up there so long this morning, but—"

"Oh, that was entirely all right," our C.O. breaks in. "We enjoyed it immensely. The weather was fine and we had a very nice ride out of it."

"Well, I'm very glad of that. There was absolutely nothing about after you chased that bandit back to France, but you know that convoy was right there passing within a few miles of the French coast, and I felt that I just had to keep some one over it. There wasn't a plane in the sky on the other side, but still if no one was on patrol and some Hun *had* slipped out and taken a crack at it the Navy just never would have forgiven us; and I shouldn't blame them. So I thought, as long as you boys were in the air, I'd keep you around over it for a while instead of sending someone else."

"I'm really glad you did," our C.O. assures him. "We've hardly done any flying lately, and that sort of thing helps to keep us from getting rusty. It's a nice day, and we were just as comfortable sitting around up there as we would have been sitting around in the pilots' room on readiness; and we were a lot less bored."

I think to myself, "Is it possible that this same man we're standing beside now was the voice in our headphones that ruled us many miles away in that weird world above the clouds only an hour or so ago?"

None of us is gifted with even a fraction of the imagination we need to realise what we do when we're on patrol, what miracles we perform as part of the day's work! We were so big and fast and terrific, streaking about above the clouds out there, so completely detached from the earth, yet obeying this man's quiet distant voice; and the C.O. terms it "sitting around up there." Man's accomplishments have outstripped his capacity to comprehend them!

We spend the afternoon in various ways. We are on call, but can do anything we like as long as we stay on the airdrome. I spend some time in my room practicing on my accordion. Percy joins me with his, and we work on some pieces together. Then our C.O. brings his, and the three of us work together for a while. Percy and I are just learning, but the C.O. is a good player. The C.O. and I work on a homemade arrangement of "Carry Me Back to Old Virginny" which I've worked out from the way my mother used to play it on the piano, and which the C.O. is very fond of.

After an hour's pleasant practice together we break up. The C.O. has to go to his office and take care of some work, and I have an appointment with Norman to practice on the "Link Trainer."

This is an American invention for pilots to practice blind flying—piloting by instrument. It consists of a little mock airplane mounted on a pedestal, with the closed cockpit and controls of an airplane and a complete layout of instruments. An intricate arrangement of motors and connections causes it to behave just like an airplane, and a recording attachment records on a sheet of paper the course that the student is theoretically flying.

I find Norman in the billiard room with Elby, and after they've finished their game Norman and I don our caps and Irving jackets and walk through the camp to the Link Trainer building. We take turns instructing each other in the trainer for about half an hour each. The one who is student climbs into the tiny cockpit, closes the hood so he can't see outside, and starts the motors. Then he pilots it by the instruments before him, while the one who is acting as instructor assigns the courses that he is to fly and orders him to make climbs, glides, turns, and so on, all by a little telephone arrangement.

By the time we've finished this and returned to the mess it's tea time, and we join other officers who are drifting into the dining room. Our "tea" consists of toast and marmalade or jam, two or three kinds of cake, and of course tea.

After that I wander back to my room, light the fire in my fireplace, and sit down in front of this friendly little centre of warmth to write a letter home:

Dear Mother and Dad: Just received your letter . . .

It's beginning to get dark, and my batman comes in and puts up the black-out blinds in front of my windows. They are wooden frameworks that fit the window frames, covered with heavy black cloth to keep any light from showing outside.

My letter finished, I wander back to the lounge, feeling restless. John and Tid are there, reading the evening papers, and I join them. It's just after six o'clock now, and the six o'clock news is being read by the B.B.C. announcer. He is saying something about an enemy bomber that:

> .....crossed the southeast coast this morning and came inland a short distance, but turned back without dropping any bombs, and returned homeward across the Channel pursued by our fighters."

A little later some one tunes the radio over to the German radio station at Bremen. The German "news" in English is being given, by the familiar pontifical voice of "Lord Haw Haw," as he is called—the Englishman who turned traitor and works for the Nazis:

> This morning, bombers of the German Air Force attacked the British naval dockyards at Chatham, causing great devastation among docks and shipyards and destroying a British cruiser. They also attacked military objectives at Southend and Folkestone, wreaking terrific havoc. Immediately after this raid a British convoy attempting to pass through the Straits of Dover was attacked by our bombers, and a destroyer and six merchant ships totalling thirty thousand tons were sunk.
> A formation of twenty-five British Spitfires were guarding this convoy, but they fled at sight of our bombers. However, one of our bombers pursued them and shot down two of them. The complete destruction of the British Royal Air Force is now nearly finished; and it is definitely known that the few remaining British pilots are so exhausted and terrified that many of them refuse to take to the air when ordered to go up and intercept our airplanes.

We are only half listening, as we have been discussing whether we should go by bus down to R———, the nearby suburb of London, to take in a movie. John has just yawned and remarked: "This inaction is getting me down. I surely wish those Huns would come over and give us a scrap once in a while!"

We finally decide in favour of a movie instead of supper, and getting our overcoats and caps we leave the mess by the back door and take a short cut out of the camp to the bus stop near by. The Havana Theatre is showing Bette Davis in *All This and Heaven, Too*, and we are soon losing ourselves in the happiness and romance and sweet sadness of this great picture.

Donald Duck snaps us out of it afterward and keeps our sides splitting with his adventures on a camping trip; and at the end we rise with the rest of the audience and stand at attention while "God Save the King" is played.

Outside after the show, we half feel our way along the darkened streets to a restaurant we know, where we have a light lunch to make up for the supper we missed.

A crowd of airmen are waiting for the bus at the stopping point when we get there, many of them from our squadron. We watch the numbers on the various busses that come down the street, until ours comes. Just two dim little lights approaching us along the dark street, and when they are close we can make out the towering outlines of the big double-decker bus, with the number "123" in dim blue light on the front, which means it's the one we want.

We swing aboard and climb the little winding stairway to the upper deck, and feel our way to seats in the gloomy interior, which is very dimly illuminated by little blue lights. Maybe two dozen airmen fill most of the seats up here, and the huge vehicle trundles off through the darkness.

As the bus sways along the lonely road the smooth whining rhythm of the motor is background and accompaniment for snatches of soldiers' ditties and ballads as some of the boys break out in song. Cockney and Irish and Yorkshire and Welsh and Scotch voices, strong and throaty, blend in songs of, home and sweethearts.

Finally the bus slows down for the airdrome, and the spell is broken.

We clamber out and pass through the sentry gate after being identified, and make our way by the familiar short cut to the back door of the mess. It's misting a little, and no German planes have been over, so we guess that the weather is "closing down" and there won't be any flying tomorrow. We are only supposed to be at "fifteen minutes available" in the morning anyway, not being scheduled for readiness until afternoon; so we're pretty sure we can sleep late in the morning.

We bid one another goodnight, and I go to my room, take a bath, and go to bed. Another day of war, such as it is for us at this period, is over.

CHAPTER 12

We Stage a Comeback

One night late in December it was especially blitzy. No bombs were dropped near us, but there were Huns droning back and forth overhead continuously for several hours. The anti-aircraft kept up an unceasing racket, and even Alfy joined the chorus more frequently than ever before, making the boys drop their ale tankards and spill their sherry in the lounge during the evening, and afterward breaking our sleep pretty frequently.

Once during the night the droning of a German machine suddenly swelled to a long agonised moaning that ceased suddenly at its very peak, and afterward we learned that it was a Junkers 88 that had been hit by anti-aircraft fire and had dived into the ground not far away.

Next morning we knew what it was all about. The great fire raid had been made on the City of London, causing England's worst fire in several centuries.

There was still no resumption in daylight activity, and during the lull we speculated a lot on its meaning. We wondered if the Huns were getting ready to start a big offensive, and most of us thought it inevitable. They had learned that on long drawn-out air offensive operations over our territory their losses were all out of proportion to their winnings in combat with us. Therefore it seemed logical to expect them to get organised for a concentrated short offensive to try to get control of the air over southeast England, the first necessary step before they can commence the one and only campaign which if successful may win them the war—the invasion of England.

The lack of German air activity in daytime seemed ominous, and we wondered when there would be a change, not knowing at first that we were to take matters into our own hands and make the first change—that we British fighter pilots, who were supposed to have been annihilated and driven from the air by the overwhelming hordes of Prussian fliers who were set upon us last summer and fall, were to show how badly we were beaten by striking the first offensive blows of the new year!

So that you will understand what a significant step it was for us to take the offensive, let me remind you of the status of the R.A.F. in the summer of 1940 when the great Battle for Britain began. Without a doubt we were greatly outnumbered. Obviously then we had to make every machine and pilot count, and could not afford the extra risks involved in fighting over the enemy's territory, where all pilots shot down would be lost because those who escaped alive would be captured, and where damaged machines that had to force-land would be lost also, together with their pilots. We could only afford to fight on our own ground, where we could keep losses to an absolute minimum. It would be a tremendous step for us to go on the offensive, significant because it would mean we had grown enough to be able to afford such risks, and doubly significant if it came now on the heels of the enemy's abandonment of such operations.

Often we longed for the time we could go on the offensive and give the Hun some of his own medicine, and wondered if it would come soon. We had been on the defensive so long that it was hard to imagine what it would be like going over enemy territory, but we grinned in anticipation of making the Nazis spend long hours "at readiness" as we did, taking off at unexpected times to go up without knowing where to expect the enemy or in what numbers.

So when the big news came shortly after the first of the year, it was like the answer to a prayer for most of us. We were to initiate things with a daylight bombing raid on a target in northwest France! A formation of bombers was to be escorted by several squadrons of Spitfires and Hurricanes, and our squadron was included.

There would be no attempt to sneak through and get away without being intercepted, for the main object of the raid was to get the Huns to come up and do battle. To add to the sting of the raid two squadrons of Hurricanes were going to "shoot up" the St. Inglevert airdromes, a cluster of airdromes that are used by the Nazis as front-line fighter bases. By this is meant they would attack with machine-gun fire, strafing personnel, gun positions, vehicles, and parked airplanes.

"Zero hour" was noon one day early in January. All morning we sat around in nervous anticipation. We speculated a lot on how well prepared the Huns would be to meet us. One thing we felt sure of was that, if they intercepted us at all, it would be with an enormous mass, for we had never seen them offer to do battle without at least a three-to-one advantage in numbers.

This sounds like boasting, I realise, but it's absolutely true. Any R.A.F. fighter pilot will tell you the same, and boasting is anything but a fad in the R.A.F. On the average these boys are by far the most modest fellows I've known, and I've knocked about quite a bit. The average of them has less to say about the time he faced a dozen Messerschmitts alone (as most of them have) and came back with half his tail and an aileron shot away, than the average American commercial pilot whom you can hear around any big city airport telling about the time he flew clear across Lake Deepwater with a spark-plug wire on one of his nine cylinders getting looser and looser.

One of "B" Flight's pilots, a very young-looking fair-haired kid whom we called "Toss," was particularly excited. He sat or stood around all morning, grinning from ear to ear in anticipation, and saying: "We're for it. We're for it now! We'll have a party for sure this time!"

We took off for our rendezvous at the appointed place and time. Circling slowly we fell into our prearranged position with the other squadrons of fighters and the bombers, and in a few minutes we were sweeping down across the Thames Estuary, cutting southeast over Kent, across the cliffs near Dover, and out over the Channel. We must have been a formidable sight to the German observers on the coast of France as we approached, for as far as I know this was the biggest British formation that had ever flown in war. There were over a hundred machines—not nearly as many as the Nazis had used in their big raids on England last summer, not as many as my squadron had often faced alone; but we made a pretty good-sized cloud just the same, and it was certainly more than the Nazis had ever had to face before!

We were to enter France from the north, between Calais and Dunkirk where the coast runs almost east and west. We flew eastward almost parallel with the coast until we were about by Calais, then started swinging in. I had had trouble with my fingers getting cold on the way, but now that we were nearing France I found that they weren't bothering any more. My circulation had speeded up enough!

As we started coming in over the coast black puffs of smoke began unfolding here and there in the air about us, as if by magic. The Germans have very heavy concentrations of anti-aircraft batteries along the coast, and they were going full swing. By the time we crossed the coast the air about us was well peppered. None of their shots came close though, so we didn't have to change course. This was reassuring, and I began to feel more at ease.

Now that we were crossing into a foreign country, I had an impish desire to call out on the R/T and ask the boys if they all had their passports ready. I would have, if we hadn't been told not to "do any natting over the R/T" until the raid was over.

The two squadrons of Hurricanes that were to attack the St. Inglevert airdromes detached themselves from the formation about the time we entered France, and went down. They would do their attack at very low altitude. All of us were scanning the sky closely now, watching for the expected horde of Huns who we felt would be coming to intercept us.

I began to speculate on the confusion at the Nazi airdromes, when for the first time in the war they were getting a real alarm. I imagined Nazi pilots having to rush out from dinner, from bed, from the bar, and from wherever else they might be—the confusion of getting transportation to their drome, and all the other difficulties incidental to an unexpected call to arms. "Hurry, we're being invaded!" "Where's my helmet?" "Where's Hans?" "Run and get Wolfgang out of bed—if he's sober!" I almost forgot my business of watching for them in my speculations on what excitement our appearance must have caused among them. It made me feel good. They were getting some of their own at last!

We kept swinging around in a gentle right-hand turn, first to the south, then southwest, then west, so that finally we were headed home again, although we were now well inside France. Still we could see no signs of enemy planes.

The bombers were passing over their target now, and I began to think they hadn't dropped their bombs yet, for there was no sign of any smoke in the target area. Suddenly a series of volcanic explosions began occurring all about in the target area, with debris flying up and great clouds of smoke following. They had dropped their bombs all right, but I'd forgotten it would take a little time for the bombs to get down to the ground. It looked to me as if they'd covered the area pretty thoroughly, and very accurately.

We passed a little south of the St. Inglevert airdromes, the ones that the Hurricanes were "shooting up," and I grinned at the unforgettable sight there. The twenty-four Hurricanes were making themselves look like a hundred, all milling about over the airdromes in a mass of wheeling, diving, zooming, twisting and turning machines, as each pilot dived down to machine-gun a target and then zoomed up to turn and dive back in again. It was like a bunch of bees swarming. Most of these pilots were Canadians ("Crazy Canadians," our C.O. jokingly termed them in warning us all to stay clear of them while they were on this job), and they were surely acting the part now. I wondered what would happen to any unhappy Messerschmitt that would have the misfortune to blunder into their midst! The Canadians were exhausting the accumulated steam from many weeks of virtual idleness in this attack, and making a job of it.

Now the bombers, whom we were trailing, were approaching the coast, and the air beneath them became full of the angry black puffs of smoke from anti-aircraft shells sent up by the coastal guns again. We were passing out near Cape Gris Nez, where I fought my first air battle last summer. By the time we reached the coast the anti-aircraft smoke was like a long black cloud just beneath us, with flashes from fresh explosions agitating about in it. All of the fire was too low to bother us, and most of it seemed to be erratic in direction also. Only once or twice I felt little jolts in the air from shells that exploded somewhere close beneath us.

Then we were out over the Channel again, and I realised that the raid was over and we hadn't seen a single enemy airplane. We had singed Hitler's moustache and given Herr Goring a nice little punch in his fat middle, and were getting away without even a fight! Big in its significance, the raid, as far as we were concerned, might just as well have been a little cross-country practice trip. Not one of us had fired his guns, and none of us had been fired at, except by the anti-aircraft guns which practically don't count.

It was while we were crossing the Channel on the way home that the only fighting took place, though we didn't know about even this until afterward. It appeared that three Messerschmitts followed us out over the Channel—keeping a safe distance behind and trying to look brave, thinking it was all over, I suppose. They probably planned to tell their superiors how they had routed us and chased us home. But of course they didn't know about the Hurricanes that were still behind us, making sure that everything worth while that they could find on the St. Inglevert airdromes was riddled. These Hurricanes finally got through and followed us a few minutes later, just in time to come across the three unhappy Messerschmitts, and they shot all three down into the sea.

It was a nice little trip, and it boosted our morale a lot. The papers made a big thing of it, and every one in London was talking about it for the next few days. It made people feel good to know that we were giving the Nazis some of their own, and it boosted their confidence by proving that the R.A.F. was so far from being annihilated by the German blitz that it could administer blows of its own.

Don't confuse this with the night raiding and bombing, which is always carried out by both sides when weather permits, under cover of darkness when the chance of combat is negligible; nor with small daylight bombing raids using cloud cover. Those two kinds of bombing have always been carried on by both sides. It's the raids in broad daylight, where the enemy has a chance to see the raiders and do battle to stop them, that the Nazis ceased last fall and we began with this raid in January,

The weather turned foggy the next day, and at noon our squadron was released for the rest of the day Tommy, my new flight commander, and I wanted to see the fire damage in the City of London; so we went downtown and spent the afternoon there.

The City of London is a borough in the central part of London that contains the buildings of many large banking and business firms. The section that was burned out was roped off, but we managed to get in on the strength of our uniforms. It was a ghastly sight—silent streets lined with empty stone skeletons of once magnificent buildings, the fire-blackened walls still standing with blank windows and nothing inside but heaps of brick and rubble. All about was the haunting smell of burned wood. We were shown through the ruins of the Guildhall, London's once magnificent city hall, scene of countless historical events; and we told the official who showed us through it that each of us would remember this the next time he got a Hun in his sights. There was no possible military objective anywhere in the vicinity, and it was truly "an act of vandalism by the greatest vandal of all time."

One scene I don't think I'll ever forget, as an example of the indestructibility of the British spirit. Near the outskirts of the area which was burned out we followed a street on one side of which all the buildings were burned. Most of the buildings on the other side were burned out, too; but sandwiched in between two large buildings that were completely burned out so that only the walls stood, we saw a little ladies' dress shop that had somehow been saved. The walls outside were black from the fire; the windows, cracked, and the window frames, scorched. Bricks and rubble blocked the street in front of it.

But the sidewalk was swept clean, and that little shop, with ghastly fire-blackened desolation all around it, burned-out stone buildings towering around it on both sides of the narrow street—that little shop was still open for business, and doing business, with its windows filled with a neat display of ladies' dainty underthings!

Weather of course interfered a great deal with the operations of both sides through the winter, but the R.A.F. let few opportunities pass to follow up their initial daylight air offensive. Practically every day of good weather R.A.F. fighter squadrons made sweeps over France, sometimes escorting more bombing raids and sometimes just going by themselves, but always giving the Nazis a chance to do battle if they would.

Our squadron wasn't always on these sweeps, or raids, for the work was rotated among a number of squadrons; and I didn't necessarily go each time our squadron went, because we now had plenty of spare pilots and the work was rotated among us. There's little formality about the distribution of flying duties in an average R.A.F. fighter squadron. The spirit of the boys is such that all want to do their share, and it's run like a big family, with the C.O. permitting the boys to work out their own schedules usually, subject to his approval.

When there is a 100 *per cent* reserve of pilots in the squadron, usually about a third are away at any one time, either on leave or on forty-eight-hour passes; and for the most part the pilots arrange among themselves who is to work on what days, who is to go on leave when, etc., making a schedule that will be most suitable to all while allowing for an equal distribution of work.

Our squadron went on a number of raids and sweeps during January and February, over Belgium as well as France, and even parts of Holland. Never on these sorties did any of us get a chance to use his guns. The same was true of most of the rest of the squadrons. Occasionally a few Huns would approach our formations at high altitude and watch for a chance to drop on a straggler, but there was never a sign of any real attempt to do battle. Nor did they make any offensive sweeps of their own until late in February, when they began sending a formation over very high once in a while, to scurry home as soon as our fighters reached their altitude and they saw they would have to fight if they stayed any longer.

Thus the winter went on, while we pilots flew a little and loafed a lot, always wondering when the big blitz would start again.

One foggy morning a section of three of our machines was sent out over the North Sea after a bandit. They were Jimmy leading the section, Toss, and John. John came back ahead of the rest, and when he taxied up it was easy to see why. His guns had been fired, his bulletproof windscreen was badly mangled, and there were big holes in his wing and fuselage.

They had intercepted a Junkers 88 bomber (a larger type than the Junkers 87 dive bomber), and its rear gunner had done this to John's machine with cannon fire. The other two boys soon came in, to say they had both fired on the Junkers but finally lost it in the clouds. They thought it was going down but of course couldn't claim a victory. However, a few hours later they got confirmation. An SOS from the crew had been intercepted, stating that they had crashed in the sea and abandoned the airplane and were floating in their life raft.

A little later a German ambulance airplane flew to the spot and picked them up, the R.A.F. making no attempt to interfere. So that established the victory, and it was awarded to the boys as confirmed—one-third to each pilot. It was the first engagement any of us had had in the new year.

CHAPTER 13

Interlude

Early in the winter our C.O. had told me he was trying to get me an opportunity to go home on leave; and quietly through the winter he had been working on it. Even when prospects began to look good I couldn't believe it, and I said little about it in my letters home except that I had an application in. Somehow it didn't seem possible that I could leave while this war of which I was part was still going on, and actually live again in the old kind of world with no enemies and no black-outs and no bombing nor readiness periods nor patrols, and with good coffee and cars running on the right side of the street. I said I wouldn't believe it until I was on the boat!

Late in February an order came transferring me to a new squadron. I hated to leave the old bunch whom I knew so well; the order had come with little warning, and I had to leave right away; so I avoided farewells as much as possible and got off.

My new squadron mates were fine fellows like all the rest of the R.A.F. They took me on a party the first night I was with them, and in twenty-four hours I was feeling right at home.

Their work was a little different, and there has been some publicity about their, or rather our, activities. However, I won't go into that now. They used the same type Supermarine Spitfires that my old squadron had, and I got along all right.

Only a few days later a message came through to the squadron's headquarters:

Pilot Officer Donahue report to Embarkation Officer at ——— not later than ———.

I knew what it meant: my trip to America, which had been only a dream, was to become a reality!

The message gave me three days' notice, and during the next two I spent my spare time packing the things I wanted to take, making last-minute preparations, and pinching myself to prove that I was awake and it was really happening. I was to leave on the noon train, and the last day I did the early morning patrol with Tony, my flight commander.

As I took off on what was to be my last flight in an indefinite time I uttered a little prayer that I might finally find a Hun. I still hadn't used my guns since the engagement on Armistice Day!

We cruised across the Channel into France in hope of "scaring something up," and I watched the sunrise from above clouds over Dunkirk at twenty-five thousand feet. We hadn't found a sign of life in the air when Control called us and warned us that "you're getting your feet pretty wet"—which sounded like a hint that he'd feel better if we were closer home.

So we headed back. As we neared the English coast, Control told us a bandit was approaching us from the south at about eight thousand feet. There was a heavy bank of clouds at that height, so we knew the bandit must be approaching in them. They ended about five miles south of us, so that if he kept coming our way he would shortly break out into clear air where we could see him and perhaps intercept him. It undoubtedly was a bomber trying to get to England without being seen.

We approached the edge of the clouds, and Control said, "The bandit is very close to you now."

I switched on my gun-sight and turned my firing button off safety, watching the edge of the clouds closely and fervently hoping that my prayer would be answered and a bomber would make its appearance; but minutes went by, and no Hun appeared. Then Control called and told us the bandit had gone back towards France. Hearing new voices over the R/T, I knew that it was the next patrol coming up to relieve us, telling Control that they were in the air. Then Control called us and told us we might land; and regretfully I took a last look at France and switched off my gun-sight and put my firing button back on safety and turned back to our base.

At the last minute before I left the airdrome for the train I remembered promising to bring home some pieces of a German plane for souvenirs; so I hunted and found some pieces of a Messerschmitt dumped behind one of the buildings, tore off a few strips of metal wing-covering, and packed them in my things.

The voyage was rough and seemed endless. I am a poor sailor, and though I managed to eat my meals pretty regularly I found that there were a bunch of rules which my stomach dictated for me: principally that I couldn't concentrate my gaze on one thing while the ship was rolling; and that prevented my reading. No radios can be used on ship either, for it is found that ships can be located by radio impulses that radio receivers themselves send out sometimes.

We were cut off from the world except for daily news summaries which were received on the ship's wireless and typed out and posted in the passengers' lounge; and for the sight of the other ships in the convoy. I would stand out on deck by the hour watching the waves and the other ships and trying to read the signals flashed back and forth between the ships by means of signal lamps.

One Sunday forenoon the weather was absolutely lousy. It alternately rained and snowed and sleeted. Waves broke over the front of the ship as it heaved and tossed, and nearly drenched those of us who were on deck. Visibility was very low, and we could scarcely see the other ships in the convoy.

We passengers were never informed of our position; but we had been sailing so long that we didn't see how we could help being nearly "there." Also some unusual activities of the crew suggested that something was afoot. Looking off to our port I saw what looked like a low dark cloud nearly hidden by the mist, and I watched it for several minutes, until I knew it couldn't be a cloud, because it had trees on it!

This is supposed to be a story of war, so I'll go lightly over this interlude of peace. I was to have about a week at home, and I planned to spend it getting in some good exercise on my father's farm, to make up for some of the loafing I'd done through the winter.

I didn't get in much work. A crowd met me at the train in my home town, and I found myself almost a celebrity! I had more invitations than I could possibly accept to speak at various gatherings and over the radio. The Commercial Club of St. Charles gave a banquet in my honour and presented me with a wonderful gold wrist watch and my mother with a bouquet of flowers. The Kiwanis of Minneapolis gave me a silver loving cup. Friends were coming to see me all the time, and I was deluged with letters—even to receiving fan mail! Most of the week I was in a daze, everyone was so good to me.

The lights at night were as strange to get used to as the black-out had been when I first went to England. Especially when I was inside a brightly lighted place at night and opened the door to go out, absently expecting to see nothing but darkened streets and houses and little dim lights on cars, I would be bewildered for a moment by the bright street lights, neon signs, and blinding headlights of cars flashing by!

It was also strange being in civilian clothes again, for I was unable to wear my uniform: according to international law I must be interned for appearing in the uniform of a belligerent nation. It was strange too, to see so many young men in civilian clothes, and no British uniforms—and to walk down the street without having to reply to salutes continually. The few uniforms I did see looked very odd, after being used to seeing British and allied uniforms for so long.

I found it hard to realise the change in popular opinion that had taken place in the United States in the few months I was gone, and the widespread awakening to the peril which the many-phased Nazi march of conquest holds for America; though in the papers I occasionally saw strange manifestations of it.

A pilot officer in the Royal Air Force, such as myself, earns the equivalent of about $88.00 per month, out of which he must pay for his meals, keep up his uniform, and pay about $6.00 per month income tax. It was hard to believe that, among a people ninety per cent convinced that their safety depends on England's victory, factory workers engaged in industries vital to that victory were striking and delaying production and jeopardizing England's chances.

The average American aircraft factory worker certainly earns more than the British pilots flying the aircraft he builds, and works much shorter hours. Yet I read of their striking for still more pay, though every day of strike by workers in aircraft factories means that boys who are fighting their battles will die for the want of the new equipment. The more airplanes and guns and tanks America can furnish England now, the fewer she may have to produce for herself *and man with her own sons* later, for England can be depended on to use them to the greatest advantage against the common enemy.

If Germany wins this war there will be no "American standard of living" such as we have known. America will be forced to impoverish herself and her people in the greatest armament race in history to forestall the inevitable Nazi encroachment in the Western Hemisphere; and in that program there will be no room for maintenance of the old living standards against the Nazis' advantage of slave labour from defeated countries. It seemed foolish for Americans to be using methods to raise their standard of living which jeopardize their very existence as Americans—standard of living and all!

I did manage to spend a little time working on my father's farm, and it was strange to be doing the familiar tasks I knew so well on the farm just as if nothing had ever happened, while in my pocketbook I carried a little piece of pasteboard that read:

Return Ticket
Southern Railway
LONDON
(Charing Cross)
to
F———

CHAPTER 14

The Watch over the Channel

I arrived back in London early in the morning of the 17th of April. The sky was cloudless, like the morning in July when I first saw London. In other ways it was a painful though dramatic contrast.

On that other morning the city had been peaceful except for preparations for what was to come, and the air was fresh and clear.

This was the morning after the greatest bombardment that London had received, and the sun was a red ball glowing feebly through the haze of brown smoke that covered the city. Fire fighters were working everywhere; streets were roped off, littered with broken glass and scattered brick and masonry and other rubble; fire hoses lay all about. Piles of rubble marked where buildings had stood the day before.

Other buildings still stood, burned out or burning out inside. Here and there was a great pit in the middle of a street, with dirt and rock scattered all about and water from broken mains flooding the street. Firemen were still working heroically against the flames of buildings struck by fire bombs; and A.R.P. workers toiled in the debris of buildings hit by high-explosive bombs, to rescue persons trapped inside.

The London firemen are my heroes there. The risk they take in fighting fires during air raids is terrible, for the whole scheme of Nazi bombing is to have the first planes of the raid loaded with fire bombs and manned by the best crews, who locate the targets and set them on fire, so that the machines that follow with the high explosive bombs have only to aim at the fires.

The firemen attack these fires unflinchingly, knowing that the fires they are fighting are targets for more bombs. Their casualties are very high and their work exhausting, but nothing seems to stop them.

I remember particularly one rather youngish man, in the uniform of the Auxiliary Fire Service, drinking a cup of tea as he leaned against a mobile canteen that was stopped close to the burning building that he was working on. It was nearly noon, and he had obviously been up all night. His uniform was drenched, torn, and plastered with mud from brick and cement dust. His blond hair was matted and tousled under his steel helmet. His face was grimy and smoke-stained, and his nose bloodied, and he seemed a little groggy; but he was grinning just the same. Like a boxer standing back in a neutral corner, along about the twelfth round.

Waiting for the train that would take me to my squadron, I entered the crowded restaurant at the station and sat down for tea. A lady sat down at the same table, looking tired and a little stunned. She told me that she lived just outside London, but had a little restaurant in town. She had spent the day winding up her business as best she could, because her place had been blasted to bits the night before. And she was only one of many. Those Americans who would rather wait and have war come to them, than let their sons fight abroad, could take a lesson from that and many things much worse that I saw that day.

The trainman at the gate looked a little curiously at the crumpled and battered return ticket that I showed him. It was nearly two months since I had used the first half of it.

It was swell to get back to the squadron, though I felt a little bit like a prodigal after being away so long. The boys were all tickled to see me and to get the cigarettes and other things I had brought from America. They were throwing a party in the mess that night, so that I couldn't have arrived at a better time.

I was glad to learn that they had had some very successful operations while I was gone. "Killer" McKay, as the newspapers call him, had added a bar to his Distinguished Flying Medal, having got his twelfth confirmed victory. Two of the boys had been badly wounded though, and at least one of them, Sergeant Mann, is not expected to be able to fly again. He was awarded the Distinguished Flying Medal while in the hospital.

This boy had been shot down for the sixth time. His machine was badly shot up and his engine wrecked over the Channel, but he managed to glide back over land. Then when he was only about two hundred feet up, too low to bail out, his machine caught fire and he had to force-land it in a farmer's field. He crawled out of the cockpit then, and in spite of the fact that he was terribly burned, he took his camera out of his pocket, carefully adjusted it for light and distance, and snapped two pictures of the blazing wreck, after which he staggered across two fields to the farmhouse!

As you may recall, this is not my original squadron. I was posted to it a few days before I went to America. Naturally I wanted to get in touch with my former squadron and find out how they were; and I did so, by telephone, the first night.

The news I got didn't help me to sleep well that night, and clouded my otherwise joyous return to action. If there had been heavy fighting while I was gone, as in the blitz of August and September, 1940, I should have known that I couldn't expect the boys to be all right. But I knew the fighting had been slight, with both British and German casualties comparatively minor, and I had high hopes that my old bunch would be unchanged. The news I got was hard to take.

Pip and Norman are both gone. John is missing, but there is a possibility that he is alive, a prisoner of war. I hope so.

Nearly as hard to take as the deaths of Pip and Norman was the news that the C.O., whom we idolised and who had done so much for me, including making my trip to America possible, is a prisoner of war. That news was a source of joy to the boys when it came, because they had seen him shot down over France under circumstances that seemed to make it impossible for him to get out alive, and they had sadly given him up for dead.

We hope that he will be treated well, and from what we hear of the treatment the Germans accord their prisoners he probably will. According to an international agreement they are required to give their prisoners the same food *and pay* as they give the equivalent ranks in their own forces. This is checked up on by the Red Cross.

Just before I went to America on leave, Gillies and I were patrolling at low altitude one morning when we sighted a set of fifteen vapour trails very high up, coming across from France. As we were too low and too few to do anything about it we just watched them and, when they were nearly to the English coast, saw one turn around and go back, apparently with engine trouble. They were Messerschmitt 109's on offensive patrol.

When they got over England we were right under them, and three of them came down towards us; we thought we were going to have a fight, but they went away again. It was an insignificant occurrence, and I thought no more about it.

Then a day or two after I got back from leave, Gillies showed me a picture from *The Aeroplane* of a formation of German planes making vapour trails, and I recognised it as the formation we had seen, includ-

Vapour Trails
English Channel and coast of France in the background of this photograph, taken with long-focus lens and infrared plate.

ing the one which turned back!

I'm sorry I can't tell much about the work of my present squadron, because it's very interesting. However, it is different from that of other fighter squadrons, and to a certain extent secret. I'll quote from what one London newspaper was permitted to say about us recently. This is from a write-up in *The People*, headed "Britain's Cavalry of the Air":

> Air Station, South-East England, Saturday The Spitfire pilots at this station think nothing of a little before-breakfast "singeing of Hitler's moustache" raid. They are a kind of cavalry of the air, scouting in front of the main forces and operating almost entirely over the Channel or enemy territory.
> These young pilots, spearhead of our attack—their work is mostly offensive—have a different job to the rest of the R.A.F. Our bombers may go out on specific jobs, our fighters on interceptions. But these Channel patrols are up harrying, probing, prying, making lightning machine-gun raids and generally being a nuisance.
> When they go off on a routine "reco"—reconnaissance flight— they never quite know what they will find. They are liable to drop in for a lot of unlooked-for trouble, and generally come out of it very well. . . .

The white-capped waves of the French coastal waters were rocketing backwards a few hundred feet below us, and just over our heads, five hundred feet above the sea, scattered fluffy clouds were billowing past. Heavier clouds obscured the sun. It was very early on a dull murky morning a few days after my return from America, and Tony (my flight commander) and I were doing the dawn patrol. We were flying low over the sea about three or four miles north of the French coast near Calais, heading westward for home after having been out near Dunkirk. What we had been doing there will have to be left untold, but my thoughts were mainly on whether the cooks would be up yet in the mess when we got home, so that we could get breakfast. I hate flying before breakfast, and was wishing it was possible to get something to eat early on mornings when we did the dawn patrol.

Control had just warned us over the R/T that there were six or more bandits near us, but it didn't worry us much. He is always anxious when we're in enemy territory, and frets a lot over nothing. We are ever on the alert against surprises, and if we ran into too many Huns we'd just pull up and lose them in the broken clouds close above us. I didn't even turn on my gun-sight or take the firing button off its safety position. I can do that in a second nowadays.

We flew abreast of each other, wide apart, so that we could watch each other's tail. I took a few seconds to check my engine instruments and fuel supply, and when I looked back again I got a little jolt.

Two Messerschmitt 109's were streaking along just above the water a few hundred yards behind us, coming up for a surprise attack! They were camouflaged dark, with their noses painted yellow. Behind them were six more in close formation.

I called out over the R/T "Bandits astern," and waited just long enough to see Tony zoom upwards towards the clouds, indicating that he'd heard me. Then I too zoomed up, switching my gun-sight on and my firing button to the "Fire" position. I still didn't know if there was going to be a fight.

The clouds were so scattered that they gave scant cover, and I pulled on up above them and turned one way and then the other to keep anything from getting on my tail. A moment later the pair who had been closest behind us popped up through the clouds ahead of me, which meant that they had overshot me because of the turns I was doing, and the fight was on!

I took a snap shot at long range at one of them, and it was swell to hear the bedlam again and smell the powder smoke and feel a Spitfire shudder and slow from the recoil as the guns roared. Then I let him alone and took after the other, which had swung across in front of me. I chased him about among the clouds for a wild minute or so, shooting at every chance, as he twisted and ducked about trying to lose me. Twice I saw small pieces fly back off his machine as I was firing, and I finally lost him in the clouds.

Zooming up above the clouds again I saw three or four others near me, and maneuvering about violently to keep any of them from getting on my tail, I got a short "beam" shot at one as he crossed in front of me and then took after another and chased him a little way and got a short shot at him just before I lost him in the clouds.

For a moment I found myself alone, but then another popped up through the clouds in front of me, coming straight towards me head on. He was about fifty feet below my level and about three hundred yards in front, and if he pulled up his nose a little he could shoot at me. But he made no attempt to do so—just flew straight ahead, while I lost no time in nosing down until my sights centred on him and letting him have it until I had to break off to avoid a collision. I started to turn around to follow him after we'd passed, and saw when I looked back that he was no longer flying straight and level but was going down in about a forty-five-degree dive, with black smoke rippling back from under his fuselage. The realisation of what I'd done awed me a little. I swung on around as he disappeared through a very thin cloud and followed him right down under the cloud but wasn't in time to see him crash. There was no sign of him. Then I stooged around under the clouds for a minute, hoping to see some signs of wreckage in the sea. I was sure he had crashed, for he was so low when I last saw him that he couldn't have straightened out before hitting the sea. Even if he had I should have seen him in the air above the sea.

Then a formation of six came along low over the water, probably the same six that had been behind the two who first tried to attack us, and I decided there were too many people here and pulled up into some heavy clouds. When I last saw them they had made no move to follow me, and they may not have seen me.

I had a little difficulty in flying in the clouds then. My compasses were spinning like tops, and my "artificial horizon," which is the main instrument used in blind flying, leered at me from where it lay, almost upside down over in one corner of its cage. It always goes haywire in a dog fight and takes a while to start working again. Finally my "directional gyro" compass quieted down so that I could hold a straight course by it, though it wouldn't tell me what course it was until I checked it by the magnetic compass; but by flying straight and level for a little while I got my magnetic compass to steady down also—and found that I was steering in the direction of Holland.

When finally I got turned around and headed for home, I broke out of the clouds and didn't need the instruments any more anyway.

All this time I had practically forgotten about Tony, not having seen him. In a dog fight it's everyone for himself, and each pilot is too busy to think about anyone else. Now I anxiously called to him over the R/T, asking if he was all right. My radio wasn't tuned right, and I didn't understand his reply; but it was a relief to hear him anyway. I answered back, "I cannot understand your message, but your voice sounds very good!"

On the ground we got each other's stories, and I found that I'd given him some anxiety. He had heard my warning at the start, and had pulled up through the clouds just as I had, turning about to avoid being attacked from behind. But he must have turned in a different direction, for he saw no more Huns; nor did he see me. After a moment he went back down under the clouds but couldn't see any signs of life there either, and he began calling me to find out where I was. I must have had my receiver tuned very badly, or have been just too intent on my work to hear—perhaps a little of both; anyway I never heard him, and when I didn't reply after several calls he asked Control to try to get me.

Control called me several times without getting any answer, and Tony began searching the sea for me, presuming that I was shot down and reflecting how heroically I had warned him of the danger with my last words! Tony said that Control finally called him and told him in the most doleful tones, "I am afraid that I can get no reply from him."

And then a minute later he heard me calling him, and it was like a voice from the dead!

When he learned that all the time he was so worried about me I was having the time of my life in a swell dog fight that he had missed out on completely, he was more than disgusted.

I was hoping to be credited with a confirmed victory on the strength of having seen the 109 going down so obviously finished, but couldn't say I'd actually seen it crash, so that I was only credited with a "probable." If it had been near our own coast I'd have been all right, for then observers on the coast would probably have seen it crash. Later we learned that radio messages had been picked up from the squadron leader of the German formation at the time, calling one pilot for several minutes, and then asking all the other pilots in the formation if they had seen him; and all of them answered that they hadn't. So, although I could only count it as a "probable" I felt that it was at least a "very probable"! I was also credited with a "damaged" in addition, on the strength of having seen pieces flying off the second plane that I fired at; so it wasn't such a bad job of work to get done all before breakfast anyway!

That just about brings the story up to date. It's the best account I can give of my war experiences, subject to the restrictions of censorship, and I hope it has been half as interesting for you to read as it has been for me to live it!

Perhaps I should wind it up by touching on the emotional side; I've thought of it. But it might look melodramatic, and I think I'll just leave that.

I'm writing in our pilots' room, wearing my Mae West and flying boots. It's a clear sunny afternoon in May, and Gillies and Perkins and

I have just had a pleasant walk along a winding, shaded country road, lined with bluebells and violets. Somewhere overhead we could hear the distant moaning of Messerschmitt 109's on offensive patrol, but the other flight was on duty then and so we thought nothing of them. It's Saturday, and we met some little school kids out on a tramp, all six to eight years of age. They paid no attention to the Messerschmitts either, smiled at us shyly and impishly as we passed them, and went on chattering after we were gone.

I can hear some 109's overhead now, and I know that somewhere up there, trying to locate them, is the patrol which Chris and I shall be relieving in another half-hour.

If I step outside the door and look southeast I can see the French coast all the way from Dunkirk down to Boulogne, resting along the farther edge of the clear blue expanse of water which bounds the no man's land of the air war.

In the great deep blue sea of air above this water, eerie and scary, the watch over the Channel carries on.

Last Flight from Singapore

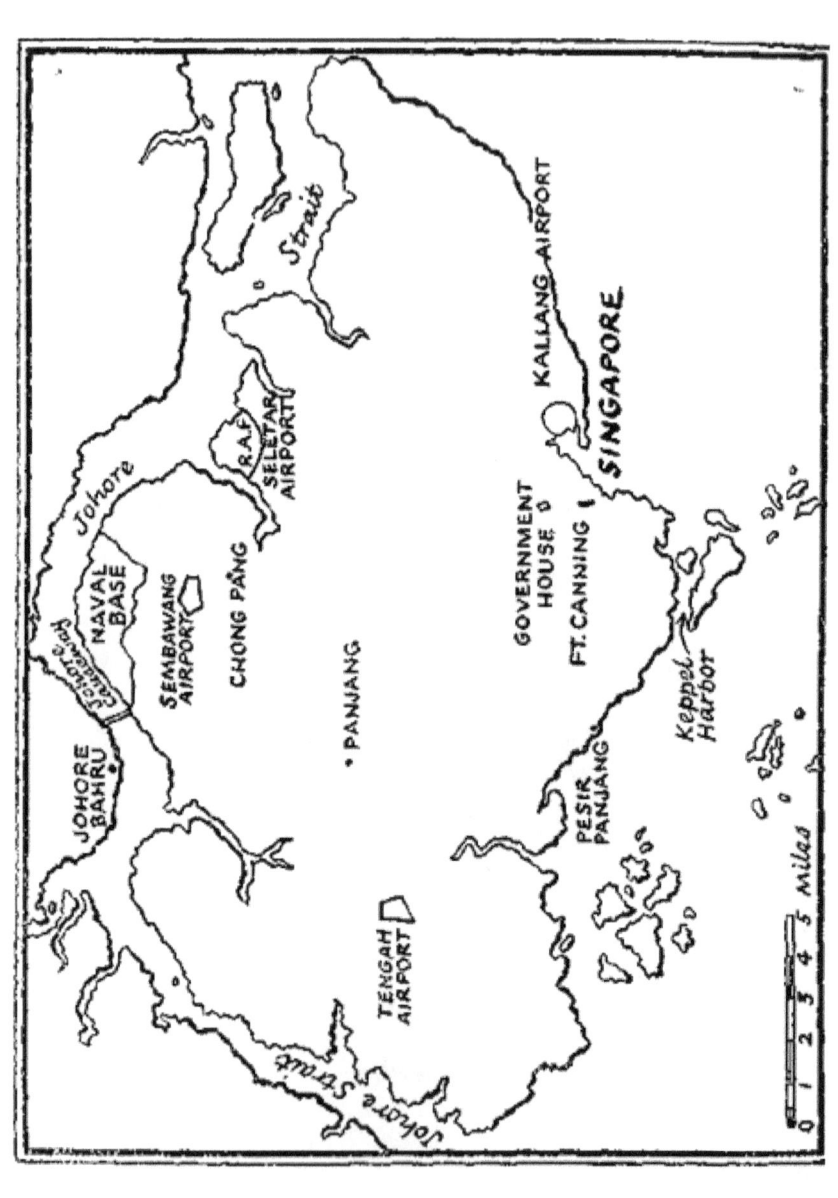

Contents

Parting	153
Impatience	162
Our "Road to Singapore"	166
At the Front	175
Island under Siege	185
Into the Fight	194
Beginning of the End	214
Evacuation	227
Stewie's Escape	235
War over the Jungle	241
The Battle of Palembang	250
A River Massacre and a Frightened Pilot	262
"We'll be Back"	274

CHAPTER 1

Parting

I suppose if I had accomplished anything really worth while during the fighting in Singapore and Sumatra, I should now suspect that fate had something to do with my being there, for it was certainly quite by chance that I was sent. However, my accomplishments in the Far East proved to be so small and my attempts at accomplishment so regularly crowned with frustration, that there could hardly have been any design about it.

It all really started with an invitation I received to a party back in England, last autumn (1941)—started with that, and ended with my evacuation from Java in a hospital ship, after being wounded in "the greatest military disaster ever suffered by British arms."

This invitation came from D———, an airdrome about a hundred miles from where I was stationed. The party, it read, was being given as a farewell for the officers of 300 [1] Squadron, who were preparing to leave for overseas service. "300 Squadron?" I thought. "Why, that's Squadron Leader T———'s gang. I *must* see him if he's going overseas; I'll have to take that in."

Squadron Leader T——— had once been my flight commander and was an especial friend of mine. He must have had me invited.

So it was that I knocked off work at noon of the day of the party, having arranged to take twenty-four hours off and to borrow a little training plane for the trip to D———.

I was pilot in a Spitfire squadron at that time, doing reconnaissance work over the Channel and Northern France, a job in which I was completely happy. I was at a pleasant station with a swell bunch of fellows, and the work was most absorbing and exciting, with frequent opportunities for us to accomplish something and break into the *com-*

1. This is a fictitious number.

muniqués.

I was in extra high spirits that noon and couldn't help whistling gaily as I stripped off my Mae West (life-jacket), hung it on my nail in the pilots' hut, and put on my collar and tie (which are never worn when we're flying, because they interfere with looking around). Calling a gay "See you tomorrow!" to the fellows, I hurried outside, mounted my bicycle, and pedalled away. A fifteen-minute ride, following the macadam taxi strip around the edge of the airdrome to the gate and then up a winding tree-lined country road for a couple of miles, brought me to the house where we were billeted, and I hurried upstairs to change clothes.

The exhilarating feeling of looking forward to a full twenty-four hours of relaxation, free from dangers and responsibilities, was enhanced for me just now by pride in the memory of having done a little good work during the morning. Alan and I had been nosing along the French coast about mid-morning, the cannons and machine-guns of our Spitfires loaded for anything we might encounter.

This time it had been a German motor launch of some sort, and the picture as we went in to attack was still fresh in my mind—the boat dead in my sights a few hundred yards ahead as I came in, skimming low over the sea. Then the terrific barking of my cannons and the roar of my machine-guns as I pressed the firing button, the glimpses from the corners of my eyes of wicked white flame lancing the hot grey smoke-clouds whipping back from my cannon muzzles, the exciting stench of gunpowder smoke; then the sight of my first shots striking, falling a little short and throwing up great showers of spray that nearly hid the boat; then the rest of my bullets striking home—brilliant white flashes of cannon shells, and the red sparkle effect of scores of explosive machine-gun bullets, dancing up and down over the bow and the low bridge, and over the queer little square superstructure with a big swastika painted on each side.

Then I was breaking away in a violent turn to avoid colliding after I'd closed to point-blank, and turning in my cockpit to watch Alan following in with his attack, his distant Spitfire looking wicked and panther-like from in front, as only a Spitfire can; seeing the row of little lights break out, flashing along the front of his wings, and the twin streams of grey cannon-smoke puffs ripping back from his machine like taut strings of soft grey beads; then the answering clouds of spray thrown up about the boat by his bullets and the blinking of white cannon-shell flashes all over its hull. We didn't dare wait to see what became of the boat, but we wouldn't have given much for its chance of remaining afloat very long!

After that the two of us—scooting for home side by side and low down over the waves as hard as we could go, engines bellowing raucously at full throttle, and controls stiff with the speed; squirming in our cockpits to look furtively backwards for signs of 109's (Messerschmitts) in pursuit, feeling for all the world like a couple of kids who'd just stolen a watermelon! For we were only two, and we'd got away with this in clear weather without cloud protection along the part of France where the *Luftwaffe* had its greatest concentration of fighters, hundreds of them. Besides, we had done this right under the noses of the coastal anti-aircraft guns, and so quickly they didn't have time to fire a single shot at us!

As no signs of pursuit appeared we breathed deeper and deeper, until finally the French coast had faded away behind, and then the lighthouse tower of Dungeness slowly emerged from the haze ahead of us, looking beautiful and friendly because it meant that we had got away with "another one."

Upstairs in my room now, I shed my rough blue "battle dress," and after bathing and cleaning up, donned my "Sunday best" uniform which my batman had laid out, freshly pressed, with buttons polished and gleaming. Taking the overnight bag which I'd already packed, I left the house and pedalled back to the Mess, hoping I wasn't too late for lunch.

I almost didn't make the trip to the party after all—in which case I wouldn't be writing this story—for a strong north-west wind was blowing, and over the lunch table, Moses, just down from a patrol, told me he thought I'd have trouble making it to D———. He'd noticed thunderstorms and low cloud in that direction. So after lunch I rang up John, our duty pilot, asking him for the weather to D———, and he confirmed what Moses had told me. Thunderstorms, with fog right down to the ground in places, blocked the route, and there wasn't a hope of getting through for the time being.

As a result I just about decided to call off the trip and ring up Squadron Leader T——— to tell him goodbye on the phone; but then I thought I'd wait and see if the weather might improve. It did toward mid-afternoon, and John rang me up to tell me that Operations said I could try it if I liked, so off I went.

Even then I nearly didn't make it, for after I'd flown about fifty or sixty miles the weather got thick and dark all around. A thunderstorm loomed ahead with white curtains of rain hanging to the ground. I was miserably cold already in the open cockpit of the little Moth biplane, and sick of shivering, my face blue and my nose running, and of bouncing around in the rough air which tossed the little trainer about like a chip; sick above all of the slow speed—exasperating, since I was used to streaking about the countryside at two and three hundred miles an hour in Spitfires.

So I almost said "Nuts to it!" again and turned back; but then I saw a lighter patch ahead on my left and decided to make a try at it. By swinging off my course and edging close to the London balloon barrage I managed finally to get by the bad area, and then it was clear sailing the rest of the way to D———, where I landed triumphantly.

There I found more bad luck in store for me, for Squadron Leader T——— was gone; not only that, but there was no party either!

The duty pilot gave me the news, as soon as I reported to him in the watch office and told him what I'd come for. "Well, I'm awfully sorry about this," he said. "Didn't you get our wire? We telegraphed everyone who'd been invited and told them the party'd been postponed. You see, the boys who are going overseas have all had their embarkation leave extended and they aren't back yet. Yes, Squadron Leader T———'s away, too. I don't know just when he expects to be back."

Well, that *was* something. I'd completely wasted a trip up here just because of a telegram that somehow did nut reach me. It had been a darned cold trip, too.

I rang up the local Operations Room, and got permission to return to my home airdrome as soon as my machine was ready.

The "Station Duty Flight" (a crew of mechanics whose job was to care for visiting planes) were refuelling my airplane and checking over one of the magnetos which had bothered a little on the way, and while waiting for him to finish their work I stood around toasting myself In front of the wall-type electric heaters in the little watch office, for I was chilled through and through.

Presently one of the mechanics came in to tell me the news. "I'm sorry, sir, but I don't think we can get that magneto fixed for you today. There seems to be something wrong inside it, and we'll have to take it apart."

"All right," I answered, "it doesn't make much difference. I'll stay here overnight then." And so I did.

All these chance occurrences that led up to my staying at D———

that night, also led to my living the rest of the events of this story; for next morning before I left, Squadron Leader T—— returned from his leave, and in the ensuing visit talked me into joining the rest of his squadron to go overseas.

Not directly; but he told me that he'd like to have me with his squadron, and I said that, for my part, I was game, if he could get me transferred. So he rang up the officer in charge of postings at Group Headquarters, who said that the time was very short, but if I were willing to forgo embarkation leave he'd do what he could about it and let us know. So we let it stand that way. I flew back to my home airdrome, and after telling my C.O. and the other pilots of my squadron that I might be leaving them soon, I went to work.

Squadron Leader T—— hadn't entirely talked me into volunteering for overseas service; I'd thought of it occasionally before. It was mainly that the opportunity was presented to me at a time when it sounded particularly attractive. Winter was fast approaching with its weeks of foggy weather and inactivity in England, while big things appeared to be in the offing abroad. Japan wasn't in the war yet, of course, but Hitler's armies in Russia had reached the north-eastern shores of the Black Sea and a drive down through the Caucasus Mountains looked imminent; besides, we'd heard rumours and opinions (which soon proved correct) that one side or the other would be starting something big in Libya before long. It seemed likely that the squadron would be sent to one or the other of these areas and that we'd have a chance to write some history wherever we went.

A couple of days after my meeting with Squadron Leader T——, the officer in charge of postings telephoned me that my transfer had been arranged and that I was to report at D—— in two days' time. It was what I wanted, but I realised with a shock that it was going to be very hard to say goodbye to this place and to the pals I had worked and flown and fought with all these months. They seemed to feel the same way about it, too. Some of us drove to Dover that night, to take in a vaudeville show at that famous old theatre, the Dover Hippodrome. It was my last night out with the gang.

The Huns staged a dive-bombing raid on Dover while we were on the way. We could see the anti-aircraft bursts in the sky and the great yellow flashes of the bombs below, so we parked for a few minutes on a hill overlooking the town, watching the display and listening to the drone of engines, the explosions of bombs, and the barking of anti-aircraft guns, until it all quieted down again, and we drove on.

During the show I got all the fellows to autograph my programme, and kept it for a remembrance of my last night out with them. The performance consisted of dancing and other numbers by the "Saucy Lovelies," humorous acts and monologues by Hal Monty, music by "Butch and Buddy"—a couple of air-raid orphans I picked up in a Liverpool shelter by the manager of the show. There were also juggling, "Poses by Eve" (enough said), and other numbers.

I had one or two patrols next morning, which I don't remember much about, except that I flew with a strange heavy lump in my breast. When noon came, my flight was off for the rest of the day. But I took one more hop my way, as a sort of farewell jaunt with my old Spitfire. I'd had the same machine for nearly six months—ever since it was brand new—and I felt very attached to it.

I'd had the words "Message from Minnesota" painted on its side, because that is my home State.

I took off, and flew up and down the middle of the Straits of Dover for a while, flying above and below and through a blanket of thick, fluffy clouds that covered most of the Straits, hoping someone might come out from the other side for a fight. Then I spent a little time searching around the French coast for a couple of" bandits," which Control told me (*via* radio) were patrolling in the Cap Gris Nez area; but I didn't see anything of them and finally Control informed me they'd gone back inland, so I gave up and headed homeward, taking one last look across at France as I circled my drome before landing. Someone else would fly my airplane from now on, and he'd remove the name I had on it. But I consoled myself with the hope that soon I'd be flying a new "Message from Minnesota II" somewhere, anyway.

That afternoon I packed. Next morning, one of Squadron Leader T———'s pilots came down to fetch me in a training plane and I flew to D——— with him, planning to return later and get my heavy luggage by train.

At D——— I found that all the pilots of my new squadron were back from their embarkation leave, and I had a chance to get acquainted with them. There were three other Americans in the crowd, two Californians and one from Florida, all swell fellows. The Californian boys were Don G——— and Red C———; the latter was to become the squadron's first ace. Kleck, who came from Florida, had quit a good Government job in Washington to join as a recruit the Royal Canadian Air Force. There were five New Zealanders also, besides boys from Australia, Rhodesia, Canada, and as we put it, "even a few Englishmen," who were generally known as "the foreigners."

All were getting "shots in the arm" from a doctor that day, and I joined them in "sick quarters" to get the first of a series of shots for yellow fever, tetanus, typhoid, and other tropical diseases, with the result that I nursed a sore arm for a day or so.

The next couple of days I spent doing some practice-flying to get acquainted with the Hurricane fighters this squadron used, as I had never flown Hurricanes before; and after that I got a couple of days off to wind up my affairs.

The first of these two days I spent in London, taking (are of some financial matters and shopping for various things, including a "tropical trunk"—all steel for protection against insects.

Before I left London the next morning I stopped in at the American Eagle Club for a cup of coffee, and here met Tex M——, a friend of mine from Waxahachie,

Texas, who had been flying in the American Eagle Squadron. He told me he had just been posted to Singapore and was on embarkation leave, prior to sailing. I told him I was going overseas, too, but didn't know where, and we wished each other luck.

I took a train for my old squadron's base, arriving in late afternoon. It was cloudy and blustery and chilly, with a few snowflakes in the air, and when I got out to the drome, in a taxi, there seemed to be little going on. I visited my flight's dispersal hut first, to get a few belongings I'd left there, and found that the flight were off duty and only a couple of boys around.

All the Spitfires were standing in their dispersal bays,[2] like tired cavalry horses asleep, each as familiar to me as an old comrade, bringing me memories.

There was Paddy's old machine, "N," which had always been lucky. Paddy had shot down at least two 109's with it. Chris was using it the day he was out on a recco (reconnaissance flight), and surprised a formation of three 109's over Le Touquet, dropping on them out of the sun and shooting down two before they knew what had happened, and then coming home so excited he couldn't talk, having completely forgotten to finish his recco! Gilli was flying it the day he blundered into a whole bunch of 109's in a thick haze low over the sea north of Nieuport, shot down one, damaged a second, and got away unscathed,

---

2. Dispersal bays—individual parking-spaces, usually walled on three sides for protection from bomb blast.

leaving the rest dog-fighting with each other in their confusion.

There was Chris's old machine "P," Gilli's "U," Roy's "V," Alan's "T," and all the rest, including "S"—the one everybody hated because it didn't perform as well as the others. And of course there was my own "O," my "Message from Minnesota," which I knew and loved the best. Personalities, all of them, to me; for one of us will fly another's airplane when his own is laid up for repairs, checks, and so on, and I knew all the peculiarities of each.

There wasn't one in whose cockpit I hadn't experienced unforgettable thrills and scares, flown through unbelievable scenes of grandeur and beauty among and above the clouds. And how often I'd seen each of them taxi-ing back to its place after a flight across the Channel, displaying evidence of a battle fought or a target attacked—the tattered remnants of what had been fabric covers for the holes until they were shot away, fluttering about the holes for the machine-guns in the wings, and the ugly bared cannon muzzles, dirtied with powder-smoke, their covers likewise shot away. Sometimes it was I who taxied in with my machine bearing these signs, my heart still pounding, while I grinned behind my oxygen mask with an amount of pride proportional to whatever it was that I had accomplished.

And now it was all over. I was saying good-bye to it all and to them all, and it was very hard. Sergeant Y——, also an American, was flying my machine now.

He came around while I was there and said he was going to taxi it across to the hangar for a thirty-hour inspection, and I asked him if he'd mind my taxi-ing it over for him. He said O.K. So after I was through collecting my things I climbed into the cockpit of my old friend, started up, and taxied across the field. When I stopped in front of the hangar and shut off the engine, I thought I should make a ceremony of leaving it for the last time, then realised how foolish I was, and jumped out and walked away without looking back.

The wind was still blowing and the sky overcast that night as I rode along the dark highway and through the blacked-out city with the friend who drove me to the station, and my heart was heavier than ever. I'd planned to stay overnight and take a morning train, but a telephone call at supper-time informed me that our date of embarkation had been advanced and that I had to take the train right away.

It meant I hardly had time to say goodbye to any of my pals, which was probably just as well because I know I'd have broken down. I wanted at least to see Chris, and I'd made a hasty trip to the country house where he and his wife were staying, but had found it dark, silent, and empty save for their little dog, "Rocky," who alone answered when I knocked, and who barked his goodbye as I walked back across the lawn. They had gone away somewhere for the afternoon and evening, not knowing that I was coming.

When I got on the train, I could hardly keep my eyes dry as I fumbled my way into one of the darkened compartments and slumped down, utterly miserable, beside a couple of soldiers going on leave, who moved their rifles to make room for me on the seat.

Hoping to see something familiar, I pulled the curtains aside for a last look after we got out of town, and as if the elements sympathised with me I found that the clouds had blown away and that the countryside now was bathed in brilliant moonlight. The airdrome was out of sight from the railway, but "Old Baldy," a high, rounded hill that was a landmark beside it, was plainly visible and I took a long last look at it, trying to photograph it in my memory. Then I replaced the curtain, resolving to keep my mind in the future.

CHAPTER 2

Impatience

I suppose that if you rounded up a score of two-year-old colts from a Montana range and penned them in a half-acre corral for a few weeks during the fresh new days of spring, you could get an idea from watching them of how we fighter pilots felt and acted during our long imprisonment aboard ship.

Accustomed as we were to flying an hour or two in going from one place to another, this business of spending days and even weeks between stops was appalling. We read until our eyes ached, played cards, argued endlessly about everything from air tactics to women's suffrage. Our tempers grew shorter until we were constantly flying off the handle at one another over insignificant little things, so that our C.O. was at his wits' end trying to keep the peace—and still our voyage had scarcely started!

The lazy, ambling motion of our ship, with its top speed of fully fifteen miles an hour, was exasperating. Didn't it know we had a war to fight? I spent so much time leaning on the rail, watching the endless acres of waves crawling past, and wondering how there could be so many of them all in one ocean, that I thought I'd be developing a permanent stoop.

I suppose it was only natural that we started seeing Gremlins. These are the little men, about four or five inches tall, who live in the sky and have been a legend in the R.A.F. ever since the first pilot took off with a hangover in the last war, saw one perched on his windshield making faces at him, and swore off Paris night clubs and French champagne for the duration.

I heard about them shortly after joining the R.A.F. and asked a pilot of the last war, who was adjutant at my station, if he could tell me what they looked like.

"Well," he said, "it really depends on what sort of shape you're in when you see them, old boy. Of course you modern pilots don't drink, so you're always in the same shape. Why, as I remember, they're rather sly-appearing little chaps, with long white beards, dressed in green waistcoats and tall green hats. Most of them don't intend to be mean, just playful—except the one I used to see in peace-time, perched on my pillow on mornings after a night out in town—"

He shook his head reminiscently. "That was a wicked one, absolutely ferocious to look at, too. He had a little sharp dagger that he'd waken me with by poking me just above the eyes. I'd start to raise up, and '*Bam!*' he'd hit me on the back of the head with a hammer twice as long as he was. Then the little blighter would run down to the foot of my bed and sit there laughing at me. I'd growl at him and tell him to hop it, but he'd just sit there and make a face at me. I'd close my eyes and try to sleep again, and a minute later he'd be back, to give me another working over!" He shook his head again. "That one was a regular outlaw, but most of them aren't too bad if you treat them right."

I think I should add here that these little fellows are credited with many unusual gifts, including great strength and the ability to fly—supposed to be due to their special diet of spandule, or aerial seaweed (airweed).

If you ask a student pilot about Gremlins, he'll probably tell you of the ones who hide in training planes during flight. When the student is coming in to land, they all run out to the end of one wing and, just when he's about to touch down for a perfect landing, give a great heave upwards, tipping his machine over so that the opposite wing hits the ground. Or the ones who cause crack-ups by moving trees or telephone poles in front of you when you're gliding in to land, or push other airplanes into your way when you're taxi-ing on the ground. Or the tribe known as the "Ground Wallopers," who are responsible when a student bounces on landing; they shove your control stick forward or backward just as you're touching down, causing you either to hit the ground too hard or else to zoom up too high and pancake.

Another gang of them have an ingenious and destructive prank, which they sometimes work even on experienced pilots. Two of them stand by in your cockpit, out of sight, while you're flying, and when you move the lever to lower your wheels in preparation for landing, one of them sneaks up and throws the lever back into neutral so that your wheels stay up, retracted. Then the other one, hiding behind your instrument panel, rewires the position indicator for your wheels, so that it shows "Wheels Down" when in reality they're still up, and you glide in for a perfect crack-up, landing your plane on its belly.

After the dust clears away, while the crash truck is approaching and you're still sitting in your cockpit, gazing stupidly at your bent or broken propeller and wings, the two little fellows jump up on your windshield, stick their tongues out at you in a final gesture of insolence, and vanish, leaving you to figure out how you're going to explain it all to the C.O. At least, that's how some pilots claim it happens.

There's no end to the kinds of tricks they'll pull if they have it in for you. They hide behind your compass and hold magnets by it, causing the compass to point the wrong way, and you get lost. They steal your maps, hide in your radio set, and bang on it with hammers so you can't hear any messages. They sneak into your gas-tank and drink up your gasoline, steal the bullets from your machine-guns and put in corks, paint Messerschmitts on top of your cockpit hood to scare the life out of you, and so on, until they've driven you half crazy.

The first one was discovered on the ship by our C.O. one evening when we were all gathered in the Officers' Ward-Room (lounge), with most of the ship's officers. One of the officers, who was called Dinty, was just going to sit down in a comfortable chair when our C.O. grabbed him and called out in alarm, "Look out—Don't sit down, Dinty! You'll squash him—Look!" He was pointing at the middle of the seat, and we all looked. Sure enough, there was the cutest little Gremlin, about middle age, curled up fast asleep, his head pillowed on a tobacco-pouch which the navigator had left there.

Dinty, who of course couldn't see it because he wasn't a pilot, was absolutely bewildered. He gazed first at us, then at the chair, then back at us—all grouped around and staring.

Someone said, "S-sh—We mustn't wake him up!" and that was too much. With a frightened expression on his face, Dinty retreated to the bar for a quick one.

The Gremlin awoke presently, to follow us when we went down for supper, where he amused us while we were waiting to be served, by cavorting about the room, climbing up on the table and running up and down its length, until he finally tripped over a spoon and fell head first into a glass of water. Ambrose rescued him then, lifting him out tenderly by the coat collar with his thumb and forefinger, and setting him out to dry on an empty plate—all to the complete consternation of the naval officers present!

After that, we were frequently visited by one or more of them. One night, two of them were playing about the Ward-Room, with all of us watching, and they climbed into the recess in the wall in front of a porthole. Kleck got an inspiration and called, "Look out! They're trying to open the porthole!" Whereupon we all rushed in stop them, for the portholes must be kept tightly closed it night to prevent any traces of light showing. Sure enough, the two little chaps had hold of the big brass wing-nut, one at each end, and were just going to start unscrewing it!

Our C.O. reprimanded them severely, while they listened, with heads hanging and guilty looks on their faces, no doubt wondering if it wouldn't be best to lock us in our cabins. Then we showed them the proper way out for Gremlins—through the ventilator pipe.

We never learned what our original destination was to have been, for one of the great events of history, which was to change it, occurred while we were docked at a port of call.

We heard the news on a Sunday evening when most of us had been away from the ship, attending a movie put on in a shed by the docks for the ship's company of a large warship that was docked near us. Returning to our own ship after the show we were met on the ladder by Red (one of the two Americans from California), his face flushed with excitement, shouting the electrifying words, "America's at war! The Japs have raided Hawaii! Here, read this!" He was waving a wireless message in our faces. It was a general message to all British ships and read:

"Commence hostilities with Japan Repeat Japan at once."

CHAPTER 3

Our "Road to Singapore"

I felt dazed and overwhelmed. After all the fighting that we Americans in the R.A.F. had been through, believing that we were helping to make this unnecessary, it had come at last, all in a twinkling, and our country was committed to take part in the slaughter.

In the Ward-Room we drank a toast with the British officers, to our new alliance. Then later, at midnight, we gathered around the radio to listen to detail after terrible detail of the world-shaking events that had happened in the last few hours.

Everyone was subdued— we Americans because of the tragedy it spelled for our country and the others, because we felt it would lengthen the war to have Japan added to our enemies. The only bright side for us Americans was knowing that we wouldn't be outlaws any more in the eyes of our own country— as we were when I went home on leave to the States the previous winter and wasn't allowed to wear my uniform.

We remained in port for several more days, and it was during this time that Don, the other Californian besides Red, got separated from us. He had a chance to do some flying one day, and in the course of his trip his plane force-landed in a neutral country and he was interned. We never saw him again.

He was to escape finally; and months later, on America's Memorial Day, I was to lay a wreath against a wooden cross with his name on it, erected beside a hole in a little paddy-field in a Ceylonese jungle, where he had crashed on Easter Sunday, shot down by Japanese fighters in the defence of Ceylon.

Finally we put to sea again, and there followed many more monotonous days. We pilots had to do "gun watches" on the ship, providing the crews for two of the ship's pom-pom anti-aircraft guns, working in four-hour shifts. Personally, I have always felt that anti-aircraft guns should be abolished, and Kleck grumbled that this was like asking Charlie McCarthy to take care of a pair of woodpeckers; but we endeavoured to subordinate our sentiments and do the job properly.

Actually, we found it rather interesting to learn how to operate these things, after the considerable experience which some of us had had in dodging their fire. The Germans use this type of gun as well as the British, and Vic, for example, still bore scars on his face from one which he failed to dodge.

We sailed into warm tropical seas, where we changed from our blue uniforms into light "tropical dress" of open-necked khaki shirts, khaki shorts, and tan-coloured *topees* instead of caps; and we slept in hammocks on deck because it was too hot in our cabins.

At night the sea was "phosphorescent," one of the wonders of nature which most of us had never seen. Every disturbance in the water caused little flaky green lights to flash beneath the surface, so that the water churned from the ship's sides seemed full of fireflies. Every white-cap was a shower of fiery little green jewels; every fish left a trail like a small green sky-rocket in the darkness, and the wake of the ship was like a great convulsive mass of coloured fire.

It was on one of these nights, while on watch, that I got my first torpedo scare. I had been leaning over the rail by my gun for a long time, idly watching the lovely show, when suddenly I thought I heard a hissing noise, hooking up, I was terrified to see a huge trail of phosphorescence coming in a straight line toward the ship, scarcely a hundred yards away. I just seemed to freeze, inside and out, as if hypnotised by the sight, as it streaked on, cutting just beneath the waves and straight for the middle of the ship. It came straight as a die until less than twenty yards away, when it suddenly executed a sharp turn, in the most unorthodox manner for torpedoes! Then it started following along beside the ship so that I could see its outline, illuminated by the phosphorescence, and I recognised it as a big porpoise!

When my breath came back, I called the other boys to look. Soon we saw not one porpoise but several; then more and more joined up until there were all of fifty swimming beside us, mostly in pairs, gambolling about and converting the dark water for two or three hundred yards out into a fairyland of curving, swirling green sky-rockets. They followed along with us for fifteen or twenty minutes, one of the weirdest and most beautiful shows I've ever seen. Then, little by little, they dispersed and disappeared into the darkness.

Another morning Kleck mistook a piece of floating wood in the distance and shouted "Periscope!" at the top of his lungs, with the result that "Action Stations" was sounded on the ship's alarm system and everyone was in an uproar, including the captain, who'd been taking a bath in his cabin and came bounding up onto the bridge with less dignity than speed, clad only in a bath towel.

We were still in complete ignorance of our eventual destination, when finally we were transferred onto a fair-sized warship, along with the pilots of another squadron, which I will call 175[1] Squadron; they are to play a part in the rest of this story.

We now were able to guess that we were being taken somewhere in the Far East, although no one knew. Then, after we had been at sea for a couple of days, we pilots and all the ship's company not on duty were assembled on deck one evening for a lecture.

It began with a talk by the first lieutenant, on the Far Eastern situation. Using a large map for reference, he showed us where the Japanese had attacked in the Philippines as well as in Borneo and other islands, and reviewed the situation there. Next, he pointed to where they had invaded Burma and were working toward Rangoon, and last of all to Northern Malaya, where they were pushing down the long Malay Peninsula toward Singapore, at its southern tip. Everything hung on Singapore. If it fell, the enemy would be able to conquer the Dutch East Indies, which would give them the rubber, tin, and oil that they needed to continue the war.

Then the captain spoke, outlining for the benefit of his crew the work which the ship was to perform in this many-sided campaign. We thought it was a considerate gesture on his part to take his crew into confidence this way—the sort of thing that probably accounted for the wonderful spirit we had already noticed among the entire personnel of his ship.

But we pilots were impatient to learn what was to become of us. It was obvious that the ship was taking us in some place out there, but there were a dozen theatres of operation where fighter squadrons would be needed. Naturally, our highest hopes were that we might get to Singapore itself.

The captain gave us the answer to that, too, at the close of his talk. "Our Royal Air Force guests are going to leave us at——" he named a place in the Dutch East Indies, "where they will get their airplanes. I

---

1. A fictitious number for the squadron.

understand they are then to fly the rest of the way to *Singapore, which is their destination!*"

A cheer went up from our crowd. We all wanted action, and now we had drawn the jackpot!

About all I remember of the trip across the Indian Ocean is that the sea was always smooth and the days were always hot, sultry, and endless. We didn't ever have ambition enough to see Gremlins any more. Our one diversion was swimming, in a canvas pool rigged up on the quarter-deck, which served to cool us off a little. But we were thankful, anyway, that we were on a fast ship, making twice the speed that a trooper would have. On the evening before we pilots were to be disembarked, the captain gave a brief talk over the ship's loud-speaker system, stressing the idea that the eyes of the world were focused on the battle we were joining, and bidding us "goodbye, good luck, and good hunting!" We were quite impressed, and I hoped fervently that our squadron would make a good name for itself in the events to come.

Each of our squadrons was up to full strength of twenty-four pilots (giving a reserve of 100 *per cent* over the normal flying strength of twelve), so there were forty-eight pilots altogether; and the forty-eight were now divided into three groups of sixteen for the trip to Singapore.

I am not permitted to say where we disembarked and got our airplanes. Suffice it to say that on a sunny morning a few days later the sixteen pilots of my group landed on the municipal airport of Batavia, the principal city in Java, all of us flying brand-new Hurricane II fighters.

This airport was a stopping-point in peace-time for K.L.M., the big Dutch airline, and they had a modern passenger terminal, complete with restaurant, waiting-room, and bar where I got the first Coca Cola I'd tasted since leaving America.

We had lunch, and then took off on the next leg of our trip, a flight of three hundred miles or so north-west to a jungle airdrome in Sumatra.

It was a beautiful trip, for the sun was out and the fertile, well-cultivated farmlands of Java appeared rich and green as we cruised over them. There were scattered fluffy clouds under us at low altitude that glistened softly in the sunlight and set off the beauty of the landscape underneath. Then the sea-coast, the beautiful blue-green, and the white-capped waves gleaming in long lines of snowy crest as they collapsed majestically along the beaches far below us, in all the splendour of colour that you see in Technicolor pictures of South Sea islands.

On out across the sea for half an hour or so and then Sumatra, a far different kind of country from Java. This was where everyone said, "If you ever have a forced landing, you've just had it!" No cultivated farmlands here. No sign of any kind of civilization. Just endless dark flat jungle stretching off into the steamy horizon in all directions, broken only at great intervals by some silvery stream winding its way across our course and off into the distance. Many, many miles of this, until at last a broken patch appeared ahead of us, and as we neared this it took shape as an airdrome cleared out of the jungle—our stopping-point.

As we circled the field before landing, I noticed a strange type of four-engined bomber parked on the ground. It looked like pictures I'd seen of the American Flying Fortress bombers, and I wondered if it could really be an American plane out here in the war zone. I knew America was in the war now, but somehow I just couldn't connect the Stars and Stripes and American uniform with the awfulness of real fighting.

But when I landed and taxied past the bomber, I saw that it really was so. There were the American insignia of white star over red and blue circles on the sides of the fuselage, seeming very strange to me now after having seen only British and German insignia for so long. There were the strange, light-tan uniforms and caps of U.S. Army officers and men around the machine, and they gave me a queer thrill. The men were starting their engines then, and before I had time to park my machine and climb out, they were already taxi-ing down the field to take off, so I didn't get to talk to them. I was told they didn't belong here and had only landed for gas.

It was too late for us to go any farther that day, so after getting our airplanes serviced and put away, we prepared to stay for the night. This airdrome was simply a couple of enormous runways cleared in the jungle, which grew thickly right up to the edge of the field on all sides. Little "bays" for parking airplanes were cut back into the trees, so that when a machine was parked and a few branches thrown over the top it was effectively concealed from the air.

The R.A.F. were just getting established here, and the Officers' Mess was a large wooden shed with concrete floor, and wooden benches and tables for us to eat at. We lined up at meal-time and drew tea in tin cups from a big boiler, and dipped stew from another boiler into tin plates. Bread, margarine, canned strawberry jam, fresh bananas, and pineapples completed our fare.

We slept in camp cots and learned the intricacies of enclosing ourselves in those overhung mosquito-netting affairs which all beds have in tropical places; you've probably seen them in the movies. It's not as difficult as it looks, I found; the sides simply tuck in under the edges of the mattress all around, so that to get in you just pull out one side of the netting, then tuck it back under after you're inside.

The air had been very hot and muggy when we landed, but during the night there were little rains accompanied by some thunder and lightning every hour or so, and it became comfortably cool. However, by the time we got up next morning it was hot and steamy just as before.

That day the weather was too questionable for us to continue to Singapore, so we lay over, and most of us spent the day working on our airplanes. Our machines were brand new, having just been shipped out from England, and there were numerous things to take care of before they would be in fighting condition.

Among other things, all the machine-guns were heavily coated inside and out with a special grease to resist corrosion on the long sea journey. I spent most of the day working with some armourers on my airplane, removing and disassembling its twelve guns, carefully cleaning all the parts in gasoline, greasing, and oiling the parts properly for service, and then reassembling, installing, and loading them.

We worked beside the airplane, sitting on empty gasoline cans, retreating under the wings to work during the frequent showers that swept across. And while we worked, by chatting with these armourers who had all been in the fighting zone in Malaya until recently, I gradually assimilated some of the picture of what lay ahead for us.

It was from them that I first heard of the new Navy Zero fighter ("Navy-naughts" as we called them at that time), which is to the Jap air force what the Messerschmitt 109 is to the *Luftwaffe*. These fighters, while not as fast as our Hurricanes, were a sleek little job none the less, with great manoeuvrability and an exceptional cruising range. They carried extra fuel tanks under the wings, that could be jettisoned for combat, and they could operate more than three hundred miles from their bases. They were usually armed with light and heavy machine-guns, although some had twenty-millimetre cannons. While our fighters were a match for them individually, we had to expect to be badly outnumbered ordinarily when we engaged them.

One of the armourers, a sergeant, had been an air-gunner on Lockheed bombers until recently, and it was from him that I got most of the information about the Navy Zeros. He had destroyed one of them in combat himself.

They told me the Jap bombers seemed to be good machines, too, and could fly at more than twenty thousand feet with full bomb loads. Much of their bombing was directed against airdromes; the raids usually being carried out by three squadrons of nine planes each in one wing—twenty-seven in all. They flew in beautiful close formation, and when attacking airdromes they did "pattern bombing," all letting their bombs go at once so that they plastered the whole area evenly.

They said the raids were terrifying affairs, but caused surprisingly few casualties. The soil in Malaya and Singapore is so damp and soggy that there is little blast effect from even the heaviest bombs. Ordinary small "slit trenches," three or four feet deep and a couple of feet wide, were all that were used normally for shelters; and often heavy bombs had landed within a couple of yards of a trench and the men suffered nothing worse than a shower of damp earth. In addition to their heavy bombs the enemy dropped lots of devilish little "anti-personnel" bombs, about fifty-pounders, which exploded just as they touched the ground, and threw shrapnel in all directions. The latest news was that the enemy were less than fifty miles from Singapore Island, and the only airdromes we had left were the four that were situated on the island. It looked as if we had a tough fight ahead of us, which, after all, was just what we wanted.

By the following afternoon the weather had improved enough so that we could go on, and we took off on the last leg of our trip, another three hundred and fifty miles to Singapore itself.

There were two Blenheim bombers making the trip with us, and by previous arrangement we simply followed in formation with them, letting them find the way because they were better equipped for navigating. After taking off, we grouped around them in sections of four, circled the airdrome once to get organized in formation and headed out across the jungle again—this time nearly straight north.

After the first fifty miles we began to see the coastline in the distance on our right, at first paralleling our course and then gradually angling closer; and it was a little relief to know it was there anyway, to head for in case of engine trouble. We all dreaded the thought of having to land in this jungle.

After perhaps an hour we crossed the coastline and droned out on our one-hundred-and-fifty-mile stretch of overwater flying, across the Straits of Malacca. This wasn't really open sea, as I could see on my map, for it was broken by small islands scattered along most of the way, so that we were seldom out of sight of at least one or two of them.

By this time I was getting tired and stiff from being cramped in one position and I squirmed in my seat, loosened my straps, and tried to do some primitive setting-up exercises for relief. I'd gone for so long without flying that the posture was hard to get used to again. My engine, throttled down almost to idling speed to keep pace with the slower bombers, purred endlessly on the mime note, which was broken only when I held my head to one side of the cockpit and got the *staccato* crackling of the exhausts from that bank of cylinders. Like most of the rest I flew with my sliding cockpit hood open to keep cool, for the sun was out and the air hot; we were actually crossing the equator on this very hop, Singapore being only eighty miles north of it.

This was late in January, and I thought how different it must be back home in Minnesota, where it was midwinter, the thermometer by the door of our house probably allowing zero or below, the ground frozen hard, and the countryside covered deep in snow. Right now my folks might be outdoors, bundled in heavy clothes and over-shoes, beating their hands together and rubbing their cheeks and noses to keep them from going numb.

And yet here I was at the same time, my clothes and the inside of my helmet damp and sticky with sweat, yearning more than anything else for an ice-cold Coke or Orange *Crush!* I was leading a section of four, the three others formatting on me loosely, their tiredness evidencing itself in the way each of them slowly drifted about in the formation, some times lagging behind, then getting too much speed and drifting up too far ahead. Once Artie S——came up beside me for a moment, and I could see his face, with a dopy expression on it as if he were half asleep. We had our oxygen masks unfastened from our faces to keep cooler, so I could see when he grinned across at me, and I grinned back.

After a long time the sky grew darker ahead. The Blenheims started losing altitude, and we did too—keeping formation with them. Then the unmistakable dim outline of land began to emerge along the darkened horizon, and we knew that after months of travel our destination was at last in sight. We began passing under heavy, blue-black storm-clouds that forced us to fly lower and lower, and looking ahead I could now make out a great harbour on the coast, with the dim shapes of several ships anchored in it. Singapore harbour!

CHAPTER 4

At the Front

We flew low across the harbour. Just before reaching it the Blenheims lowered their wheels to landing position to show they were friendly, so we did likewise, pausing over it that way. At the same time, one of the Blenheims shot off a couple of Very lights in a secret colour combination to further identify us to the anti-aircraft defences; we could expect the gunners to be quick on the trigger at a place like this, and we didn't want to get them excited.

I noticed one ship in the harbour that contrasted strangely with the rest, because it was all white except for a narrow green stripe around it and large red crosses on the deck, sides, and funnel. It was the first hospital ship I'd seen, and it looked grimly suggestive there. Little did I suspect that I was to be a passenger on it within a month !

Singapore Island is roughly diamond-shaped, about twenty-five miles long east and west, by fifteen miles north and south, and our destination was Tengah Airdrome on the north-west side. We made it just ahead of a heavy rainstorm that was bearing down from the north, and though the setting sun was still shining from the west, we had to fly through a curtain of rain on the north side when we were approaching to land.

Even circling the drome we could easily see we were in a war zone, for it was spotted with filled-in bomb craters just like the ones in England, and there were quite a few unfilled ones, too, indicating that the airdrome had recently been bombed. There was a fresh hole in one end of the concrete runway that we had to dodge when landing.

After I was down I taxied to a spot as far as possible from any other plane (for dispersal in case of bombing), and hopped out gratefully. As I was stretching to get rid of my cramps, I happened to think that by rights I should have made a ceremony of climbing down from my machine, for it meant that I was setting foot on the continent of Asia for the first time.

I borrowed a screwdriver to remove the panels in the sides and bottom of the fuselage of my airplane, and hurried to untie and unload my baggage, which I had fastened in various nooks and crannies of the framework. A lorry came around to collect some of us, and we were driven to the Officers' Mess, a great beautiful building of dark-grey stone at the top of a gentle grassy incline overlooking the airdrome.

There we met the main part of 300 Squadron (my squadron), who had arrived in another group two days before. They had spent the last two days getting their machines into shape and ready for action, and were full of pep because they planned to start operating the next morning. (The group I came in was made up of the remainder of 300 Squadron and some of 175.)

The boys told us they'd had their first taste of Jap bombing the day before, after landing on another airdrome. The place was raided by a formation of twenty-seven bombers at high altitude, and while most of the boys got to cover in time, Mickey, Cam, and Ambrose were caught in the open and just managed to duck into a drainage ditch (fortunately dry) as the bombs were falling. They got showered with dirt from a bomb that landed quite close, but weren't hurt.

I was anxious to get word of my American friend from Waxahachie, Texas, Tex M———, whom I'd said goodbye to in the American Eagle Club just before I left England, when he told me he was going to Singapore. He should have arrived here ahead of us, because we had been delayed and re-routed on the way. Red C———, the Californian in our squadron, who was also a friend of Tex, gave me the bad news. Having arrived here ahead of me in the first group, Red had already inquired, and learned that Tex had been killed a couple of weeks before, shot down in battle with Navy Zeros.

After a supper served by Malay and Chinese waiters in the spacious, airy dining-hall of the Officers' Mess, a conference was held in the lounge, between our C.O. and the pilots who were to be on duty next morning. An R.A.F. fighter squadron operates as twelve airplanes, so that not all of the pilots and planes fly each time, and the work is rotated among them. This allows planes to be laid up for servicing and overhauling and provides spares to replace losses, and gives all the pilots an opportunity to rest and provide replacements for their casualties. The twelve who were to operate next day were from the first group to arrive, so that it was as somewhat of an outsider that I sat in on the conference.

Details of formation and tactics were worked out and settled on the basis of what they'd learned about enemy tactics and the capabilities of their airplanes.

They'd received lots of tips and information from other pilots who were fighting the Japs here. The standard enemy raid consisted of twenty-seven bombers flying in dose formation at twenty-two thousand feet, escorted by anything up to twenty or thirty Navy Zero fighters flying above them. In attacking these formations it was essential to act fast and try to get at the bombers before the Navy Zeros above could interfere. It was best to attack the bombers either head-on or from the side; very unwise to attack them from the rear, because of the heavy concentration of machine-gun and cannon fire from the rear turrets of all twenty-seven bombers, which focused on anyone coming up from behind.

The enemy usually staged one or two of these raids every forenoon, in addition to little raids and reconnaissance flights at odd hours throughout the rest of the day. We knew that for the time being we must expect to operate against very heavy odds, and that somehow we must try to use enough better tactics and skill to make up the difference.

That night was clear with a full moon, an ideal night for bombing, and there were so many pilots in the Mess that it was decided to disperse us in case the place got hit; so some of us piled into a lorry and were driven to a camp in a rubber estate outside the drome, where we all slept in one big tent.

Once, in the middle of the night, some of us heard a heavy explosion in the distance, and next morning (January 31) we learned what it was. Our armies had been evacuated from the mainland of Malaya, into Singapore Island itself, and a section of the Johore Causeway, a long concrete highway bridge connecting the island with the mainland across the mile-wide Straits of Johore, had been blown up. The enemy armies were now just across these straits, only three or four miles from our airdrome.

That day a B.B.C. news broadcast began with the words, "The Battle of Malaya has ended and the Battle for Singapore has begun!" We had arrived just in time to take part in the defence of an island under siege.

The twelve boys who were to be "on" next morning were up and had breakfast before daylight so as to be in readiness at dawn, while the rest of us got up at our leisure and drifted around to breakfast at about eight o'clock. Even though I wasn't flying that morning I couldn't help feeling some of the tension that I knew the others were undergoing, as they sat around the telephone in their "dispersal huts" at the edge of the field. It was more than three months since any of them had flown in action—and that had been the cautious, sparring sort of game we played back and forth across the Channel with the German fighters through most of 1941. Several had never been in actual combat. Now they were waiting to take off against a new enemy who was all out to crush us, just, as the Germans were in the Battle of Britain; so that each time they went up they were quite likely to see combat.

Alter breakfast we who were off duty lounged about for a time on the veranda overlooking the field, idly watching the scores of *coolies*, both men and women, at work filling in the bomb craters. Each carried two round wicker baskets, suspended from the ends of a stick across the shoulders. They used little implements like grub hoes to fill the baskets with earth, and then carried their loads to the craters and dumped them.

About nine o'clock someone remarked, "Oh-oh! Looks like the boys have got a scramble."[1]

Sure enough, a frantic bustling was taking place down at the drome. Pilots were bolting from the dispersal huts and racing towards their airplanes, ground crews running to help. Nearest to us, we could see Red take the bottom wing of his machine in a leap and then disappear into his cockpit. A moment of tense quiet followed, while the boys were getting settled in their machines with helmets, parachutes, and seat-straps buckled; then, down the line, the first engine came to life, its note rising to a surprised bellow almost as soon as it started, when the pilot slammed his throttle ahead rudely to get going.

Other engines joined the chorus one after another, and clouds of dust billowed up as the Hurricanes left their parking-spaces, *coolies* running in all directions to get out of the way. The field became alive with planes, all heading for the end of the runway, the pilots taxi-ing jerkily, as fast as they dared, dodging bomb craters, racing in clear stretches, slowing down again, stopping to avoid collisions or let others by, speeding up again, all in a bedlam of noise from the dozen Rolls

---

1. Scramble—the term in the R.A.F. for any flight in which fighters are ordered off to intercept the enemy.

Royce engines, each roaring fiercely in spurts, quieting momentarily, bellowing out again, and slowing once more, in response to the hurried manipulations of throttles as the pilots made their way by fits and starts across the drome.

The two leading machines arrived and turned in on the end of the runway, pausing momentarily, their mighty engines trumpeting at idling speed. Then their idling propellers became invisible and a great stentorian roar swept across the field to us, drowning all the other din, as these two machines gathered speed down the runway and were off, skimming up over the boundary, wheels rising upward and inward to their recesses in the fuselages after taking off, like pigeons folding up their legs. Others followed, one pair after another. They made a gentle left-hand climbing sweep around the airdrome, while the last ones to take off caught up and took their places in the formation; then they disappeared into the blue, climbing steeply, and peace and quiet came back to the airdrome.

A few minutes later, the air-raid sirens sounded. No planes were in sight, so we just walked around and located the trenches nearest to the mess in case we needed to know, then stood outside, waiting for developments and hoping to get our first glimpse of Japanese airplanes. We were satisfied on the latter score after a few minutes, when three fast single-engined planes, obviously fighters, flew over at about fifteen thousand feet, in loose formation, weaving violently as if they thought they were being chased. They headed away to the north, and one chap who belonged here told us reassuringly, "That's only the recco flight. The bombers will be along in a little while now."

That seemed to be all for the time being, so some of us got a ground crew and a little Farmall tractor, and drove out from the airdrome a mile or so to where a few of our airplanes, including mine, had been parked among some rubber trees for dispersal. There were so many things to be done, like installing radio and oxygen equipment as well as making engine adjustments and thorough checks on each machine before it would be ready to fight, that the ground crews couldn't take care of them all at one time, and some of them were parked out here temporarily.

We hooked the tractor onto one, and after lots of sweating and shoving, finally getting a tow from a passing army truck, we managed to get it out of the woods and up on the road.

About that time we became conscious of a heavy distant drone—not too distant, either—and looking up, we saw an enormous cluster of bombers far above, little close-grouped, silver flecks against the bright blue tropical sky! They were in close formation just like those we'd heard about—the first mass bombing formation I'd seen since the Battle of Britain, and it held me fascinated.

They were heading to pass to one side of us, so we didn't have to take cover, and we stood in the road watching them, hoping to see our fighters break in among them. However, they started turning, about that time, making a wide sweep and heading away to the north again without dropping their bombs. Apparently they had been warned of the presence of our fighters on patrol and ordered back—something which occurred quite frequently. They seldom followed through with a raid when they knew our fighters were at their altitude in time to meet them. If we could have had earlier warnings of their approach, we should probably have turned back many more raids than we did in the days that followed; but this was impossible now that we had lost Malaya and couldn't keep observers there, for the warnings we usually got didn't give us enough time to reach the altitude of the bombers before they were overhead.

After the formation had gone out of sight we returned to our job, and took the Hurricane back to the airdrome where the crews could work on it. Pretty soon the squadron came back and landed, having been unable to make contact with the enemy; and in a short time they were refuelled and back in readiness.

About eleven o'clock they were scrambled again. I had been chatting with Red in a tool-shed near our flight's dispersal hut when the word came. As he dashed out to his airplane I flung a casual "Good luck!" after him, little thinking that I'd have occasion shortly to recall it.

A few minutes after they took off the air-raid sirens sounded, but there were no signs of any enemy planes and most of us wandered up to the Mess to pass the time. After a little while we heard "that noise"—"again—the ominous heavy drone of many distant engines— so we went outdoors, took one look upwards, and then raced for the shelter trenches !

It was another formation of twenty-seven just as before, if not the same one, and this time it was heading to pass right over us. I sat in a trench with my heart pounding from running and excitement, looking up at the cluster of neatly spaced little silvery shapes drawing relentlessly towards us across the sky. Was this their bombing run? It surely looked like it. I rehearsed myself in what to do—crouch down, fingers in ears, mouth wide open, try to avoid touching the sides of the trench—and hope for the best. The next moments were very tense and quiet, all of us subdued, waiting for the warning scream of the bombs.

A battery of heavy anti-aircraft guns opened up nearby with their ear-splitting cracks, and white puffs of smoke began dotting the sky around the formation. It came on steadily until nearly straight above us, and we crouched low, knowing that it would be now if at all.

And then the moment was past and they'd gone over and no bombs had fallen. Relieved, we climbed out of the trenches again, but stayed near at hand, warily, because they might turn around and come back over. I occupied my time carpeting the bottom of my trench with dry leaves, because the ground was clamp and sticky and I'd already got my knees muddy.

They didn't come back though, and we watched them flying south and cast in the direction of the city until they were out of sight. Then we went back to the mess, and Ting and I sat out on the veranda, drinking Coca Cola. The air was pleasant, not hot, the sky clear, birds singing in the orchards around the mess; it might have been a pleasant Sunday morning in summer back home.

We wondered if the squadron would manage to make an interception this time. From the distant sounds it appeared that the bombers were now flying north, up (he east side of the island, and as the sound grew more distant we thought we could hear faintly the moan of distant engines power-diving once or twice. We strained our ears for the sound of machine-gun fire which would indicate a fight, but couldn't hear anything more.

After some time a lone Hurricane appeared from the north-east, losing height until it was near the airdrome, when its pilot opened his engine and roared low and fast across the field, rocking his wings in the victory signal. We finished our drinks and hurried down to meet him as he taxied in.

It was Red, and we saw at once that his guns had been fired, because the fabric patches were shot away from the holes in the wings in front of them. He was grinning from ear to ear as he climbed out of his cockpit.

"I got a fighter, Art!" were his first words when he saw me. "Boy, did we have a party!"

Then, after a pause to get control of himself because he was too excited to talk coherently, he went on, "We ran into a whole slew of them at twenty-two thousand feet, somewhere up in Malaya. We'd been chasing all over and hadn't seen a thing, and then all at once we did a turn and there they were, just off on our left, stacks of big twin-engined bombers.

"We sailed right through the formation from one side to the other, shooting at everything in sight. Then when I came out the other side I saw two fighters coming at me—little chubby fellows with great big radial engines in front and painted bright green all over. I thought 'All right, you ——s!' and I started climbing for all I was worth. They couldn't keep up with me at all. I got well above them and then turned and dived on the nearest one. I got real close before I let him have it, and honest you never saw anything like it. His machine just seemed to explode, with pieces flying off and smoke pouring out. He whipped up sort of, right in front of me, and then spun over sideways. The last I saw of him he was just a ball of fire going down. I gave the other one a burst, too, and I think I damaged him, but I was out of ammunition then so I dived away and headed for home."

By this time Red was the centre of a crowd of fellows, all shaking his hand and congratulating him. It was his first combat, and he had realised the good luck we had wished him before he took off.

A Brewster Buffalo fighter came gliding out of the distance, its engine dead. When about three hundred feet up, the pilot apparently saw he couldn't make the drome. He turned and disappeared behind a wood near by, and the crash truck and ambulance went off in that direction. Later we learned that the pilot had cracked up but wasn't hurt seriously. His engine had been damaged in combat and he'd glided all the way back, trying to make this airdrome, and falling only a few hundred yards short.

More Hurricanes were stringing back in at intervals now, until all except four of the boys had landed safely. When these four didn't show up after a reasonable time we began to get worried. Finally we got a call from Sembawang Airdrome, a few miles to the east, informing us that three of the four missing boys had force-landed there with their airplanes shot up, and were unhurt. They were Kleck (the American from Florida), Denny, and Mickey. The C.O. drove over to get them, returning about mid-afternoon, and after razzing them for "forgetting to duck" we listened to their stories.

Denny had shot down a bomber in flames, making the morning's score two definitely destroyed, in addition to several damaged. He had got some bullets in his engine and radiator from return fire from the bombers, so that his oil-tank and radiator went dry and his engine overheated and "seized," on the way back. He just made Sembawang, which was the nearest airdrome.

Kleck, the Florida boy, also had an exciting time. He damaged a couple of bombers in the initial attack and then turned around to chase after one that was lagging behind the rest. He was almost within range when a Navy Zero fighter jumped him from behind. The first thing he knew, showers of tracers were going by him and there were several loud explosions in his airplane from cannon shells. Then he was blinded by steam and glycol and oil spray in his cockpit, so he rolled over and dived to get away. Flames were coming from his engine and he thought he would have to jump; but the fire went out after a moment and being over enemy territory he chose to try to make it home. His engine ran intermittently, giving him a little power, although catching fire a couple of times more for short periods. He finally made it to the Straits and across them to Sembawang. The field was badly bombed, and with many unfilled craters. As he didn't have enough height to glide in on the runway, he had to land right among some craters. He bounced over most of them and then rolled to a stop at the edge of one, miraculously avoiding a crack-up.

Mickey said he "had a go" at one bomber and was attacking another when he suddenly noticed "funny little holes," as he described them, appearing around him in his machine, whereupon he dived away. His engine and radiator were hit so that he, too, was blinded by steam, glycol, and oil. Once he thought he was on fire and unfastened his straps with the intention of bailing out, but the fire didn't materialize. Then he saw Sembawang ahead so he stayed with his machine, trying to make it. When he got there his windshield was so covered with oil and glycol that he couldn't see enough to tell whether he was landing on the runway or not, and like Kleck he landed among the bomb craters. This was very bad, because he hadn't had a chance to fasten his straps again—the straps keep you from being thrown forward in a crash, so you're not so likely to be injured.

When Mickey saw the bomb craters going past his wings he retracted his wheels so that his machine dropped down on its belly and slid to a quick stop—a very wise move. By thus deliberately doing a minor crash he avoided the probability of a serious one, for if left on its wheels his plane would probably have rolled on until it hit a bomb crater. Not expecting to see anyone there whom he knew, he was quite astounded, on climbing out of his wrecked machine, to see

Denny and Kleck approaching, laughing at him; and to learn that he was the third to force-land there!

Only one pilot now remained missing. That was Bruce, a New Zealand boy, one of the finest chaps I've known and the best-liked boy in the squadron. He hasn't been heard of since, and I believe he is now listed as "missing, believed killed." Though we knew we had to expect casualties now, we felt it was too bad that he, of all of us, had to be the first.

There was a Chinese business man in Singapore who had a standing offer of a bottle of champagne for every Jap plane destroyed, so that evening Red and Denny, accompanied by some of the others, drove into town to collect the two bottles they had earned by their victories. Those of us who hadn't flown that day were to take over on the morrow, so I went to bed with high hopes of having my first crack at the Japs in the morning.

CHAPTER 5

Island under Siege

I had taken over a nice airy room in the mess that day, and once during the night I awoke at the sound of air-raid sirens. A little later, dreamily, I heard the noise of anti-aircraft guns, of two or three airplanes droning about in the distance, and then the far-away thuds of several bombs exploding.

Next morning when I got up I saw a new landmark to the east which was to remain part of the scenery for as long as I stayed in Singapore. The bombers in the night had hit and set fire to one of the great oil storage tanks near the naval base a few miles east of us. The landmark was a great sinister column of black smoke, with red flames at its bottom, rising and widening Vesuviuslike to a height of three or four thousand feet where it flattened out and stretched southward in a long dark ugly mantle as far as we could see.

I didn't get to fly that day either. My high hopes of seeing my first action against the Japs were frustrated by a new and most disappointing order which we received early in the morning. Our squadron were to leave Singapore and move to Palembang, a Dutch city three hundred miles south in Sumatra, not far from the jungle airdrome where we stopped on our way up here. We were to go there because the prospect of enemy raids on Palembang and on shipping in the Banka Straits near by had made it necessary for a squadron to be stationed in the vicinity.

We were all terribly disappointed. None of us wanted to go, for here in Singapore we were right in the middle of things, while it would be comparatively quiet, so we thought, in Sumatra. And so it was that I felt anything but sorry when the C.O. told me I was to remain here temporarily at least, in charge of a group of the boys who were being left behind. It was necessary to leave six behind because

OIL STORAGE TANK ON FIRE NEAR THE NAVAL BASE AT SINGAPORE

LOUNGING ON THE VERANDAH OVERLOOKING TENGAH AIRDROME

there were that many airplanes not serviceable for the trip—the three which had been damaged in the fight the day before and had force-landed at Sembawang, and three others that had minor troubles or damage.

The only order the C.O. gave me was to do what I could toward getting these machines into flying condition—though I'm quite sure he knew I'd have my own ideas about what to do with them after that !

The boys took off for Palembang after lunch, leaving the airdrome strangely empty and silent after the roar of their engines had died away in the distance. Ours had been the only squadron here at Tengah, 175 Squadron having taken up residence at Seletar Airdrome on the east side of the island. The countryside was quiet, the afternoon sunny and pleasant. The only sign of war was the silent, sullen black smoke-column brooding above the horizon east and south of us. I found it hard to realise that we were besieged by a great army, just across a narrow strip of water no wider than the Mississippi River !

I had inherited for my use a beautiful new 1942 Ford Sedan which the C.O. had been provided with; but Kleck, who was one of the group staying with me, wasn't to be outdone. He appeared later in the afternoon, triumphantly driving a '41 Chevvy he had promoted; it had been left behind by a bomber pilot whose unit was unexpectedly moved away!

We were able to use these cars to good advantage during the next couple of days, at the task of getting our airplanes repaired. Normally a squadron's ground personnel look after all repair work, but in this case our ground personnel weren't available. They had come only as far as Sumatra and would probably remain there, along with the squadron's equipment and spares. We were little better than orphans here.

We had the cooperation of another unit, who supplied us with a crew of men to work on our machines, and helped us in other ways, and we drove all over the island, visiting various places to procure needed spare parts and tools. This was a highly interesting way of passing the time until we could start flying again, for it gave us a chance to see what the island was like. We got a radiator here, a wing-tip there, a couple of propellers from different sources, a propeller installation tool kit from another place, and so on. We made frequent trips to Sembawang, of course, taking spares for the three machines which Kleck, Denny, and Mickey had landed there, and checking on the repair work.

Most of the island seemed to be wooded, either jungle or rubber plantations. Vegetation was rich and green everywhere, due, I suppose, to the large rainfall. The soil itself didn't look rich, being mostly a sort of light-brown clay. The roads were good, mostly black-top, and wound pleasantly through forests, rubber estates, and curious little Malayan-Chinese villages. It was here that I finally became completely at home driving on the wrong side of the road, for the traffic was left-hand as in England, all the cars, of course, having the driver's seat on the right.

The Japs weren't to launch their actual assault against the island for several days more, and most of the time it was fairly quiet except for an air raid or two each day. I spent quite a bit of time working on airplanes at the drome at Tengah, and occasionally had to leave my work to take cover at sight of enemy planes.

On one occasion I really had to run for it. I was putting a wing-tip on a machine, working alone, and was so engrossed that I failed to notice the drone of an approaching bomber formation until I had been listening to it for perhaps three or four minutes. Suddenly coming to, I looked up to see them almost overhead, a standard high-altitude raid. The nearest shelter trenches were a couple of hundred yards away, so I jumped into my car, parked beside the airplane, and started off with my wheels spinning.

As I approached the trenches I could see some Indian Army soldiers diving into them, so I knew I'd split the timing pretty close and just yanked the emergency brake handle and landed running, without waiting for the car to stop. The bombers were directly overhead. I dived into a trench with a couple of Indian Sikhs and crouched down, waiting; but the bombers passed on and no bombs fell, so I climbed out again.

The heavy anti-aircraft guns were barking furiously. All at once I heard a whistling noise as of a bomb falling, and in practically one leap I landed on my knees in the trench, in a huddle with the Sikhs again. There was no explosion, so after a minute or so we cautiously stuck our heads above ground, looked warily all around like so many gophers leaving their holes, and then climbed out.

I found I had muddied my arms and legs and cut one knee in this second leap for cover, so I drove back to the Mess to clean up. There I found Kleck in almost identical condition, his arms and legs muddied and one knee cut also. It seemed that he had heard that same noise and leaped back into the trench he'd been using, just as I did, with the same result. We made quite a joke out of being "wounded" in a bombless air raid! We didn't know what made the whistling sound that scared us, but presumed it was a dud anti-aircraft shell, falling back to earth after failing to explode in the air.

They never did bomb Tengah Airdrome while we were there, in spite of passing over it frequently. Either they went on to bomb somewhere else or turned away at the approach of our fighters. Once we saw them bomb Sembawang Airdrome several miles away—an impressive sight. We couldn't see the drome itself from Tengah, but we saw the scores of smoke-clouds shooting up in a quick procession across that section of our horizon, tumbling and swirling together to a height of perhaps three or four hundred feet. The sound came to us—awe-inspiring, heavy sustained booming and rumbling that lasted for several seconds while the earth under us shook and trembled from the distant explosions. Gradually the smoke-clouds rose and thinned away, leaving only a couple of small black columns from fires that were started.

In the Officers' Mess the Malay waiters and batmen had all run off after the news that the enemy were so near, but the two elderly Chinese cooks and "Tichi," a little Malay boy of ten or eleven who worked in the bar, remained on the job. The meals were still lavish, the only difference being that we had to serve ourselves. There was always plenty of ice-cold beer, as well as Coca Cola and other soft drinks, to be had.

We had a pleasant surprise on the third or fourth day after the squadron had gone to Palembang, when they all returned, roaring out of the south late in the afternoon and swooping low across the airdrome to let us know they'd arrived. After they landed we learned that they'd come up to escort a bombing raid on an enemy position in Malaya at dawn next morning, and I promised the C.O. I'd have three of my machines ready to go with them on the raid.

The boys' opinion of Sumatra hadn't improved during the time they were there, and they were all glad to get back and wished they could stay. There had been almost nothing for them to do in the line of flying, except some monotonous convoy patrols. The closest any of them had come to action was an occasional chase after lone bombers, snooping around ships in the Banka Straits, that ducked away into clouds at sight of their Hurricanes. They said it was hotter than before, the bugs, snakes, and lizards all doing well and thicker than ever, and the mosquitoes still growing.

I had to work a good share of that night with my crews, finishing repair jobs and doing final inspections on the three machines that I'd promised the C.O. I'd have ready. It was bright moonlight, and we worked and sweated and toiled until about two o'clock in the morning. Then with the last engine checked, the last fuel tank filled, the last gun cleaned and loaded, and the last cowling-clip fastened I told the men they could go to bed and take the morning off. Then I drove wearily back to the Mess for two or three hours' sleep myself before the raid. I was to take part in it, so naturally I was looking forward once more to getting my first action against the Japs.

It was all in vain though. A change in the situation at dawn made it necessary to cancel the whole raid, and about mid-morning the squadron were ordered to fly back to Palembang.

I was again to stay behind, but three of my pilots were to go with the squadron, taking the three airplanes that we had got ready. I tried to talk the C.O. out of taking these airplanes. It hurt our pride to see bombers coming over each day and not be able to do anything about it except run for shelter and then watch from our trenches. I had hoped that I could get started operating with my bunch and get a crack at them. But the C.O. said he was afraid he might need the airplanes at Palembang. He consoled me by saying that if I got any more planes in serviceable condition I could keep them and use them, for the time being at least.

Kleck was one of the three of my group who had to go to Palembang with the squadron this time, and he was quite put out about it. He had the same hopes I had about operating here, and he naturally didn't think he'd get any action down there in Sumatra.

He shouldn't have worried on that score. He was destined to get more action there than I got in Singapore and I was never to see him again.

That would have left only three pilots in my group, but after the squadron left I saw that two of the machines hadn't taken off with the rest. The pilots were Denny and Sergeant H———. They both had engine trouble and would have to wait over for a day or two. So for the moment there were five of us. Denny was a flight commander in the squadron and senior to me, so he automatically was in charge of our group.

By this time we were beginning to hear a little more of the noises of war. Particularly at night we could hear distant guns booming out an occasional few rounds. We expected that as the enemy got time

CONSRUCTING A BRICK DISPERSAL PEN AT TENGAH AIRDROME

to bring more of their artillery into position we'd be hearing much more. Our airdrome was only two or three miles from the edge of the narrow straits separating us from the enemy.

Towards noon of the day after our squadron flew back to Palembang we were all surprised by a visit from 175 Squadron (whose pilots came out to Singapore with us). As I mentioned before, they had been operating from Seletar Airdrome on the north-east side of the island, right on the edge of the Straits. They had been forced to take off on very short notice this morning and fly over here, when the enemy began shelling their drome!

We were all glad to see one another and had quite a reunion in the Mess, swapping accounts of what we'd been doing. They said they'd had lots of patrols and chases and had fought two or three engagements with moderate success.

It was about noon and we were all lounging on the veranda, swapping stories and waiting for lunch to be ready, when suddenly the quiet was broken by a muffled explosion, a whistling noise, and then a loud explosion, all in rapid order :

"*Whoompf—phe-ew—BLAM!*"

The building shook a little. Conversation stopped in midair. We exchanged glances, and I looked around for a place to duck.

Someone ventured, "I didn't hear any airplane!"

"*Whoompf—phe-ew—BLAM!*" The building shook again.

Someone else said, "That *isn't* a plane! "

Then a startled "Look!" and there on the far side of the airdrome we saw two thin flat clouds of light-blue smoke drifting along just above the ground, about fifty yards apart. As we looked, there was a bright flash in the ground near them and the earth shot upwards and outward in a cloud of dust and smoke. The same noise came to us a second later. We all knew what it was now without being told. The time had come for what was to be my first of five evacuations under fire in two weeks. Our airdrome, too, was being shelled !

The barrage lasted over an hour, but nothing landed nearer the mess than a hundred yards or so; and most of us ate our lunches unperturbed. We weren't going to let them spoil our last meal here, anyhow.

Joe H——, one of 175's pilots who was delayed taking off and didn't leave Seletar until some time after the rest, came into the dining-hall while we were eating. He looked quite shaken—and with reason. Just as he was levelling off to land on the runway two shells had exploded one on either side of him, throwing his machine partly out of control and nearly causing him to crash!

Through the windows of the mess we saw a low thatched-roof wooden building on the far side of the drome catch fire and begin burning hotly. A Brewster Buffalo landed, and as it was taxi-ing to the edge of the field a shell crashed beside it, turning it upside-down and injuring the pilot. Someone took my car to drive him to the dressing station. When I got it back I had to clean blood off the seat and dashboard.

The barrage ceased after an hour or so, for no apparent reason—probably because the enemy thought it was enough to show us we couldn't use the drome and because they didn't want to damage it any more in case they were able to use it later themselves.

From the Far East Command Communiqué:

Singapore, February 5. There has been some enemy shelling in the north of the island, with negligible results. Air reports show much enemy movement southward in Johore. Enemy aircraft have continued to make high-level and low dive-bombing and machine-gun attacks on the island, causing comparatively little damage or casualties. Shipping in the harbour was also attacked. An oil tanker at the naval base, which was set on fire two days ago by enemy bombing, is still burning. Hurricane fighters of the R.A.F. intercepted a large formation of enemy aircraft over Singapore this morning. One enemy aircraft was destroyed, one probably destroyed, and one damaged by our aircraft.

CHAPTER 6

Into the Fight

With the airdromes of Tengah and Seletar under shell-fire and Sembawang vulnerable to it at any time (for it was right on the edge of the Straits), there was only one place left from which we could operate. This was Kallang Airdrome, the former municipal airport of Singapore, on the south side of the island just east of the city.

175 Squadron were now ordered to move down there, and we did likewise, taking our two Hurricanes and two automobiles. The engine troubles on the Hurricanes had been remedied, but the weather was reported bad in the direction of Sumatra so that the pilots, Denny and Sergeant H——, couldn't go to Palembang yet to rejoin the Squadron.

They flew the Hurricanes across to Kallang while I drove my Ford, and Brownie and Ted took the Chewy which Kleck had promoted. We of course loaded our baggage into the two cars before leaving; in addition, I brought along a bag of things belonging to Bruce, the boy who went missing from the squadron's first engagement. I wanted to have it sent back to his folks.

Driving to Kallang I had to pass through the city of Singapore, my first visit to it. I took time off to drive around a little, looking at the sights, and then headed out east of town to the airdrome.

This was a sorry sight if there ever was one. The road entering the airdrome passed under imposing dark stone archways, now pitifully scarred and chipped by blast and shrapnel and bullets. The beautiful hangars and terminal buildings of what had once been a great airline base were barren and empty, with windows gone, walls gashed and torn. The vast concrete aprons between and in front of the hangars here were torn and pitted with bomb craters, as was the entire field.

The saddest sight of all was the remains of several Hurricanes and

THE AUTHOR'S BEDROOM, SEA-VIEW HOTEL, SINGAPORE

THE LAWN, SEA-VIEW HOTEL, SINGAPORE

Brewsters, as well as three or four trucks and tank wagons, around the outside of the field—sorry-looking, smashed and twisted wreckages, mostly burned out, the victims of bombing and machine-gun attacks. It was heartbreaking.

The Hurricanes had already arrived from Tengah and were now dispersed around the field with mechanics working on them, giving them their "D/Fs," or daily inspections. Denny was gone, so I inquired for directions to the Officers' Mess and found it a couple of miles from the drome.

But there were only smouldering ruins at the spot. The Mess had been hit and set on fire by bombs the day before, and was completely burned out. I found Denny and some of the others there, salvaging the bar stock from a refrigerator in the ruins—bottles of beer and liquor.

We didn't know it yet, but Squadron Leader L——, the C.O. of 175 Squadron, was acting fast in this little emergency. By evening he had arranged for all of us to be put up in the exclusive Sea View Hotel on the seashore several miles east of town, which was supposed to be one of the most luxurious places in Singapore. I found myself ensconced in a room which was like a movie star's boudoir in its furnishings—elaborate wardrobes, tables, dressers, cabinets—all in beautiful hardwood; expensive-looking chairs, settees (I think you call them), stools, footstools, and perhaps as many as half a dozen mirrors. I had little trouble, as you can guess, in finding room for my wardrobe of shirt and shorts when I climbed into the huge, luxurious bed. A couple of days later I learned that a small but nicely furnished sitting-room adjacent belonged with my room. Altogether, it was a strange lair from which to go forth to battle.

One side of the hotel looked out on the sea, but the main entrance was in the crook of an "L" formed by the building, and faced away from the sea onto a pretty little lawn filled with palm trees, its beauty somewhat spoiled by shelter trenches dug in it. There were several automobiles—including ours—scattered about there, too, because patrons were required to park their cars under the trees for concealment.

Dinner that evening was seven courses, served by Chinese and Malay waiters in a spacious dining-hall where we saw lots of wealthy civilians, including the first white women we'd seen in some time, wearing the first evening dresses we'd seen in months.

After dinner, Denny and I talked things over, discussing what we should do now. He was as anxious to remain in Singapore as I was.

Technically we were under the orders of our C.O., but he was three hundred miles away in Palembang and would naturally expect us to use our own initiative in what we did, now that circumstances were changing so fast.

Our most obvious course, one which didn't appeal to us, was to follow the squadron to Palembang, two of us flying in the two Hurricanes and the other three going by the first available boat. We not only hated to go back there, where (we thought) things would be very quiet, but also we sincerely felt that we and our airplanes would be more useful here during the crucial days ahead.

175 Squadron had been working hard ever since they arrived, and the pilots were getting tired. Also they were getting short of airplanes, so that they could use our two to good advantage. Reinforcements of either pilots or planes would be hard to get now. They were a swell crowd of fellows and we knew them so well from having been together on the voyage out that we'd just as soon fight with them as with our own bunch. Denny finally decided that we would offer to help them.

Next morning after breakfast he spoke to Squadron Leader L——, the squadron's C.O., offering to put ourselves and our two airplanes at his disposal if Air Headquarters would O.K. it. Squadron Leader L—— was delighted with the idea. He rang up Air Headquarters and gave them such a convincing sales talk over the phone that in a matter of minutes the plan was O.K.'d and we were officially "attached" to 175 Squadron. We also pooled our two cars with those which the squadron already had, with the result that the squadron was well off for pilots' transportation from then on. Now at last, I thought, I should surely be getting my much-delayed action against the Japs.

We all had some business and shopping we wanted to take care of, so Denny asked our new C.O. if we could have a couple of hours off to run into town before we went to work. The C.O. insisted that we should take the whole day off and not start flying until the next day.

Accordingly, four of us—Denny, Ted, Brownie, and I—piled into the Ford and drove to town to attend to our business and capitalize on our first chance to spend some time in the city and see what it was like.

The business section seemed to be very modern, and it might have been an American city except for the welter of Chinese and Malays all about and the *rickshaws* mingling with modern cars on the streets. However, we soon tired and lost interest in sightseeing as it was a very hot day, and stopped for refreshments at the Raffles Hotel, supposed to be one of the popular hot-spots of the town. There we saw an advertisement for the film *Ziegfeld Girl* at the Alhambra Theatre near by; we voted for a matinee of that in preference to further sightseeing, until the heat of the day was past.

The theatre was small, with a pleasant interior that belied a rather shabby outside appearance. The air-raid sirens sounded shortly after the picture started, and Ted and Brownie, who had steel helmets, clapped them on until the all-clear sounded a while later.

It perhaps wasn't just the show we would have chosen if we had had a choice, for though the music and lavish pageants were wonderful, the sight of so many beautiful girls was almost more than we could take after being away from feminine companionship for so long! The shock was quite rude for us when it was over; completely lost in the lovely atmosphere of American girls and song and gaiety and peace, we stepped outside into the teeming oriental traffic and the sweltering tropical sun, to be reminded that we were half-way around the world from America, with our enemies only a few miles away.

Towards mid-afternoon we returned to the hotel; there we learned to our very keen sorrow that our new C.O., Squadron Leader L——, had been killed while we were down town. He was a fine C.O., loved by all his boys, and we ourselves had known him well enough to like him very much also. Two of the other boys had been shot down but escaped injury, although their machines were wrecked.

One of the boys shot down, Joe H——, was first to tell us about Squadron Leader L——'s death. Joe himself had had a very narrow escape. He'd had his machine badly shot up by Navy Zeros and had to run for it, racing low over the sea to get away from two of them, his damaged engine running wide open with its radiator shot through and running dry, with the result that just after he got clear of them his engine "seized" and he had to force-land near the shore of an island. His Hurricane was almost torn to pieces by rocks just beneath the surface of the water, but luckily it stayed right side up and he managed to get out safely. He was picked up by a motor launch whose crew saw him land, and they brought him into Singapore harbour, where he got a ride by car to the hotel. We found him resting there when we arrived, a very shaken boy. It was he who had had the narrow escape the day before when two shells nearly wrecked him as he was landing at Tengah.

Later in the afternoon we drove from the hotel out to the airdrome to see what was going on, and there I met an old friend of mine, a New Zealand pilot, who had been stationed at the airdrome near London where I was, a year or so before.

He said he had been out in Singapore since before the fighting started, and as flight commander in a squadron of Brewster Buffaloes he had been in nearly all the fighting which went on here. He was so worn and haggard and had lost so much weight that I hardly recognized him. He said he had just been promoted to squadron leader and was going down to Java to re-form his squadron, as most of their planes had been lost and most of their pilots killed. He himself was off flying for at least a week or two because of shock from a bomb that had landed too close to him a few days before.

I advised him to try to get sent away for a rest, even if it meant losing his promotion temporarily. He looked much too tired and ill to carry on long.

With Squadron Leader L——'s death, Rickey, one of the flight commanders, became C.O. of the squadron, and Denny was made flight commander in his place. Three airplanes had been lost during the day but only one pilot, so that with the addition of us five pilots from 300 Squadron there were now twice as many pilots as planes. That meant that each of the two flights (into which any squadron is divided) had enough pilots to man all the airplanes. Rickey therefore instituted a programme whereby the two flights changed off, one bunch doing all the work while the other rested.

Because the heavy attacks usually came about mid-morning, Rickey instituted a short shift from 9 a.m. to 1 p.m. for one flight to do, to take care of these heavy raids; the other flight would be on duty the rest of the daylight hours both before and after this shift.

I was in Denny's flight and we were scheduled to do the short shift next morning, so we didn't have to get up very early. After we finished our five-course breakfasts we all sat around on the covered veranda at the entrance to the hotel, reading the morning papers and gossiping, for we still had an hour or so to kill before time to go out to the airdrome.

The distant drone of Rolls-Royce engines in the sky reached our ears, telling us that the other flight had already gone up on patrol; for the first time in more than three months I began to experience the familiar tension and nervousness, with the sickish pain in the pit of my stomach unusually strong. I suppose it was the realisation coming home that I was "in it" once more, with all the uncertainties and dismaying possibilities to get used to and subdue again into their places as normal parts of life.

Denny and I spent a little time talking over the formation we'd use and discussing the tactics we would try to employ. Because of our small number of airplanes, Air Headquarters had ordered us to operate as a squadron of eight until we got more reinforcements, to give us a better percentage in reserve. Accordingly, we planned to fly in two sections of four, Denny leading one section and I the other. If we engaged a. bombing raid escorted by fighters—the usual thing—I would endeavour to engage the fighters with my four to keep them diverted while Denny took his section into the bombers. Then the next time we'd change around, and he'd do the dirty work with his four while I went for the bombers.

As we talked and I visualised the situations we were discussing, I found my excitement increasing until my heart was pounding and my knees trembled a little—and after eighteen months of mainly frontline service, too!

It seemed so strange to be there relaxing, or trying to, in the cool quiet veranda of the hotel, nonchalantly discussing how we should go about the bizarre and unearthly business that might occur in that other eerie world miles above us before the morning was out, while ordinary civilian men and women lounged around us, finishing their coffee, reading the morning papers, chatting as ordinary people anywhere might, not planning to kill anyone—their greatest danger a probable sea voyage to Java in a few days. I had my helmet, gloves, and Mae West in my lap, having just unpacked them from my things, and their significance helped to make it all seem too incongruous to be real!

The other six pilots of our flight were sitting near by, and presently Denny looked at his watch and announced: "Eight-fifteen. I reckon we might as well get on down there."

We strolled out to where the Ford was parked among the palm trees on the lawn, and the eight of us piled in. I was wondering how long it would take me to get over feeling like a little boy on his first day at school.

As we were backing out from under the palm trees we heard the Hurricanes roar low overhead going towards the drome, so we knew the boys had finished their patrol. We could see them circling to land as we drove along, and by the time we reached the drome they had all landed and taxied to their places along the edge of the field. The pilots were heading toward the dispersal hut when we got there (we had just one hut for all of us at Kallang), and when they saw us piling out of the car they began taking off their Mae Wests and tossing them gratefully aside.

Denny looked over the list of available machines and assigned them to us while we were putting on our Mae Wests and otherwise getting ready. I changed from my shorts to a pair of slacks that I kept for flying in action (for protection to my legs in case of fire). Others had overalls; some flew with no extra protection.

I shouldered my parachute and went out to get my airplane ready. The crews were just finishing refuelling it and checking it over after its last patrol. I thought, "Ten minutes to get ready, and then any time after that," and my heart went to pounding again.

There were a number of minor things to take care of in getting my Hurricane to readiness. Because my legs aren't long enough for me to climb into the cockpit of a Hurricane easily when wearing a parachute, I placed my parachute in the seat, so I could put it on alter getting in—laying out its straps and the seat-straps in neat order so I could reach them quickly without getting them twisted. Then I hung my helmet over the gun-sight behind my wind-shield and plugged the radio lead and oxygen tube into their connections in the side of the cockpit. My gloves I tucked between the gun-sight and the windshield. There were checks to make on oxygen supply, air-pressure system, and the electric gun-sight. There were other minor little odds and ends to do that would each save a second in starting—like turning the gasoline on, unscrewing the primer pump so it was ready for use, turning on the ignition switches, and setting the throttle just right for starting. Because the field was soft and muddy I pumped my wing-flaps down a little to assist in getting off the ground quickly; and of course, being built rather small, I checked the position of my seat and raised it as high as it could be set.

Finally satisfied that I had everything ready, I made my way back to the dispersal hut and joined the rest of the boys, who were sitting in easy-chairs on the porch, waiting. My feelings seemed pretty well under control again, and I realised that I was slipping quite rapidly into my old mental attitude—combining fighting fever and resignation to "come what may." That is my best means of keeping my fears under control while in action.

I could see by the faces of some of the 175 Squadron boys around me that the strain of constant flying and fighting for the past several

The dispersal hut, Kallang Airdrome

days was beginning to tell. Our orders to scramble would come by telephone, and each time the phone rang they'd start nervously and lean forward tensely, until the orderly who answered it told us what the call was about. It rang every three or four minutes, but each call for the first half-hour was just some inconsequential message, such as someone wanting to speak to one of the mechanics or an officer wanting to speak to the armourer sergeant—and they'd all relax again.

It reminded me of Battle of Britain days in 1940, when my squadron did their readiness in a tent at Hawkinge Airdrome on the southeast coast of England; we all used to start in the same way with our hearts pounding each time the phone rang—often to learn that it was only some aircraftman reporting that he'd missed the bus back from lunch—and would we please send it back for him! After that we'd all sit back again, sighing deeply, each feeling that he'd been done out of another week's growth. Some psychologist should try to work out a different kind of alarm that would be less agonising to taut nerves than that quick, jarring ring which becomes almost nightmarish in times of heavy strain.

After we'd been at readiness for some time we heard the orderly taking a call and this time, after listening a moment, he replied to the voice at the other end, "Twenty thousand? Yes, sir."

Someone said "That's it!" and there was a shuffling and scraping of chairs as we started getting to our feet. The orderly turned to us from the phone to repeat what he was told: "Thirty plus bandits, above twenty thousand feet, approaching from the north-west. Scramble and gain altitude as fast as possible! "

I found myself sprinting towards my machine, which was near by, heard a Ford V-8 starting up and getting away fast, tyres spinning as it careened past me—my own Ford, with pilots hanging on the running-boards—the boys whose machines were farthest away using it to save a few seconds.

The alert ground crews were already starting our engines. Mine was running and the mechanic climbing out of the cockpit when I got there, and I scrambled in. There was the old feverish fumbling at parachute and seat straps, helmet and gloves—the glancing around to see if I was late and whether the others were taxi-ing out yet.

All tucked in and ready to go at last, I found my tenseness relaxing its hold a little. A moment's wait with engine idling, for Denny's four machines to taxi out ahead, and then I was following after them onto the rain-soaked field, fast but carefully, dodging the newly-filled bomb craters in which the earth would still be soft. It wasn't safe to take off in formation, because of the condition of the field, but Denny's four followed one another off quickly and I timed my taxi-ing to arrive in position just after them, with the rest of my section coming along behind me.

Denny was already a distant little silhouette up ahead, climbing and turning, over the harbour; the other three of his section following, with the last one just, leaving the ground, when I opened my throttle. There was the raucous full-throated bellowing of my own thousand-horse-power engine, the hurricane wind-stream forming a wall around the cockpit, tugging at my helmet and blasting my face when I peered out to watch for bad spots in the field; then came the surge of the airplane picking up speed fast, the growing tightness and responsiveness of the controls, and I was off and skimming up over the boundary, shoving my hydraulic control to "Wheels Up," drawing back throttle and propeller pitch controls to ease the engine. A red light showed in my instrument panel, indicating that my wheels were clear up in their retracted position. I shoved the hydraulic control over to "Flaps Up" and felt my machine sag a little as its flaps came up from their downward position so that their lifting effect was lost; I began to gain speed faster, the result of lowered wind resistance with the wheels and flaps out of the way.

Ahead of me I could see the silhouettes of Denny's four machines, climbing fast in a gentle left turn and "forming up "together in their assigned order. Below, the blue-green sea of Singapore's outer harbour was slowly curving backward beneath my wings and receding away.

I was in a left turn, too, cutting it shorter than Denny in order to catch him. Behind me the three other planes of my section were trailing, gradually overtaking me and drawing up into their places. My "number two" was fifty or sixty yards off on my right and a little behind; my "numbers three and four" were staggered off on my left and about the same distances apart. Overtaking Denny's section we throttled back and took up position two or three hundred yards away to his left and a little back. It was just a loose easy "search" formation, in which we could guard each other against surprise attacks, and in which we could either act independently as two units or close in and work together, as circumstances dictated.

The crackling of the radio in my ears was broken intermittently by the whirr of transmitters as various conversations were carried on.

Denny's voice came through, calling Control. "Hello, Rastus; hello,

Rastus! Tiger Leader calling. Have you any fresh information on the bandits? Over."

A second later the distant controller's voice came back in reply:

Hello, Tiger Leader, Tiger Leader! Rastus answering. Thirty plus bandits now twenty miles northwest of island, above twenty thousand feet, still coming this way. Over!

We climbed furiously, whipping our engines hard, the noses of our airplanes pointed steeply upward, reaching lip and up toward that strange world of thin cold air above us. Denny was leading us wisely in a long sweep out over the sea south of the island, where we could be "up sun" of our enemies.

Hello, Green One. Green Two calling. One of your wheels is down a little. Over.

Green One and Green Two were the two pilots on the left of me in my section, and glancing over at the nearest of them I saw the outline of one of his wheels half-way down out of its recess in the bottom of the fuselage. Then it disappeared up into place.

Brownie was Green One. His voice came over the R/T (radio telephone) now. "Thank you, Green Two. Is it O.K. now?"

Yes, it's O.K. now, Green One.

We roared onward and upward, the sun growing brighter and the air clearer. At ten thousand feet it was getting chilly, so I slid my transparent cockpit hood forward, closed, and the cockpit was suddenly quiet with most of the racket and the wind shut out and the noise of the engine reduced to a heavy drone.

Singapore Island was now a miniature in brilliant tropical green far below, landscaped with miniature jungles, orchards, fields, roads, villages, and towns, with the miniature city and harbour on its south coast, all partially screened by a layer of low broken clouds sprinkled over it like hundreds of tufts of white cotton fluff, pretty in the bright sunlight.

It was dwarfed by the green expanses of the great Malayan Peninsula which half swallows it in the hollow of its southern tip into which the island fits, and by the endless reaches of warm blue-green sea stretching in all other directions. Over it ran the long dark mantle of smoke from the oil fire, stretching from its source on the north side, down across and southward out over the sea into the southern horizon.

My altimeter reached the fifteen-thousand-foot mark, and about that time I pulled the control which "changes gears "on the engine's two-speed supercharger so it will give better power at high altitude, and also opened the oxygen regulator valve on my instrument panel to start it feeding oxygen into my face-mask. We kept climbing hard, still out over the sea a way, in a gentle left-hand sweep.

Control came on again. "The bandits are just north of the island now, altitude twenty-two thousand or above."

It didn't sound so good. We'd be very lucky if we could reach their altitude by the time they were over the island. Starting a fight with a disadvantage in altitude is one of the most reliable ways of committing suicide. Denny seemed unperturbed, and continued the sweep. He knew there was no use going in to meet them until we had enough height.

Finally when our altimeters read twenty thousand he turned and led us in toward the island, still climbing hard, chancing that we could gain enough altitude before we met them. It would have been much better could we have waited until we had twenty-five thousand feet or so, for then we could come in with a definite advantage in height; but there just wasn't time enough for that. As it was, we still had another two thousand feet to gain just to reach the height of the bombers. If my section were to engage the fighters, which would be above them, we needed considerably more altitude than that or we might have a bad time. But there was no choice.

We came in over the city, still climbing hard. Twenty-one thousand feet now, still another thousand to gain at the very least. Control came on again:

> The bandits are over the north-west part of the island now, flying south, still at twenty-two thousand and above.

Denny had us climbing so steeply that my air-speed indicator showed less than one hundred and twenty miles an hour of forward speed, and my controls felt sloppy, as if my airplane were nearing a stall. I'd turned on my gun-sight and switched the safety ring around my firing button to the "Fire" position long since.

We turned left and headed westward, hoping to cut them off. Our formation was getting very ragged. It's hard to keep good formation in the thin air at high altitudes in which the airplanes tend to wallow around loosely, and now every pilot was tense, watching all around for first signs of the enemy, not paying much attention to formation-keeping.

I noticed that one of the machines in Denny's section which had been lagging behind the rest had now disappeared entirely. Engine trouble, I presumed. That left only seven of us.

Twenty-two thousand feet at last, and we were over the south-east part of the island with still no enemies in sight. Denny led us in a left turn, until we were heading south.

For all my keenness to get into battle, the cry, when it came, jolted me.

Bandits to the left—tally-ho!

We wheeled into a steep left turn at the cry, and I saw them, in the distance to my dismay, a weird cluster of silver insects sticking out starkly against the blue, heading away from us toward the city. I felt like crying as I realised the situation, for somehow they had got around past us while we were trying to head them off. Now we would have to chase them, and they already had a good start.

It was a weird chase. At that height you hardly seem to be moving, even at three hundred miles an hour or more. We seemed to just hover there while our engines screamed and bellowed, "flat out," boring away at the thin air trying to overtake the enemy formation which we could see poised against the sky ahead of us like a surrealist painting, with above them the tiny silhouettes of several fighters wheeling about. They seemed to have passed over the east part of the city and were now going flat out for home.

As we neared the city I noticed that we were back down to twenty-one thousand feet, and our quarry seemed to be even a little lower, which meant they must be diving slightly. I recalled what other pilots had said about them:

> After they drop their bombs they stick their noses down and go like a bat out of hell. If they've got a good start on you then, you haven't a hope of catching them.

I didn't know whether or not these had dropped their bombs yet, but they obviously had their noses down, if they were losing altitude this fast, and they certainly seemed to be going some, too.

Suddenly a shower of little white objects like snowballs streaked past me from ahead, terrifying me because I thought they were some new kind of tracer bullets, and I looked around wildly for the enemy that was shooting at me. All I saw were the other Hurricanes though, and they seemed unperturbed. I couldn't imagine what was going on. It only lasted for a brief second. I wasn't to learn the explanation until after I landed.

We kept up the chase for a long way up in Malaya, following the bombers down and down, gradually gaining on them but not fast enough, for they finally made the safety of a cloudbank and we had to let them go. It was disappointing, but one gets used to disappointments in air warfare.

We didn't realise what the target of the raid had been until we were nearly back. Coming over our airdrome at three or four thousand feet, with the layer of low broken clouds making a sort of carpet just under us, I noticed through the spaces between the clouds a very light pall of thin blue smoke floating over the field. Then when I came through beneath the clouds the truth sank home as I saw that the airdrome was littered with dozens of fresh bomb craters!

Light-blue and grey smoke was still wafting from the doors, windows, and eaves of the great hangars below. Near one hangar a Brewster Buffalo was burning furiously, wreathed in scarlet flames, with volumes of stormy black smoke rolling upward—obviously hit by an incendiary bomb.

So it appeared that our enemies, not content with shelling us out of all the airdromes on the north side of the island, were determined to drive us out completely by bombing this, our only base left.

Now we were faced with the ticklish problem of getting our Hurricanes down safely in the middle of all the bomb craters and debris, for there was of course no other field for us to land on. Reaching the drome a little ahead of the rest, I circled for several minutes, trying to figure out a way to land, "shooting" the field in fake approaches at low altitude from various directions just as I had often done over pastures and stubble-fields back in America in barnstorming days—trying now to work out an imaginary runway between these craters.

Finally I made my choice, a short narrow stretch between the paths of several sticks of bombs, with water standing in the low area at one end and a cracked-up Hurricane which appeared to have just landed, lying on its belly near the other end. By this time I was leading a procession of all the rest of our Hurricanes around the field, all the pilots likewise trying to figure out how to get down. I made a try at my "runway," and made it all right, with room to spare, and then the rest followed in on it one after another, and everybody made it safely.

As soon as we'd reported to Operations on what happened, some of us went out with a truck and laid out some white boards to mark our landing strip.

While doing this we found a few enemy leaflets scattered about, and I realised that they must have been the little white things that streaked past me while we were up on the chase and gave me such a scare. I must have happened to fly through a cloud of them dropped by one of the bombers. I picked one up and kept it for a souvenir.

It was in English and purported to quote from a Lisbon news dispatch. Under the word "Extra" "in large type it carried a heading, unpunctuated: "The Yankees Tender the Olive Branch Singapore Neutral Zone?" Then it read:

> Lisbon, 14th: News has been received that America has proposed her separate peace negotiations to Nippon. The proposal was made on 14th January 1942. President Roosevelt is of the opinion that Singapore ought to be declared a Neutral Zone. The Nippon is considering this peace proposal.

We arranged to have the cracked-up Hurricane moved out of our runway as soon as possible. It was the plane of Lieutenant S——, a South African Air Force pilot, better known as Stewie. I recalled the airplane that was missing from Denny's section shortly before we attacked the bombers. Apparently he was the one. He had got separated from us, found the bombers before we did and attacked them alone. He had shot one down in flames before he was himself wounded and shot down, force-landing on the drome, to be taken away to a hospital before the rest of us came back. The story of his unusual experiences on this and succeeding days is included later.

A crash truck arrived soon and took his machine out of the way, and the "runway" which we had marked off—a short narrow strip of sod in between rows of bomb craters—became our sole landing-ground for the duration of our stay in Singapore.

Three of the boys from the other flight, who were on the ground, had a narrow escape during this raid. These were Joe, Fitz, and Tom, who had been loafing in the hotel after they went off duty when we relieved their flight. They heard us take off and heard the air-raid sirens a little later. Having nothing better to do they thought they'd take a drive to the airdrome to see what was going on. They took one of the cars, drove down East Coast Road, and were just turning in at the gate of the airdrome when the sentry there shouted to them and pointed upward.

Stopping the car, they climbed out just in time to actually see the bombs coming down in a great cluster. They only had time to throw themselves flat and cover their ears before the bombs were striking. Two big five-hundred-pounders landed, each about a hundred feet from them, one demolishing a house directly across the road !

Their car was holed in places by shrapnel, and one door was wrecked, while the boys themselves were bruised and blackened with dirt, their clothes torn, and they were badly shaken up. Fitz had to be taken to the hospital for treatment of shock, but was released the same day; Joe was told to stay off flying for a couple of days.

Poor Joe! It was he who had had two shells crash beside him at Tengah two days before. Then yesterday he'd been shot down and had crashed in the sea. So he was shelled one day, shot down the next, and bombed on the third !

It was nearly noon when we landed from this patrol. There were no other scrambles before one o'clock, when the other flight came back to relieve us. We doffed our Mae Wests, took our parachutes, helmets, and gloves out of our machines, put them away, and left the rest of the day's fighting to the other flight.

From the *communiqué* :

Singapore, February 7. Enemy aircraft again raided the island this morning and bombs were dropped, causing some damage. Fighters of the Far East Command intercepted the raiders, destroying one enemy aircraft, probably destroying another, and damaging two. All our fighters returned to their bases.

At the Sea View the management were keeping a score-board of our successes, so when we came to lunch that noon we told them they could put down another enemy plane destroyed, as the result of Stewie's victory.

We were quite popular with most of the guests there those days, in spite of our rough everyday working dress which must have seemed out of place in such an exclusive hotel. Of course there were a few, the more blue-blooded, I suppose, who didn't take to us so well. Probably they thought the only legitimate officers were those they saw in peace-time at their exclusive dances, dressed in bandmasters' uniforms; so our usually boisterous return from work, in sweaty shorts and shirts (open-necked) with revolvers slung in rough service webbing, was quite beyond them.

One grumpy old codger in particular appeared to have nothing to do but sit around all day drinking pink gins and looking liverish and important. He was waiting for a boat to evacuate him, so that in addition to fighting to keep the Japs off his head now, we would quite likely have to patrol and perhaps fight over his ship later, to keep him from being sunk. His dislike for us was made obvious quite often. Some of the boys went for a dip in the hotel swimming-pool on this afternoon, and he came snooping around and tried to chase them out, saying they couldn't swim there because they hadn't been "introduced"!

Among these boys was Brownie, and he rose nobly to the situation. "Well, my name's Browne. I guess that introduces me!" he replied. The others introduced themselves likewise and went on with their swimming.

The poor fellow retired quite perplexed, which, whether he knew it or not, was a good thing for him. The boys were trying to have enough fun to loose themselves from the strain they were under and would have thrown him in if he'd bothered them any more.

That night Rickey threw a little party to celebrate his promotion to squadron leader. He was able to get hold of some champagne, and a boisterous time was had by all. I've forgotten most of what went on, but remember that about halfway through the party someone remarked that he heard the Japs had landed on the island of Bali. We were all for taking off at once and going down there to make sure Dorothy Lamour escaped.

Next day was Sunday the 8th, and our flight had the "long day"—from dawn until 9 a.m. and from 1 p.m. until dark. It was quite uneventful for us, however. We had one routine patrol in the morning, and in the afternoon I did a convoy patrol with one other pilot, escorting a merchant ship out of the harbour and down the straits towards Sumatra for an hour or so. While we were doing this escort a big raid came over, which the rest of our flight chased unsuccessfully. I saw them drop their bombs in the north-east part of the island; that is, I saw the great mass of smoke-clouds shooting up from the area as the bombs exploded, perhaps twenty miles away.

The other flight had a combat that morning, however, with an escorted bombing raid, in which they brought down at least two of the enemy. Rickey was shot down in this engagement and force-landed on the airdrome, his machine crashing through the fence on the north side, and out onto East Coast Road, where it shed its landing gear in

SIGHT SEEING IN SINGAPORE

A FORCED LANDING ON KALLANG AIRDROME

the ditch on one side, slid across the road on its belly, and stopped with its nose in the ditch on the other side. Rickey himself was unhurt—except for his feelings.

From the *communiqué* :

Singapore, February 8. During enemy raids over Singapore Island this morning our fighters probably destroyed one enemy bomber. Two other bombers were damaged. All our fighters returned to their bases.

CHAPTER 7

Beginning of the End

On the whole, enemy air activity had been small for the past few days; but the next day, Monday, they really started crowding us.

Things began popping early. We had the short shift from 9 a.m. until 1 p.m. and I was awakened at dawn by the roar of engines as the other flight took off and climbed up over the hotel and off into the distance. They came back to land after an hour or so, while we were eating breakfast—not in one formation this time, but drifting in singly or in pairs, which meant they must have been in action.

They were off again in a short time, and when we reached the drome just before nine they were still flying, so that we had to wait a half-hour or so for them.

Again they came back in scattered ones and twos, indicating they had been fighting. They looked pretty tired as they left their machines and came to the dispersal hut, but most of them were grinning triumphantly. There'd been numerous skirmishes and chases with low-flying bombers, and nearly every pilot had had one or more shots.

Sandy A——, a very aggressive pilot of 175, had got two bombers, bringing his total score to five. Sergeant H——, one of my group from 300 Squadron, had got one also, his first victory. He said he dived on a bomber which he found alone up in Malaya, and fired on it. As he pulled away he looked around furtively to see if it was shooting back at him, and was quite amazed to see it go into a spin instead. He watched it crash in the jungle! Three or four other bombers were damaged too, while our boys suffered no losses.

I took over Sandy's machine, and he warned me that it had a "runaway" gun—a machine-gun that worked all right except that it wouldn't stop firing once it started, until it used up all its ammunition. The armourers were working on it and would get it fixed up if they had time. Others of our flight took over the rest of the machines, and the boys who had been flying made off to the hotel for breakfast.

Hardly had we settled down to waiting when the telephone rang, and the message was "Scramble to twenty thousand feet at once!"

It would be the regular morning high-altitude raid approaching, and the eight of us raced to our machines. I was halfway into my cockpit before I realised something was wrong: armourers were still sitting on the wings of my airplane, working, with the big panels still off above the guns.

The armourer sergeant was looking distressed. "I'm sorry, sir, we haven't had time to reload your guns yet. Yours is the last machine we came to. We'll get them done as quick as we can."

There was no one to blame. The crews were overworked and this scramble had come too soon after the planes landed to give them time to finish. I climbed in and got set, waiting impatiently, while other machines started and taxied out. The armourers were working feverishly on my guns, snatching out empty ammunition tanks and fastening new ones in, threading fresh belts through the chutes that led into the guns. Roar after roar of sound swept across the field as the four planes of Denny's section took off, one after another in quick order. Then my own section was taking off, leaderless. I hoped Brownie would know enough to take over the lead. Of all the lousy luck!

At last the armourers were putting the panels back over the openings in the wings above the guns, and I primed my engine and pressed the starter button. The engine caught and started idling. The seven other Hurricanes were far out over the harbour now, one section of four and the other section—mine—only three, all climbing fast.

Finally the last panel was in place, the men were sliding down off the wings, and the sergeant waved the "go ahead" signal with his hands. I taxied out as fast as I dared, but by the time I was off, the others were entirely out of sight. There was nothing to do now but to go "free-lance," for there was slight chance of finding the others once I'd lost sight of them.

I abused my engine terribly climbing nearly wide open, for now that I was alone I was extra anxious to have a height advantage before the enemy got over the island.

My lot was frustration again, however, for in spite of all my furious climbing I was scarcely fifteen thousand feet up when I saw enemy planes coming in over the island. Hoping they might hang around a few minutes I kept climbing anyway, careful to stay four or five miles away from under them so I wouldn't be spotted while below them and jumped by their escorting fighters. But within a couple of minutes after I saw them they had turned away and were making northward at high speed. Out of luck again !

After that, Control kept reporting smaller formations at various altitudes, which seemed to nip in over the north part of the island for a few minutes and then go away before there was time to find them; or sometimes to do standing patrols a little way up in enemy territory.

I spent an hour or so free-lancing around, mostly at high altitude, hoping to find one of these groups when I was in a position to jump them. Two or three times I spotted a couple of fighters in the distance and carefully stalked them until I got above and up-sun. Then I went down in screaming dives to attack, only to find when I got close enough to identify them that they were Hurricanes—others of our flight, doing the same thing I was. It looked as if they must have got split up somehow, and I wondered if they'd had a scrap.

The scenery at high altitude was magnificent that morning. Gigantic tumbled masses of cloud rose to fifteen and twenty thousand feet, beautiful and awe-inspiring with their great misty mountains, valleys and chasms, with here and there a detached cloud like an island suspended by magic in the sky. It was all so enchanting that once or twice when I was waiting for information from Control I surrendered to temptation, and swooped down among them to play about for a couple of minutes, diving at their tops, careening at four hundred miles an hour through great foggy valleys and in and out of weird mystic caverns half a mile deep, occasionally shearing away to practise a few rolls.

Far off below, a level carpet of broken fluffy clouds lay over the island, obscuring most of the countryside. Through it ran the mantle of oil-fire smoke, a long belt in which the black and white clouds churned and writhed together, endlessly, like two flavours of boiling hot blancmange, chocolate and steamy white, slowly mixing.

Somewhere under the south part of that carpet would be our hotel—no bigger than a pinhead—and the old grouch who tried to chase the boys out of the swimming-pool, still sitting on the veranda, no doubt, with his pink gins and his liver and his dislike for the world. What a narrow life he led! Perhaps most of ours were short, but they were wide as we could make them while they lasted, anyway!

At last I got wind of something worthwhile. I had been sitting at around twenty thousand, when Control reported "fifteen plus bandits" just north of the island at fourteen thousand feet. This was just what I wanted, something below my altitude, and I swooped off in that direction, hoping to catch them silhouetted against the clouds below. However, I must have arrived too late, for I couldn't find anything in the area. I was getting worried that they might find me first, when I happened to spot far below, through an opening in the low clouds, the shapes of two twin-engined bombers, crossing the Straits at very low level, going northward toward home!

They were almost directly beneath me, so I peeled off in a nearly vertical dive. I had to lose sight of them on the way down, for it was only a small opening in the clouds through which I'd seen them, but I gauged my dive to break through the clouds where I thought they should be.

I was in an awful sweat, for I was in high hopes that my luck had changed at last. This was the closest I'd come to getting a shot yet. I imagine I was doing nearly five hundred when I passed through the clouds, for I had to just fly in a long great circle for a few seconds after I levelled out, to get my speed down to where I could manoeuvre. I was looking vainly all around for the bombers, but though I searched frantically for several minutes I failed to spot them. Either I had misjudged the course they were taking or they had climbed up into the clouds for concealment. I was several miles up in enemy territory when I finally gave up the search.

On the way back I spotted a truck parked on the road and put a burst into it from my guns. As I fired I was fascinated to see what looked like long weird ropes of white smoke suddenly streak far out ahead from my wings, snakily, their farther ends touching the truck or near it. It was the first time I had ever fired "tracer" ammunition. The special bullets are coated with chemicals to give off smoke, to show you where your bullets are going. The squadrons I'd served with in England never used it, but 175 Squadron did. The only times I'd seen tracers before were when German pilots shot at me, for all German squadrons use them.

When I stopped firing at the truck and turned away I was again startled, by the runaway gun which Sandy had warned me about. Now it rattled away on its own, firing at nothing, until it was out of ammunition!

About this time, Control ordered us to return and land unless we were engaged, so I headed homeward.

We'd hardly had time to get refuelled and rearmed after this flight when we were ordered to scramble again. Another big high-altitude raid was on the way, and we took off in a rush, climbing madly even before we had joined up in formation. Then after a couple of minutes a new order came over the radio from Control.

Hello, Tiger Leader, Tiger Leader! There are low-flying aircraft attacking our troops in the north-west part of the island. Detach two of your aircraft to deal with them. Over!

Denny's voice came across at once, acknowledging the order, and then he called to me. "Hello, Blue One, Blue One! Will you take your number two and take care of that? Over."

"O.K.," I answered. "Hello, Blue Two. Follow me!" And I led off in a diving turn into the north-west, leaving the others to climb on up after the big raid. My number two's name was Sergeant M——.

Control called again, urging us to hurry, and we opened our engines to full throttle as we swept down under the clouds towards the area given. As we neared it I strained my eyes trying to discern any airplanes there, or anti-aircraft puffs which would indicate their presence, but I could see neither. We arrived and circled that part of the island low down, watching in all directions without seeing anything. Finally I called Control.

Hello, Rastus. Hello, Rastus! Tiger Blue One calling. We are in the area but we don't see anything about. I'm afraid we're too late. Have you any new instructions for us?

But I never gave him time to reply, for a couple of seconds later I saw it. We were travelling north just then, toward the section of the Straits where the Johore Causeway crossed into the enemy-occupied city of Johore Bharu, and I caught sight of an airplane in the distance straight ahead, low down over Johore Bharu and travelling north.

I fumbled excitedly for the transmitter switch. "Tally-ho! Straight ahead of us, Blue Two!" I called, and laid out after it, pushing throttle and propeller pitch controls clear ahead, and this time "pulling the plug" also—a control which cuts out all governing over the engine's supercharging so that it can put out an emergency power far greater than its normal maximum.

The sound rose to an immense, strained bellowing, and in a few seconds my controls began to stiffen from the increased speed, and the countryside seemed to fairly stream past, close beneath our wings, for we were flying low down over the trees.

Crossing the Straits of Johore we streaked low across the rooftops of Johore Bharu, chasing our quarry who was now following along the main highway which leads north-west from the city up into Malaya. I remember noticing that the road was packed with military traffic—enemy trucks, buses, cars, etc.

The enemy plane had a good start on us, and at first we hardly seemed to gain on it. We started getting flak—the first Japanese flak I'd seen. There was just an occasional black puff near us at first; then soon a regular hail of it, following us right along. It seemed to make about the same-sized bursts as the British and German "medium" flak—Bofors and pom-pom guns—with the differences that this stuff seemed to have adjustable fuses so that it was timed to explode near us, and that it had no tracer effect, remaining invisible until it exploded. Ours and the German medium flak doesn't explode unless it actually hits you or reaches the end of its travel, and the shells are all tracers, appearing as red or green balls. We were so intent on overtaking our quarry that we just let them blaze away, without taking any evasive action from the shells.

At last we were gaining noticeably on the other machine, and soon I could discern its shape as that of a single-engined plane with "fixed" (non-retractable) landing gear hanging down. From pictures I'd seen I took it to be a type of two-seater fighter known as the "Army 97." It alternately flew at about five hundred feet for a minute or so and then dived to tree-top height for a way, where we could scarcely see it against the jungle. We stayed at about five hundred feet ourselves.

Behind me a couple of hundred yards Sergeant M———'s plane, guarding my tail, appeared as a vicious silhouette against a background of angry anti-aircraft puffs sprinkled pepper-like against the sky.

I think I was perhaps four or five hundred yards behind our quarry, for I remember that I already had my thumb on the firing button ready to press it in a few more seconds, when the beginning occurred of one of those nightmare experiences that last actually but a moment but live for ever after in inescapable memory.

First a bright flash of colour caught my eye. I was staring down fascinated at a green Navy Zero wheeling across below and ahead of me, turning steep left just above the tree-tops, while seemingly without any conscious decision I was twisting over viciously in a diving turn after him. I closed in, still diving, pulling my nose around until my sights lined up with him and a little ahead, leading him. Then I let him have it, the quick, shattering roar from my guns startling me, and my long white tracers reaching out to caress the graceful little green wings ahead of me with their strange red discs painted near each tip. Only for two or three seconds, and then I had to break off to straighten out of my dive before hitting the trees. Just as I was breaking off I heard a bang and felt a jolt, and saw that one of the smaller gun panels was gone from my right wing. I thought it had been shot off; but I forgot about it in what I saw a moment later.

I zoomed up hard, nearly blacking out and just missing the trees. My runaway gun was chattering away on its own irritatingly and spewing its tracers aimlessly out over the jungle. I turned left to get around at any new enemies that might be behind. And there, amid the confusion of anti-aircraft fire bursting all around, I saw Sergeant M———'s Hurricane diving steeply, obviously hit! I was right over him as he struck, in the corner of a little field, at close to three hundred miles an hour, in a terrible ghastly eruption of splintered wings and flying pieces and then steam and dust and smoke that swirled out to obscure the awful sight.

I recall circling cautiously for a moment, dazed and shocked by this and trying to take in the whole situation and see how many new enemies I had. In doing so I apparently lost sight of both the one we'd been chasing and the Navy Zero. There were no new ones to be seen either.

Thinking back on the event, I believe the Navy Zero pilot must have been above us when he saw us chasing the other Jap, so he dived on us from behind, firing and hitting Sergeant M———. Then his speed carried him on down and ahead as he levelled out from his dive, until he was below and in front of me where I first saw him. Sergeant M——— must either have been killed by the bullets or had his controls disabled, and went into the fatal dive that I saw.

A pathetic little wisp of smoke and dust rising above the trees was the last I saw of him, as escorted by the storm of anti-aircraft fire I made my way alone back to Singapore Island.

Control was telling the others about another raid coming in at high altitude, so I headed out over the sea and started climbing. I was late again though, for I saw the bombers approaching the island when I was far too low. In fact I was able to call up Control and correct him on the position he was giving for them once or twice, while still unable to do anything myself except look up at them and swear. When they were almost over the island they turned away and headed out seaward. Later I learned that some of the others chased them and got in a few shots, damaging two or three.

After they had gone away I did a little free-lancing again but nothing more turned up, and finally Control ordered all of us to land. I was down before the rest, and when the others landed and came up to the dispersal hut I had to give them the news of Sergeant M———'s death.

I hadn't known him well, but the mute faces and glistening eyes of some of the boys told me how much they thought of him. I wondered if any of them felt it was my fault.

Late that afternoon, Denny, Ted, Brownie, and I drove into town to take care of some business, after which we stopped in at the Raffles Hotel for a drink. Ted had a brother who was a captain in the Singapore police force, and while we were there he dropped in and joined us. It was from him that we heard the incredible news.

The enemy had *forced the Straits of Johore* during the preceding night and landed *"in force"* on the north part of the island!

There was supposed to be heavy fighting going on in the jungles and rubber estates around Tengah Airdrome now. No one seemed to know what it meant or how serious the situation, but it sounded ominous. That explained the sudden spurt in enemy air activity this morning!

I realised that the orange crush I was drinking didn't taste good any more. The siege was over and the enemy inside our gates. Was the thing we couldn't let happen, really occurring? Was Singapore falling? I didn't know much about military strategy, but it seemed to me that if we couldn't hold them at the Straits we had slight chance of holding them anywhere on the island.

Apparently this news had been broadcast at noon, but we hadn't listened to the news. It failed to interrupt the evening dance programme at the Raffles, however; for before we left, the orchestra men were collecting on the platform.

Back at the Sea View that evening we learned from the boys of the other flight that the afternoon had been a field day for them. The island had been teeming with small groups of bombers and dive-bombers, mostly unescorted, at low altitude. Everyone in the flight had got at least one crack at them, and they had destroyed five or six as well as getting a bunch of probables. Sandy, the boy who had got two in the morning, got another in the afternoon to make his score three for the day, six for his total score to date. They lost two machines, but the pilot of one got away unhurt and the other escaped alive although badly wounded.

By now we could hear distant artillery fire most of the time. That night it was louder than ever, with the explosions of shells sounding closer.

From the *communique*:

> Singapore, February 9. An enemy force in strength succeeded in landing on the western shores of Singapore Island last night. They are being engaged by our troops. Fighting continues.
> Hurricane fighters of the R.A.F. supporting our troops successfully intercepted enemy raiders today, destroying three, probably destroying three others and damaging thirteen.
> In a later patrol our fighter aircraft wrecked an enemy truck during a road strafe.

By now we were all looking forward to the next day in anticipation of good hunting. No doubt there'd be lots of bombers operating in close support of enemy troops, flying at low altitude where we could get at them easily.

Our hopes were all dashed, however, by a new order that came through for the squadron that night; they were to take off all their flyable Hurricanes at dawn and evacuate them to Palembang, in Sumatra (where 300 Squadron were)! It had been decided not to risk losing all our Hurricanes at once, as we would do, should this, our only remaining airdrome, get bombed any worse or come under shell-fire from the advancing enemy. Also there was a pressing need for more airplanes at Palembang.

This last gave credence to a disquieting rumour we heard from someone that night—that Palembang had been heavily raided during the past two or three days and that 300 Squadron (my squadron), who were defending the place, had been badly "beaten up" by overwhelming numbers.

There were eight machines to go, and the pilots who flew them were all taken from regular 175 Squadron pilots, so we five attached pilots from 300 Squadron were among those staying behind. Those who went were met in the dispersal hut next morning by the "A.O.C.," the officer commanding all the air forces in the area. He talked to them a few minutes before they left.

He told them he understood their keenness and desire to stay on in Singapore, but he gave them a picture of the situation. He said that, during the day before, more than two hundred and fifty enemy airplanes had been over the island; that we had hunted and fought them all day, only eight strong ourselves, but that we couldn't expect to keep up such a pace. So he was sending the airplanes to Palembang, where they were just as badly needed now as here, and where the operating conditions were much more favourable.

We others didn't mind being left behind. There were rumours that a fresh squadron might come up in a day or so, if the military situation got stabilized. If there was any chance to do some fighting we wanted to be in it. Singapore just *couldn't* be allowed to go under!

About mid-morning we five from 300 Squadron drove out to Operations—which were in a large house commandeered by the R.A.F. a couple of miles from the hotel—to see what we could learn.

The Operations Room had apparently been the living-room of the house. A sort of stage about three feet high was erected at one end, where the controller and operations staff sat behind a counter which contained at least a dozen telephones and microphones, and bristled with switches and connections.

It overlooked the "operations board," a huge map, several feet across, of Singapore Island, Southern Malaya, and the surrounding sea and islands. Positions of all "plots" of our own or enemy planes were marked by little blocks of wood on this board, moved about by assistants wearing telephone headsets, on the basis of information they received on their phones. This was how the information on enemy aircraft was put into picture form for the controllers. It was from here that our air operations were directed—the controller speaking to us in the air with one of the microphones and ordering us about on the basis of the situation as he saw it pictured on this board.

The controller on duty this morning was Squadron Leader C——, whom Denny knew quite well. He had been C.O. of 300 Squadron back in England during the preceding spring and summer. We found him at his post in the Operations Room, though there was nothing for him to do—there weren't any airplanes for him to control now.

He was seated at the counter, idly watching the plots of enemy aircraft on the board below him, as the assistants moved the blocks of wood about. We saw one marked "Thirty plus, 22,000 feet" a couple of feet north of the edge of Singapore Island on the map; an arrow, showing its direction, pointed south. There were three or four other blocks representing smaller formations scattered about.

He could tell us little, except to advise us to hang on and wait for orders. He'd heard little of how the fighting was going this morning.

Someone remarked that he'd heard Tengah Airdrome had been captured. "Is it?" the squadron leader asked. "Let's call them up and see!" With a little grin he picked up one of his telephones, which was a direct line to Tengah. The line was ominously silent.

We drove back to the hotel and loafed about. After a while a nurse came around, looking for someone with a car who would help evacuate some other nurses from a hospital a few miles away which had come under shell-fire. Denny became chivalrous and volunteered. He drove off, looking a little sheepish and answering with some defensive retort our rude remarks about his motives.

He came back inside of an hour with six nurses in the car, all in varying stages of fright. The air-raid sirens sounded just then and they all made for the shelter trenches among the palm trees out on the lawn. We pilots sat on the grass around the trenches and chatted with them while a formation of bombers droned across far above, escorted by the white puffs of heavy anti-aircraft shells around them.

Soon the all-clear sounded and the nurses climbed out of the trenches. One of them, a frail-appearing little lady, seemed to be having quite a time to control herself. She was trembling all over and weaved a little when she started to walk.

"Somebody ki-ick me under the chi-in!" she asked in a quavering but resolute little voice, and we all laughed. She was wearing a soldier's steel helmet, which alone was enough to make us laugh, it looked so funny in contrast with her meek dress and mouse-like demeanour.

We invited them into the lounge adjacent to my room, and Denny produced a bottle of Johnnie Walker that he'd rescued from the ruins of the Officers' Mess at Kallang. We had a boy get some glasses and gave them each a drink or two. It did them a lot of good and they soon relaxed and forgot most of their fright.

The frail little lady who had asked to be kicked under the chin told us that she'd spent her honeymoon in this hotel years before. She said she was a planter's wife and had lived near Kluang, a town fifty or sixty miles up in Malaya. That was the first I'd heard of Kluang except as the location of the nearest enemy-occupied airdrome to Singapore.

Finally they took their leave, Denny driving them to the hospital to which their patients had been moved.

The day was bright and sunny now, the sky clear except where the mantle of oil-fire smoke stretched across, augmented now by that from a second fire which seemed to be burning near the original one. Enemy planes were operating over the north part of the island in large numbers, but seldom came over far enough south for us to see them. It was fairly peaceful yet except for the distant rumbling of artillery. We could see several large ships riding quietly at anchor in the harbour as if nothing was wrong. We thought it a miracle that they hadn't yet been bombed.

The enemy might be approaching and the number of guests rapidly decreasing, but the hotel routine went on as usual. At four in the afternoon the same friendly little Chinese boy brought tea and cakes to my room, grinning happily and jabbering unintelligibly and good-naturedly the while. Supper in the evening consisted of seven courses as usual, delicious and expertly cooked, complete with French names on the menu that always made the dishes a surprise for us when they were brought on.

The guests who still remained were dismayed when they learned that our Hurricanes had left. It must have seemed a very bad omen to them. We told them we hoped a new squadron would arrive shortly. They commented to us, as others had, that one of the biggest helps to the morale of the people during the last few days of frightening news and frequent air raids had been the sight of our little band of Hurricanes taking off and climbing up over the city time after time each day to engage the enemy. No matter how bad the news, as long as they could see the R.A.F. still flying they felt there was hope.

From the *communique* :

> Singapore, February 10. The enemy has maintained continuous dive-bombing and machine-gun attacks on our forward areas in the western sector throughout the day, as well as high-level bombing attacks by large formations of aircraft.
>
> London, February 10 (AP). The Vichy radio broadcast today a Japanese *communiqué* saying that all British airdromes on Singapore Island had been captured.

That night the artillery fire was definitely much closer, so we knew the battle was going badly. A sullen red glow lit up a large part of the sky north of us. One battery of two heavy guns had started operating near enough to shake the hotel each time they fired. All night long the more distant rumbling was interrupted every few minutes by the vehement booming of this pair, like two doors being slammed in another part of the building.

As always in Singapore, I slept with my revolver under my pillow, and this time I kept my doors locked too. But my only intruder was the grinning Chinese boy who brought in my cup of tea early next morning.

Two of the boys had been detailed the night before to get up early and be driven to Seletar Airdrome on the north-east side of the island, to bring back a couple of damaged Hurricanes which had been fixed up so they would fly. They turned up again before breakfast, having done their job, and told of a creepy trip going over there in the darkness, being stopped and examined frequently at the point of bayonets along the blacked-out road, scared each time that they'd run into an enemy trap, until they could see who had stopped them. They said the airdrome had been captured the afternoon before, but our troops had retaken it in the evening. They were preparing to blow up the field as soon as the boys had taken off.

And still it was cool, quiet, and peaceful where we sat on the veranda of the hotel, that morning, only a few miles from the fighting—less, for all we knew. The artillery fire had quieted down with the coming of daylight. Denny and I were enthralled for a while watching an exotic, dark-haired English girl clad in shorts and a light sweater, exercising with two greyhounds among the palm trees out on the lawn. She was swinging a cloth about for them to leap at. Her movements and theirs were so graceful that I thought she must be a dancer, but someone said she was a nurse. It seemed that either she or the approaching enemy and the terrible fighting must be unreal. It just didn't make sense—but neither did a lot of things, in the last days of Singapore.

The Singapore morning papers came at breakfast-time just as usual, though we could now see a fire started by shell-fire in the north part of the town. We read them just as usual over our lavish breakfasts. I still have the copy I bought that morning, the February 11 issue of the *Singapore Free Press*. Printed and got out full-size while the enemy were almost inside the city, it gives all the local and world news. Its front-page editorial calls on its readers to be "determined and defiant."

CHAPTER 8

Evacuation

After breakfast, Denny, Ted, Brownie, and I drove to the airdrome to see what we could find out, but no one seemed to know anything. We'd hoped there'd be news of the fresh Hurricane squadron which we had heard was coming, but Tom W——, who was doing duty pilot (looking after the phones, etc.), said he hadn't heard anything.

A couple of new fires were pumping black smoke into the sky north of us, and the familiar high smoke-pall looked much heavier than before, frightening. It was drifting right across the city, most of which was darkened by its shadow. Was that an omen?

I climbed up on the side of a dispersal pen and snapped three views with my camera, one west, one north-west, and one north. Only the first one, showing the harbour and south part of the city, is innocent of smoke.

An air-raid warning was on but we weren't paying attention, until we heard the familiar heavy droning from above; then we all made for some trenches. When we reached their safety we looked up and spotted the bombers, a standard formation of twenty-seven, slowly drilling across the sky above us but passing a little to one side, so we knew our airdrome couldn't be the target. They were passing over the harbour and south part of the town, a couple of miles away.

All at once someone called out and pointed towards the city. In the harbour near the docks several great columns of water were rising majestically to a height of perhaps two hundred feet. Then dozens of smoke-clouds shot up in a row across the dock area, swirling stormily together while the awful staccato booming of the explosions reached us, shaking the ground under our feet.

I got out my camera and took another snap of this area, to contrast with the one I'd taken a few minutes before when there were no smoke-clouds.

We hoped that none of the ships in the harbour were hit. I learned later that they weren't, but a lot of damage must have been done to the docks and near-by buildings. A couple of good-sized fires got going there within a few minutes, putting up a lot of black smoke.

Finally satisfied that there was nothing we could find out here we piled into the car and drove out to Operations, to see what we could learn. We found our friend, Squadron Leader C——, on duty again when we arrived, sitting at his post overlooking the operations board which showed nothing but plots of Japanese formations, just as we had found him the day before.

He was speaking to someone over the telephone, and we caught the words as we came in: "—I refuse to have anything more to do with air-raid warnings. You might just as well keep the warning on permanently!"

He bid us good-morning as he replaced the receiver, then pointed his thumb at the phone and snorted, "A.R.P. just on to me about air-raid warnings! With more Jap formations around than you can shake a stick at. *I* can't tell them when one's going to nip in and take a crack at the city! "

We laughed sympathetically.

"Got any news for us yet?" Denny asked.

"No, I haven't heard anything," the squadron leader answered. "Tell you what,"—he reached for another phone—"I'll talk to Air Headquarters and see if I can find out anything."

He asked the operator at Air Headquarters for a certain official, and a discussion followed for two or three minutes. Midway through the conversation he turned and spoke to Denny. "Do you know how many Hurricanes there are at Kallang Airdrome that can be flown?"

"Three," Denny replied. He was counting the two which had been flown over from Seletar Airdrome early this morning, and one other which had been fixed up at Kallang.

The squadron leader passed this information on over the phone. At the end of the conversation he turned to Denny with the verdict: "You're to take the two other most experienced pilots with you and fly the three Hurricanes down to Palembang!"

So that was that. Our part in the battle for Singapore was over!

Brownie and I were the other two to go with Denny, and when we drove back to the hotel we parked the car close to our rooms and began loading our bags into it. I still had Bruce's bag which I was keeping to send to his folks and I loaded it in with my things. We weren't hurrying, as we might have if we had known what we were going to learn shortly; it was perhaps an hour from the lime we left Operations before we reached the airdrome accompanied by Ted, who was seeing us off.

As we drove up to the dispersal hut Tom, the boy who was doing duty pilot, came running out to meet us. He had his overalls and Mae West on, and looked very excited.

"Where've you fellows been all this time?" he demanded. Then, not waiting for an answer, "We've got to hurry. The Japs are almost here! I'm going with you; they've got a Brewster fixed up so it will fly and I'm taking it—if I can figure out how it works. Squadron Leader C——'s called up three times in the last twenty minutes, asking if you'd got here yet. He kept saying, 'Tell them they must hurry! Tell them they haven't a minute to waste!' He was awfully excited."

We rummaged hastily around in the hut, looking for maps of our route.

"So that's how it is," Denny remarked. "I reckon things must be getting bad fast at that rate!"

"It sounds as if Squadron Leader C——'s seen the Japs," I suggested. "They could come right past Operations without noticing it was any different from another private house."

We had trouble finding maps of Sumatra. Denny finally got a pretty good one, which he would use because he was leading us, and I got part of an old naval chart that showed the coastline of Sumatra and the River Musi which ran from the coast inland to Palembang. I stuck it in my pocket for emergency.

All three Hurricanes we were taking were in questionable condition, having been patched up and put together hurriedly, but the hardworking New Zealand ground crews were doing all they could for them. Whatever we accomplished in those last few days of operations at Kallang, we owed largely to these ground crews—who worked night and day and through bombing and machine-gun attacks, never losing spirit and always keeping our machines in shape if it was humanly possible. The ground crews at Kallang Airdrome were a real fighting bunch, as grand as those who earned an undying reputation at Hawkinge and Manston, the R.A.F's front-line refuelling and rearming bases during the Battle of Britain. Each of us picked a machine and began carrying our bags to it. Mine was in a dispersal pen about fifty yards away; to save distance I climbed over the back of the pen, taking my parachute, helmet, and gloves on the first trip. Tossing them into the cockpit I hurried back for another load. Ted was helping us get our things unloaded from the car. He and the rest of the fellows were going to try to find a ship on which they could travel to Palembang. All at once we heard a sharp explosion from a grove just north-east of us, and then an answering explosion overhead. Looking up we saw a round black cloud, a couple of hundred feet high, over the middle of the airdrome. "Oh-oh!" I thought. "So they *are* almost here!"

I lugged three bags over to my Hurricane. Where to put all my things was a problem, for I couldn't possibly take time to hunt for ropes and tie them in, and if they were loose in the wrong places they'd foul the controls. Perhaps we shouldn't be taking time to put in our bags at all.

The gun in the grove fired again, and another shell burst over the drome.

I had borrowed a screwdriver, and working feverishly I loosened the panels in the side of the fuselage of my machine and took them off. I managed to get a small bag on the floor under the control cables. There was a large removable tray in one place, containing emergency rations, water, and first-aid equipment for use in the event of a forced landing in the jungle. I loosened this, jerked it out, and tried to stuff into its place a parachute bag full of clothes and things. But there was no bottom to the cavity left by the tray, and I saw despairingly that the bag wanted to sink down and rest on the control cables just below.

Another explosion came from the gun in the grove. This time the shell burst right above us. I ducked under the tail for a moment to escape any shrapnel bits. Wondering how many more minutes we had, I hastily unstrapped the tins and boxes of supplies and water from the tray I had taken out, then put the tray back in place, empty. By dint of a lot of shoving and squeezing I got a second bag in on top of the tray, quite secure. Two of them taken care of. For the rest I'd have to take the big panel off the bottom of the fuselage and jam them in on the bottom framework, under the elevator and rudder cables, hoping the cables wouldn't rub too hard or catch on them.

I looked for my screwdriver to take off this panel, but it was gone, and I started going in circles before remembering that Brownie had borrowed it for a moment.

And then I heard the sound that froze me inside—the unmistakable cracks of rifle-fire, and close—not more than a quarter of a mile away!

Denny was putting his things into his machine twenty or thirty yards away, and we exchanged sickly grins.

"I reckon we'd better hurry," he remarked, which I thought should take a prize for understatement. I'd have to make the rest of this darn quick!

I sprinted back after the last two bags, which were still in the car, and then—horror of horrors—the car was *gone!*

Now I *was* running in circles! There wasn't a sign of either the car or Ted. Had he got scared and pulled out? I was agonised, for one of the bags was Bruce's. I hated to leave mine and couldn't leave his.

I ran over to Brownie's machine to get my screwdriver. He said Ted had driven over to the hangar for something and would probably be back in a minute. I'd just have to wait. I had locked those two bags in the trunk of the car; all the rest had been piled in the back seat. Ted obviously didn't know about those in the trunk.

Down in the field a little way we could hear the whine of an American inertia starter speeding up—Tom was trying to get the Brewster started. I took the screwdriver back to my machine, replaced the side panels, then took off the bottom one, and stuffed my third bag in the bottom of the fuselage.

Over the city a couple of enemy reconnaissance planes were cruising peacefully, at low altitude.

It was torture to wait. I climbed up beside the cockpit and began to turn the gas on and fix everything else so I could start up quickly. Denny, finished with his packing, stood by his airplane watching me, trying to conceal his anxiety.

"You almost ready?" he asked, with a good attempt at a matter-of-fact tone. To Denny, the worst sin he could commit would be to ever "flap" or appear excited.

"I can't go yet, Denny," I told him. "Ted's driven over to the hangar with the car and it's got Bruce's bag in it. I've got to wait!"

The cracking of rifles was growing in volume, and seemed to be getting a little closer. Occasionally a bullet or two whined close overhead. The fence and shrubbery on the edge of the airdrome made it impossible for us to see what was happening on the other side.

A little biplane with British markings came cruising over at three or four hundred feet, and I recognized it as a training machine that had been left at Tengah Airdrome. Some Jap pilot must be taking a ride in it!

The enemy gun in the woods, which had been putting shells over the airdrome, sent two or three after the little plane, the gunners assuming that it was one of our pilots, I suppose. I thought it would have been a good joke on them if they'd hit it.

Over the city the two recco machines still cruised around lazily.

Bizarre? I'll say it was! Everything I can remember about that morning is bizarre !

Finally Denny called, "Here's your car! "

Ted was just driving up in front of the dispersal hut. I raced over frantically, unlocked the trunk with the duplicate set of keys I had in my pocket, and jerked the precious bags out. Then I tore back to my machine and started stuffing them in the bottom of the fuselage.

Tom had his Brewster started now, and was taxi-ing out to the end of the "runway." A couple of ground-crew chaps, who had arrived to help, told me to get in while they put the panel back under the fuselage for me. Good fellows. They were sticking with us to the last, Japs or no Japs.

I clambered up into the cockpit, and when I got my straps and helmet fastened, turned to look at Denny, who was in his cockpit waiting. He leaned ahead to press his starter button, and his engine came to life. I carefully measured two strokes from my priming pump, pressed my own starter button, and felt a thrill of relief as my engine caught instantly. "Anyway, it starts," I thought. We taxied out, picking our way carefully among the bomb craters and soft spots until we reached the end of the runway, where Tom already waited for us in his idling Brewster. Brownie followed in his Hurricane. Pausing to let Denny start off first, I looked back furtively, half expecting to see Jap soldiers entering the drome and getting ready to pot at us; but all I saw were Ted and two or three other pilots and some ground-crew chaps in a little knot around the car, probably discussing what to do. As Denny's machine rocketed down the runway I turned and opened my throttle, following him.

We made one circuit of the airdrome after we took off, and were followed by Japanese anti-aircraft fire—the first time I was ever shot at by enemy anti-aircraft fire over my own drome !

I had my camera in my pocket, and while we were making this circuit I took a snap of the north part of the city, where a huge ugly fire was raging among a lot of buildings. We turned and headed southward out over the sea. When we were out two or three miles I took another snap over the tail of my machine—presumably the last air picture of Singapore, outside of any taken by the enemy.

My final memory of Singapore, as it appeared to me looking back for the last time, is of a bright-green little country, resting on the edge of the bluest sea I'd ever seen, lovely in the morning sunlight except where the dark tragic mantle of smoke ran across its middle and beyond, covering and darkening the city on the seashore.

The city itself, with huge leaping red fires in its north and south parts, appeared to rest on the floor of a vast cavern formed by the sinister curtains of black smoke which rose from beyond and towered over it, prophetically, like a great overhanging cloak of doom.

THE LAST AIR PICTURES OF SINGAPORE

CHAPTER 9

Stewie's Escape

I think this would be a good place to tell the story of Stewie (Lieutenant S——), the South African boy of 175 Squadron who was shot down on the day Kallang Airdrome was bombed, as described in Chapter VI. This is almost word for word as he told it to me nearly a month later, on a hospital ship in the Indian Ocean. After writing it down I read it back to him, and he O.K.'d it:

You remember when we were scrambled that morning and climbed up after the big raid that was coming in at twenty thousand feet or above? Well, I was leading a pair on the right of the formation, in Denny's section, and when we started getting up around twenty thousand feet I noticed my engine wasn't running right and I couldn't keep up with the rest of you. So I signalled my number two to leave me behind and go on with you, and I kept falling back until you were two or three miles ahead of me. All at once I looked off to the left and saw this mass of bombers coming in from the south-west.

They were a little lower than I was, and I called out 'Tally-ho!' and went after them. I guess you were so far away by that time that you were never able to get close enough *to* attack, but I was just right. I came in behind them, making for the nearest and coming in at him from the left and behind. The whole bunch started shooting at me and there were dozens of tracers coming from all directions, mostly seeming to converge just in front of me. Boy, it was just as though they were laying a smoke screen! I held my fire though, until I was right up close to this fellow; then I let him have it from almost point-blank range.

His rear gunner packed up and quit firing right away. Then

smoke started coming back from the fuselage, and I turned so my fire was going into his left engine, which began smoking right away. I thought, 'Well, this guy's had it!' So I turned to attack another and just then '*Wham*' I got it! The explosion threw me sideways in the seat and just seemed to stop my plane in midair. Then my cockpit was full of oil and steam and glycol and stuff so I couldn't see, and I thought this was no place for me; so I peeled off and dived for good old Mother Earth!

"I knew my leg was hit, because there was blood all over it, but it didn't hurt and I felt all right. However, I was still in an awful pickle when I tried to land, because there was so much oil and glycol and stuff all over my windshield that I couldn't see ahead. I decided to try to make it 'wheels up.'[1]

I could see the field when I was circling it, by looking out the side of my cockpit, but when I was making my approach to land, coming straight towards it, I couldn't see the field at all because of the stuff all over my windshield. I could tell by the buildings and high trees on each side where it should be, and I just steered in between them and hoped. I came in real fast, trusting to luck that I'd miss the bomb craters, touched down at well over a hundred miles an hour and slid to a nice stop in the middle of the field.

I got out and looked at my airplane. By luck I'd landed in the one place on the whole field that wasn't full of fresh bomb craters. I sat down in front of my machine, and after a couple of minutes a car drove up with a wing commander and some other officer in it. I said, 'Sorry, boys, they got me!' which must have sounded awful silly. They laughed and told me to get in, and drove me off to the hospital.

I was operated on that afternoon. They fished a piece of explosive cannon shell out of my hip, from right up against the bone.

That evening Rickey came around to see me. He told me that the bomber I attacked had gone down in flames and was officially credited to me. Was I glad!

That was on Saturday, and of course you know the Japs landed on Singapore Island the following Monday. You can imagine

---

1. A wheels-up landing is always safest with fighter planes in emergency, the plane sliding on its belly after it lands, which causes it to stop in a short distance and usually with only minor damage.

how I felt lying there in the hospital, with them coming! Then Tuesday night and Wednesday morning I could tell by the artillery fire that they were getting close. I never felt so helpless. There was a big gun only a little way from the hospital. It started working early Wednesday morning, making a terrific racket, shaking the building every time it went off. Then, what was much worse, the bombers started coming after this gun, some of their bombs just missing the hospital. It was terrifying.

About mid-morning on Wednesday we heard rifle and machine-gun fire just outside the hospital. I figured this was the finish. I had an orderly bring my revolver, because I was going to shoot myself when the Japs came in.

All at once Doc M—— came running into the ward where I was, all out of breath. 'How do you feel?' he asked me. 'Not so bad,' I told him.

I felt like a drowning man grabbing a lifebelt. 'Would I ever!' I said.

'Well,' he asked me, 'can you walk?'

'Sure,' I answered, and I jumped out of bed to show him and promptly collapsed on the floor. My leg wouldn't do a thing. Then I saw a broom in a corner and got it and managed to hobble around the room a little, using it for a crutch. He looked pretty dubious but finally said I could come along.

The other fellows in my ward were all too badly off to be moved. I'll never forget the look of utter despair in their eyes when I last saw them as I was going out.

There were five of us that the doc had collected. We all got into an ambulance that was full of shrapnel holes and had its windows smashed, and we drove off.

On the way into town we had to stop because of a bombing raid. The doc, who had been riding in front, came around in back to encourage us, but he seemed more scared than we were. We could see his teeth chattering. One stick of bombs dropped in a line right across us. I could see the first three explosions coming towards us, the third one real close. Then the fourth landed the other side of us !

After that was over we drove on as near as we could get to the docks. The doc was taking a chance on being able to squeeze us onto a medium-sized merchant ship that was getting ready to leave. We had to walk about half a mile to the dock. I was using that broom for a crutch; and no kidding, I was just sweating with agony when I got there.

We were in luck. There was still room for us. I got put in the Fourth Assistant Engineer's cabin, along with an R.A.F. engineer officer who had lost one eye, so we called him 'One-Eyed Ike.' There were more than two thousand people on board, mostly European civilians, men, women, and children. It was a refrigerator ship, and they turned off the refrigerating machinery so that some of the people could stay down in the hold. The rest had to stay on deck, except for a few of the wounded who were given the ship's officers' cabins.

About six o'clock that evening the ship pulled away from the dock and anchored outside the harbour. Then about seven o'clock next morning we sailed, in convoy with another merchant ship, with a light cruiser for escort.

We got our first attack about ten o'clock that morning. Several of us were chatting together, talking about how lucky we were to get away, when the call was passed along, 'Enemy aircraft approaching.'

After that there was pandemonium. A big bunch of planes, mostly dive-bombers, came over and most of them made for our ship because it was biggest. We were in narrow waters yet so the ship couldn't manoeuvre to avoid the bombs, and they fell all around us, shaking the ship and almost lifting it out of the water sometimes. Each time after a close one we listened for the sound of the ship's engines. We knew as long as they kept running we weren't hit seriously, and boy, they were running so hard they sounded as though they were coming right up through the deck! I heard afterwards that during this attack they got three knots more out of the ship than she had ever been able to do before!

The gun crews on deck were wonderful. They let off with everything they had at every plane as it came over—pom-poms, Lewis guns, tommy-guns. There were even chaps firing with rifles and revolvers. They got two bombers definitely destroyed and three probables out of thirty-some planes that attacked us. One small bomb came through the roof of a cabin about ten yards from ours and exploded, killing the fellows in there. The concussion knocked an electric fan off the wall in our cabin. It fell on One-Eyed Ike, who was lying face down on the floor, and I had to laugh because it lay there on top of him, still running, as if it was getting electricity from him! The bomb started a fire, but they called for volunteers and got it out in a little while.

Two chaps were brought into our cabin to die who had been on a gun-post that got hit by another small bomb. They were so mangled that they had to be carried in blankets. The blood was soaking through the blankets and running all over, and the nurses gave the men morphia to ease them out.

The nurses were wonderful and shielded the patients with their bodies each time the bombs fell. Most of the bombers machine-gunned us as they passed over, but they didn't cause many casualties. One fellow got a bullet that went right through his chest from front to back without hitting any vital spot. They just covered up the two holes and he was all right.

After this attack we had a two-hour respite, and by the time the next one started we were out in open water, where the ship could manoeuvre. I had been moved down then to the bottom of the hold, so I couldn't tell what was going on myself, but the others told me what happened. It was a high-level attack by sixty-seven planes, and it lasted for more than two hours. We received most of the attention, just as before.

Each plane dropped its bombs in a stick after a careful run. The captain was credited by all with saving the ship, for he kept watching the bombers through his binoculars, and each time one came up on its bombing run, and he saw its bomb doors swing open, he'd call out ' Hard a port!' or ' Hard a-starboard! ' and the ship would turn as sharply as it could—which was just enough to mess up the aim.

One stick of them went off so close to us that the bombs lifted the ship way up, almost clear out of the water, and damaged it some. Another lot were much closer yet, just grazing the ship's side, and would have blown in the whole side of the ship and sunk us, but they all failed to go off. Either it was a miracle or the pilot forgot to fuse his bombs. There were many more near misses, too.

It was tough on us down below, because we didn't know what was happening or when the next ones were coming. We could hear and feel the explosions. Each time we'd listen for the sound of the engines afterwards, and when we heard them we knew we were still all right.

Finally it was over and we were still going strong. Most of the passengers had been on the top deck all the time, and had spent the time singing hymns and songs to keep from going nuts. Now that it was over they all had a communal prayer of thanksgiving, and then took up a collection to buy a plaque for the ship in commemoration of all this. They raised about twenty-five hundred Singapore dollars and gave it to the captain, who made a little speech of thanks.

We had no more attacks after that, and next day we arrived in Batavia. I got off and was hobbling along the wharf planning to get to a hospital when an army doctor came along and said to me, 'Why don't you get aboard that hospital ship docked over there? Then when they sail you'll be all set.' So I did as he suggested, and here I am!

So ended Stewie's adventurous escape to fight again.

CHAPTER 10

War over the Jungle

To go back to where I left off at the end of Chapter 8. The four of us in our patched-up airplanes now headed out across the Straits of Malacca. When we were eight or ten miles out I noticed that my engine seemed to be working very hard to keep up with the other machines. Then I realised that I hadn't retracted my wheels yet—I'd been so busy looking back and monkeying with my camera that I had forgotten all about them! I raised them hurriedly, feeling embarrassed and hoping the others hadn't noticed, and my airplane speeded up at once so that I was able to ease my engine considerably.

We'd been warned that our airplanes were in very ropy condition, having been patched up and put together so hastily; and I found this was no exaggeration concerning mine. One of my wheels wouldn't lock in its retracted position and kept dropping down. I had to raise it every couple of minutes. The position indicator light for my wheels wasn't working, so at first I could never tell for sure when this wheel was clear up. Then noticing a hole in the bottom of my fuselage right by the place where the wheel came up, I found I could tell by the amount of daylight coming through the hole whether it was clear up or not.

My air-speed indicator registered zero at all times, and the airplane was "out of trim" so that I had to keep holding the stick to one side to keep it level. However, the engine purred nicely and the oil pressure and radiator temperature were normal, so I didn't mind the other faults.

Denny also appeared to be having trouble with his landing gear, for one of his wheels kept coming down the same as mine. And Tom, in his Brewster, flew for the first ten or fifteen minutes with both his wheels clear down. His trouble was just that he couldn't find the right gadget to raise them with, not having flown a Brewster before. Brownie seemed to be getting along all right in his Hurricane, although afterwards he said his propeller pitch control wasn't working, so that his engine just ran at any speed it felt like.

Everything went smoothly for the first forty-five minutes, and we were well on our way across the Straits of Malacca. In another fifteen or twenty minutes we should reach the coast of Sumatra, and an hour or so after that would bring us to Palembang.

Then Denny, who was leading us, suddenly began waggling his wings as a sign of distress, and headed downward and left toward an island a few miles in diameter, which we were nearing.

I took over the lead of the remaining three. Denny was obviously planning to force-land on this island, so I followed after him with my three, to see where he landed and whether he made it safely. We circled around above him while he made a couple of passes at a small field in one part of the island; but this seemed to worry him. He came back up alongside me, motioning me to go on, so, regretfully, the three of us headed on southward.

In a few minutes we struck the coast of Sumatra. We had to follow it southward now, until we came to the River Musi leading inland to Palembang, all of which had seemed very simple so far. But I had only followed the coast a short distance before I realised that I might soon be in difficulties. The crude map which I had picked up in the dispersal hut for emergency was an absolute menace—it showed only the one river going inland, with hardly any details by which I could identify it, whereas there seemed to be fully a dozen rivers leading in from this section of the coast! Picking the right one was going to be a most delicate matter.

To make matters worse the weather was getting bad, with the ceiling down to a thousand feet and thunderstorms and rain scattered all around, so I didn't have the visibility I needed to discern the course of each river. We didn't have enough gas to allow for errors in navigation; if I picked the wrong one we'd be sunk.

There's something frightening about being unsure of your way in an airplane. You can't stop and debate over your map as to which is the right way before going on. You're going, and fast, whether you've decided which way to go or not, and whether you're headed right or wrong, so your decisions are forced. I had terrible thoughts of our three precious fighter planes lost and crashing in the jungle somewhere, the result of my faulty map-reading.

One after another I passed up these rivers, each one because it didn't seem to check with the one on my map from what I could see of it, until I had gone by several and it seemed I surely must have gone far enough. I began to wonder helplessly if one of those I'd passed up had been the right one, and if so how I'd ever be able to find which it was if I went back now.

Then out of the rain and mist ahead another appeared which seemed to take the right direction in from the coast, curving like the one on my map, so I turned inland on it, praying I wasn't making a mistake. Within a few minutes I saw a couple of steamers on it, so I thought I must be right. And a little farther on we came in sight of Palembang itself. I gave one of my biggest sighs of relief!

There was a large storm raging to the north of town where the airdrome is located, but in view of our limited gasoline supply I decided not to wait for the storm to pass over. The jungle airdrome where I had landed before on the way from Java up to Singapore was only about fifty miles south-west from Palembang, and as the weather looked good in that direction I led on towards it. I wanted to get my three machines down safely and as quickly as possible, and I didn't care where!

A few minutes more, following the little old-fashioned railway (Sumatra's only one, I believe) that twisted and curved roughly south-west from Palembang, and we were circling to land.

As I was taxi-ing towards the watch office, I thought how much had happened in the two weeks since I landed here before, when the American Army Flying Fortress was here. It seemed a much longer time.

The weather at Palembang was reported to be worsening, so we stayed overnight. We were anxious for news of 300 Squadron, because of the dismaying rumours that we'd heard while in Singapore, and I questioned everyone I met to see what I could find out. No one seemed to know definitely how they had fared, although all agreed that they must have had hard fighting as Palembang had been raided heavily. One or two had heard rumours that the squadron were wiped out completely.

Next morning, with our airplanes refuelled, we flew back and landed at Palembang. A man drove out in a car to meet me and point to where I should park my machine, and I saw it was Squadron Leader T——. At least he was all right, I thought thankfully. He picked us up in his car and drove us into town, where we met several more of the boys in the hotel where they were staying.

It was a joyful reunion, everybody shaking hands and shouting and pounding each other on the back. We hadn't known which of them to expect to see alive and they hadn't known what had become of us.

They weren't wiped out by any means, but they'd lost most of their airplanes. They'd had very heavy attacks for three days running, fighting against vastly superior numbers—the enemy capitalizing on their shortage of aircraft by sending successive raids one right after the other. In this way they sometimes caught the boys while they were on the ground refuelling and rearming after one battle and were able to destroy some of their machines on the ground.

A lot of the boys had gone missing, but several turned up again after having bailed out or force-landed in the jungle and made their way back. Kleck, however, was among those definitely killed.

175 Squadron were operating here now, with the eight Hurricanes they had brought down from Singapore two days before. Some of our own planes which had been slightly damaged were just about ready to go again, and the boys hoped to start operating a few machines themselves in another day. Several were absent, having gone down to Java to pick up some new Hurricanes and bring them here. Three or four were now resting up from exposure and minor injuries from getting shot down and finding their way back here. They had some rather wild stories to tell.

Cam, for example, had been shot down and had crashed in heavy jungle a long way from Palembang, but managed to extricate himself from the wreck quite unhurt, though shaken. Some natives came around soon, appearing reasonably friendly, and they indicated that they'd take him to civilization in return for the gasoline in his tanks. Considering this quite a bargain, he wrote out a slip of paper, saying they could have all the gasoline they found, and gave it to them. None of them could read, but they seemed to trust him all right.

They were very interested in the wrecked Hurricane, climbing all over it and inspecting it carefully. Cam was afraid that sooner or later one of them might accidentally fire the guns. He spent quite a while trying to show them by signs that they mustn't meddle with the firing button. He says he gathered them all around and then acted as though he were going to press the button, then shook his head and waved his hands, saying, "Bad! Very bad! Mustn't do!" He repeated the performance until he was sure they had the idea. Then he started off with those who were to take him to safety.

They made their way to a river where they got into canoes and paddled off, but their progress was very slow and constantly interrupted. About every half-hour the natives would meet some friends in other canoes, whereupon they'd stop and all pile into each other's boats and sit cross-legged, jabbering to each other, for an hour or so. His rescuers would point at him and jabber to their friends and laugh, saying what sounded to him, "Look what we've got! Isn't he funny?" And he would beam back at them. He said he felt called upon to sit cross-legged, too.

He said, "I'd make signs that I was thirsty, and one of them would say, 'Thirsty? All right—have a drink'—or what sounded like it. Then he'd take a gourd and scoop up some filthy muddy water out of the river and give it to me!"

Frequently they'd stop at some native village along the river and go ashore for a visit, all sitting cross-legged and jabbering by the hour, while Cam smiled at everyone and tried to look interested. Meals were gourds of rice, so filthy it made him sick to his stomach.

After four days of this kind of travel they arrived at a village where he was able to get in touch with the outside world by a radio set. He was told to stay where he was, and soon a Dutch Army car arrived—the village was connected with the outside world by a road of sorts—and he was driven back to Palembang. He was still quite weak and shaken from his ordeal when we met him. Mac also had a bizarre experience. He had been out on a shipping escort with Junior, and on their way back they ran into twelve Navy Zero fighters. Junior was never heard of again. Mac got chased into some clouds, and when he came out he found himself totally lost. When nearly out of gas he picked a swamp close to a river and force-landed there. All fighter pilots are now provided with little collapsible rubber dinghies, packed into their parachute cushions, and Mac took his and made his way to the river. There he unpacked and inflated it, climbed in, and started paddling downstream.

These dinghies aren't built for speed, and Mac found his progress very slow. Presently he saw a canoe tied to the shore with no one in attendance and paddled over to it. He couldn't find anyone around, so he pinned a ten-*guilder* note to a nearby tree in payment and paddled off in his new purchase. After a time he met up with some natives in canoes, who escorted him to a village near by, where he was shown to the chief's house. There to his amazement, right in the heart of the jungle, he was treated to ice-cold beer from a refrigerator and put up in a huge room with the biggest and most luxurious bed he'd ever seen!

He stayed there for a couple of days, living elegantly on imported European foods, which the progressive-minded chief kept in stock, until he was rescued.

Not all the stories were pleasant. The saddest was that of Roy K——, a very young Canadian sergeant pilot, from Toronto. Vic, who was Roy's flight commander, told me about it that evening after dinner in the hotel where we boarded, while we sat toying with our coffee and watching the funny little wall lizards on the high ceiling of the dining-room go about their trade of keeping the mosquitoes and other insects cleaned up.

I wish I could reproduce Vic's words the way he told it, speaking slowly and haltingly, his voice starting to quaver once or twice, pausing occasionally to get control, his eyes blinking and watching the ceiling, avoiding mine. For Roy was a wonderful kid and Vic had been his very close friend.

He told me that Roy was wounded in the leg during a battle. His airplane was shot up badly, but he managed to get back and land all right. Then while he was taxi-ing across the field his damaged machine caught fire. The gas-tanks must have been holed, for it was all ablaze in an instant; and because of his wounded leg Roy had trouble getting out. By the time he got clear he was badly burned about the face, legs, and arms.

He was taken to the Dutch hospital at Palembang, where he seemed to do all right for the first twenty-four hours. Then shock set in and he started weakening. Vic went to see him as often as he could get time. He visited him about eight o'clock in the morning on the third day, promising to be back again at four in the afternoon. Something told him that morning that all was not well, for the doctors were letting Roy have morphia to ease the pain, something they had refused him before.

Vic was very busy that day and was delayed slightly in the afternoon, so he didn't arrive at the hospital until a few minutes past four. There he found, to his grief, that Roy had just passed away.

The sisters told him that Roy held on desperately until four, waiting for him to come, because he wanted so badly for Vic to be with him when he died. But when Vic didn't arrive on time his strength gave out. Just before he passed away he looked around at the sisters and begged, "Someone please hold my hand and call me 'Roy' before I die!" One of the sisters took his hand and called him "Roy," and that was how he died, halfway around the world from his home in Toronto.

The weather in Sumatra was hot and stifling as before little local thunderstorms occasionally breaking the heat for short periods, after which the sun would come out brighter and hotter than ever and the air would be stifling again, heavy with moisture from the steaming ground. We speculated a lot on how long it would be before the enemy tried to take Sumatra, and we weren't to be long in finding out.

The morning of the day after I arrived at Palembang the raid sirens sounded just before breakfast. A few of our boys were already out at the airdrome, doing readiness with what machines we had serviceable, along with 175 Squadron. Those of us who weren't on duty drove out to the drome to see what was going on.

We found that our boys and all of 175 Squadron were flying. The fellows on ground duty said that some Navy Zeros had been over about half an hour before and all our planes had gone off after them. They and the Navy Zeros had disappeared, so presumably our boys were chasing them somewhere.

The ground chaps were very concerned about a Hurricane they had seen shot down. They didn't know who the pilot was. It had been approaching to land, they said, with its wheels and flaps down, when two Navy Zeros dived on it. The first one, in pulling out of its dive, snapped its wings and crashed, but the second one shot the Hurricane down. Some thought they'd seen the pilot bail out, but no one knew yet. At present some low clouds over the airdrome obscured all view of what was going on above, but we could hear no noise.

Just then Scotty, a big husky chap from Alberta, walked into the dispersal building—and what a Scotty! It was he who had been piloting the Hurricane that was shot down. He had escaped by a miracle, bailing out at less than five hundred feet, and landing in the jungle a mile or so away. He was dirtied and dishevelled and still very dazed, wearing an expression on his face as if he'd just fallen out of bed!

He had just arrived from Java, ferrying a new Hurricane for the squadron. Quite a reception! It was too bad that his machine was lost so quickly, but it cost the enemy an airplane and pilot both, so we couldn't call it a bad trade.

After a few minutes we heard airplanes droning somewhere overhead, hidden from the airdrome by the low broken clouds. Occasionally there was the quick crisp roll of a burst of machine-gun fire in the sky, with more droning about and the sound of first one engine and then another power-diving.

As we had nothing to do at the drome we decided to get away from it before any bombing started, and we walked up the road a couple of hundred yards, sat down on a grassy bank, and awaited developments. We hadn't long to wait, for we suddenly found ourselves flat in the roadside ditch as if drawn there by magic, while the anti-aircraft guns went berserk at a single bomber that was approaching at about four hundred feet, beneath the low clouds.

It let go a stick of four bombs and we counted the earth-shaking booms, one after another, each one closer to us. Then the bomber was passing over the road and we cowered low in case they tried to machine-gun us. As soon as it was a safe distance away and the guns were chasing it up into the clouds on the other side of the drome I rose half out of the ditch and got a snapshot of the huge white clouds of smoke from the bombs as they drifted across the road about a hundred yards away. All four bombs had fallen well outside the airdrome—the poorest bombing I have ever seen, considering the low altitude from which they were dropped.

There seemed to be a lot more fighters and bombers around, but the low clouds fooled them so they couldn't find the airdrome. After milling around a few more minutes they all cleared away, and our fighters on patrol came back and landed. As I remember, they had shot down two or three bombers during the melee, and 175 Squadron had one pilot missing.

After they got refuelled Brownie and I volunteered to go on readiness for a couple of the boys who had been flying. The two of us had a scramble about mid-morning, but the flight proved uneventful, as the approaching enemies turned away before reaching Palembang. We stayed up for a while, doing a standing patrol at high altitude for more than an hour in hope that they'd change their minds and come back, but the activity seemed to have ceased for the morning.

After we landed, someone else took our places and I spent the afternoon in town, doing some shopping and getting my quarters fixed up. We took our meals in the Luxor Hotel and slept across the street in what had been a sort of rooming-house, but was now turned over to us. We had to furnish our own quarters.

I had a cot, but no mosquito-net for it, and as that is most important in Sumatra it was the first thing I attended to that afternoon. I got a net and then started looking around for wires to stretch it over. While I was working on my net, a little Malayan fellow came around who did our laundry, and was a particularly good scout, always trying to be helpful. As soon as he saw what I was doing he started jabbering vehemently, picked up my camp cot and tossed it out of the room.

Then he scurried away and presently appeared carrying a small wooden bed, complete with mattress, which he triumphantly deposited where my cot had been! Then he jabbered some more and hustled away again, to reappear with some boards and a hammer. Still jabbering happily and working frenziedly, he put up a framework for my mosquito-netting in a matter of minutes. I gave him a guilder, which of course made him happier than ever, though in his case I think he'd have done it for nothing.

After that I went around town doing some shopping, getting my Singapore money changed into *guilders* (Dutch East Indies dollars), and cabling my folks back home that I was safely out of Singapore.

Instead of *rickshaws*, in Palembang they had a queer sort of tricycle conveyance which the *coolie* rode on and pedalled. You sat in a wide seat, over the axle, which carried two passengers. This seemed to be quite an improvement over *rickshaws*.

Most of us took in a movie that night, in the theatre next door to the hotel. You might say there was something prophetic about the picture in a reverse way. The title was "He Stayed for Breakfast." Most of us didn't.

Chapter 11

The Battle of Palembang

From what I have since seen of the newspapers published at this time, I gather that the Battle of Palembang did not receive a great deal of prominence in the news, although it represented a major step in the enemy's conquest of the Far East—the main step between Singapore and Java. The final stages of the now-certain fall of Singapore were still occurring when Palembang was attacked, and I presume the eyes of the world were still on Singapore.

We ourselves, realising that the Singapore show was all over but the shouting and that Sumatra was the obvious next battle zone, were "digging in "in our own way, ferrying up new aircraft from Java and getting damaged ones repaired, in anticipation of the blow. Alas, we had little time, and the blow came even before Singapore had surrendered!

I was on dawn readiness next morning, which was Saturday, February 14—a gloomy, misty sort of morning, with sullen hangings of low cloud drifting across the airdrome. Tudor, our engineer officer (chief mechanic), and his men had been doing themselves proud in getting damaged machines repaired and new replacement machines fixed for combat. As a result, we had eight airplanes in 300 Squadron that morning, less than a week from the time the squadron's equipment had been virtually wiped out. 175 Squadron had gotten some new airplanes also, and I believe they had a full twelve that morning. Anyway, there were enough Hurricanes dispersed around the field at readiness to make an imposing show after what our squadrons had been through. When the light improved I got up on the nose of my airplane and took a snapshot of part of the array.

Towards nine o'clock both squadrons were scrambled and sent out together on a patrol over the Banka Straits, a hundred miles or so

Huge white clouds of smoke from bombs.

Tudor and his men repairing a damaged machine

Hurricane at the Jungle Airdrome, Sumatra

north-east. We spent half or three-quarters of an hour out there uneventfully, flying among and above tumbled masses of low broken cloud beneath a thick sullen overcast. A Jap invasion fleet was supposed to be approaching, so we heard; but it apparently hadn't got this far at least, for we saw no ships.

Our C.O. who was leading the formation finally called it a day and led us back towards Palembang. As we neared the city we had to come down through a lot of cloud, and in doing so our formation got broken up so that, when we came underneath, the two squadrons were separated.

I was leading a pair to the left and behind the C.O. Looking back I could see several machines a couple of miles behind, and one of them seemed to be diving toward another that was lower down. I was just a little suspicious, not enough to call out a warning, but keeping my eye on what was going on back there, until it was too late. Four long thin white lines suddenly reached out ahead from the plane that was diving, converging on the one in front of it—tracers—and then the one in front dived away leaving a thick trail of steam and glycol smoke!

Someone was calling "Look out—bandits!" and someone else called "Tally-ho!" Everything seemed to be in confusion back there, a *mêlée* of airplanes milling around, while we in front wheeled and headed back towards them. My number two broke away to chase after something he saw. A few seconds later I looked back to see a Navy Zero diving down on me, his big stubby round nose and silver-coloured propeller-spinner identifying him as enemy even at quite a distance. Another was following him. I opened my throttle and swung around hard to face him. I was facing him before he could get within firing range and I thought it was going to be a head-on show, both of us coming straight at each other, shooting, seeing who would give way first before we collided; but he didn't seem to want that now that he'd lost his chance for surprise. Before we were within firing range of each other, he zoomed up away. His partner behind did likewise. They had all the advantage of height and speed, so there was nothing I could do about it, and I lost track of them.

There were several airplanes milling around an area two or three miles across and I joined in, intercepting different ones that all turned out to be Hurricanes when I got close enough for identification. The Navy Zeros appeared to have all left, and the skirmish was over.

It was just then that Control began broadcasting a rather unusual order:

Hello, all Tiger and Evitt aircraft! All Tiger and Evitt aircraft! Don't land at your base! Do *not* land at your base! Go and land at B Airdrome. Land at B Airdrome!

B Airdrome was the jungle airdrome south-west of Palembang. I couldn't understand why we were being sent there, but presumed that our own field was bombed and unserviceable. I headed down the railway from Palembang and soon reached B Airdrome and landed as ordered.

After parking my machine I made my way to the watch office to join the crowd of other 175 and 300 Squadron pilots gathering there, and to hear the startling news. The reason we were ordered down here was that Palembang Airdrome was surrounded by more than two hundred parachutists, dropped there while we were away on our patrol!

And we'd wondered when the attack on Sumatra would come!

No one could learn anything very definite. The situation was supposed to be confused, with fighting going on around the drome and the city. Telephone communication with, the airdrome was dead.

Towards noon B Airdrome's Operations called for someone to do a reconnaissance to Palembang, studying the traffic along the highway to see if there were any signs of Jap troop movements down the road in our direction. I offered to go, as recco work was somewhat in my line, and it was a relief to get off the ground after the tension of waiting around for something to happen.

I scouted the road all the way, flying just above the tree-tops and getting lost once or twice by taking the wrong turns while flying in the rain, but didn't see anything that looked like military traffic coming.

There were dozens of motor cars streaming down the road. Apparently all the civilians were getting out at high speed. I could see white shorts and coloured dresses in the cars, so I knew they couldn't be Japs.

At Palembang the only indication I could see of how the fighting was going was that the Dutch had set fire to some of their big oil storage tanks, which seemed a bad sign. There was the familiar sight of frightening red flames, with angry black smoke pumping skyward and drifting over the city, nearly hiding it. It would have awed me if I hadn't come so recently from Singapore.

I returned and gave in my report, which relieved everyone because they had feared that the Japs might be attacking here right away, and we spent the rest of the day at readiness.

I was very worried about my belongings, which were all left behind in my room at Palembang, so I got to work on the telephone. After a time I managed to get the Palembang exchange and finally got through to our rooming-house there. Who should answer the telephone but Red! He hadn't been flying that morning, and consequently was among those left behind.

He said he didn't know just how the situation stood, but thought it was pretty bad. No, the Japs weren't inside the town, but he thought they were close around. He and Mac and a couple of others were getting ready to leave up the river in a motor-boat. I asked him to try to bring a little writing-case in which I had stuffed my most priceless possessions in case of just such an emergency.

It was in a small travelling-bag which I had packed with my next most valuable belongings, and he said he'd try to bring the bag and all.

Good old Red! I have never seen or heard of him since, but I've got that bag all right, thanks to him. It reached me more than two months later, Red having got it to Java and then given it to others who were leaving for India, as he stayed to fight to the last. Nearly all the films I took in Singapore were in it.

Towards evening some of our ground personnel began arriving from Palembang with the news that the battle was apparently lost, though the city was still in our hands when they left.

I think this is where I should bring in the story of Mickey N——, one of our pilots who was on the ground at Palembang Airdrome when the parachutists landed. He saw much of the battle, with experiences nearly as hair-raising as any he'd encountered in the air.

Mickey was the youngest pilot of our squadron. He had been hurt slightly in a crash a few days before and, being temporarily off flying, was doing the ground job of "Airdrome Control Pilot" that morning. This meant he had to stay on the airdrome looking after incoming and outgoing planes, taking telephone calls, and generally being on hand to take the blame for anything that went wrong. Like Stewie, he also told me his story on the hospital ship two or three weeks later:

> You remember when you fellows took off that morning to go out over the Banka Straits? Well, some time after you left a big bunch of bombers appeared from, the north, flying very low.

Escape from Palembang

We thought we were in for a real pasting, but instead of bombing the drome they just circled it.

Then we saw that they were dropping parachutists over the jungle, scores of them, in a big circle all around the drome, about a mile outside it.

I thought we were in an awful spot, because they had us completely surrounded, and I expected they'd be closing in on us right away. I rang up Operations and told them what had happened so they could warn you not to land back there; a little while later the phone was dead.

Several squadron leaders and wing commanders were there at the time, and they got all the personnel organised to defend the place. We took up positions along the road which skirts the west side of the drome, in two or three buildings there, and braced ourselves for the attack which we all thought would begin in a matter of minutes. I suppose there were a couple hundred of us all told, including the ground personnel of our squadrons who were on duty. Nothing happened for a while. There wasn't a sound from the jungle, and we kept getting more and more tense as time went by.

Pretty soon we saw you chaps coming back from your patrol over the Banka Straits. We could see some airplanes milling around in the distance and heard several bursts of machine-gun fire, so we knew you must be having a scrap of some kind. Then one Hurricane came in, streaming glycol smoke, and landed. That was Ting. He had his radiator shot up, and said he'd been jumped by a couple of Navy Zeros. Then we saw most of you heading off south-west, having heard Control, I suppose, warning you not to land here.

But then we saw that two Hurricanes were coming back. They came in and landed. I expected to see them picked off by snipers from the jungle while they were taxi-ing back up the runway, for they were right out in the open of course. However, nothing happened. I ran out to tell them to get going, but by the time I got to the pilots they'd already stopped their engines and were climbing out of their cockpits. They were Bertie and Kelly. They hadn't heard the warning not to land here, and when I told them what had happened you should have seen them move. You never in your life saw two chaps get back into their machines and take off so quick!

Then, horror of horrors, right when we expected to see Japs coming out of the jungle at any moment, in came *four* Hurricanes and landed ! They were new reinforcements for us, being ferried up from Java, and of course they had no radios installed so they couldn't hear any warning. As soon as they landed some of us piled into a car and tore out onto the field to warn the pilots. We told them to turn around and take off as fast as they could and go down to B Airdrome, but they all said they couldn't. They didn't have enough gas. They'd had bad weather all the way up which made them fly around a lot, and their tanks were almost empty.

So there was nothing for it but to get a petrol tanker out on the field and fill them up, hoping we had time. You know how the jungle comes right up to the airdrome on all sides there, so you can imagine how conspicuous we felt working out in the open on those Hurricanes, knowing there were a couple of hundred or more Japs with rifles and tommy-guns in that jungle ! We fairly tore around, and we got those four Hurricanes refuelled in what I bet was an all-time record. Were we relieved to see them safely away again and to get back under cover !

Some army officers came around after a time and inspected our positions and gave us advice. They had their headquarters back about a mile or so along the road to Palembang. We asked them if they'd made any contact with the enemy yet and they said no, except for shooting a few while they were coming down in their parachutes. They hadn't seen anything of them yet, and thought they might be infiltrating down towards Palembang, which was eight or ten miles away.

We waited and waited and nothing happened, and the tension of just sitting there not knowing what to expect or when to expect it was almost as bad as being attacked and having it out. Finally a couple of the army officers came to tell us they had orders to retire to Palembang, to defend the city, and they advised us to do likewise. With our telephone wires cut, we couldn't get in touch with Operations for orders, and we decided to take their advice.

There were lots of cars and lorries to go, and I caught a ride with an army doctor. We started off ahead of most of the rest and drove along without incident for the first two or three miles. Then we rounded a corner and saw a couple of wrecked cars in the road about a quarter of a mile ahead.

'Oh-oh,' the doc said. 'This looks like an ambush!' He put on the brakes, and just then there was a terrific explosion in front of the windshield and I felt something stab into my neck. Next thing I knew I was lying face down in the road, coughing and gagging on blood in my throat and mouth, with blood all over my clothes, too. The explosion must have been a hand grenade.

I thought sure I was dying. I couldn't talk or breathe or do anything except gag on blood that kept flowing into my throat as well as outside, from my wound, and I expected that if I didn't die the Japs would be along in a minute and shoot me anyway. But nothing happened right away, and after a bit my ears stopped ringing so much and I was conscious of a voice calling me in a loud whisper. 'Hey! Come on and get down in this ditch—quick!' It was the doc calling me. I opened my eyes and saw I was a few feet from a ditch at the side of the road. I gathered all my strength and half leaped and half fell over into it and huddled down by the doc. The ditch was about three feet deep.

I still thought I was dying. The blood in my throat made a rattling sound when I breathed, and I remembered the phrase about death rattling in one's throat, and thought that was it. The doc must have thought so, too, for he kept reaching over and feeling my pulse.

In a few minutes we heard another car coming. It stopped a few yards up the road from ours and we heard the occupants scrambling out and making for the ditch. Then pretty soon we heard the Japs coming out of the jungle and onto the road, and I thought, 'Now it's coming!'

We heard them talking and heard their footsteps on the road, and then they came up to our car, which was only three feet from the edge of the ditch we were in! They walked all around it, jabbering to each other, opening and shutting the doors, and apparently giving it a general once-over. I knew it would come now, because it could only be a matter of seconds before one of them glanced down and saw us, and I was trying my best to look like I was dead, lying with my mouth open and the wound in my neck showing. Once one of them jumped right across the ditch without noticing us. I just couldn't believe it when I heard them walk away after a little while.

However, they didn't go far, and they kept coming back. It was evident they were taking up stations around here for the time being, for they kept walking up and down the road and in and out of the jungle and all around, jabbering back and forth to each other. Then one of them standing near us in the road called out excitedly and several others came running, and my blood froze! 'Now they *have* found us,' I thought. But it wasn't us. It was two other fellows a few yards up along the ditch from where we were—the ones who'd scrambled out of the car that came after us. They put two bullets into each of them, and after each report there was a sickening '*oof!*' from the one who was hit. Then at the last report the doc himself moaned and jerked, and I thought they were shooting us now, but he'd just done it involuntarily.

Pretty soon we heard a lorry coming. It stopped a little way up the road. We heard the door open and the driver getting out, and then his voice, pleading, 'Don't shoot me, you—! Don't shoot me!'

Then a shot, and silence.

It began to rain, and all I thought was, 'Thank God! A little concealment!' But it stopped again soon.

After a time some Japs came along in a Dutch armoured car they'd captured. It stopped near us and there was lots of jabbering and running about, and then we heard it drive up and start pushing against our car. It was pushing it sideways, towards us, and we thought they were pushing it into the ditch, which would mean it would fall right on us. But they stopped pushing it when the wheels were just on the edge of the ditch. Apparently they just wanted room enough to get by. Another three inches and it would have toppled in on us.

Finally, after we'd lain there for over two hours, we heard machine-gun and rifle fire from up the road and bullets whining overhead, and striking around. The Japs withdrew from around us down the road a way. For a time we were in a no-man's-land between the two fires, but finally our forces got to where we were, and we were able to come out of our cover.

Our forces were composed of soldiers and R.A.F. chaps from the drome, at the head of a long column of lorries and cars, making their way toward Palembang. The going the rest of the way was slow and we were almost continually under fire. The

Japs kept falling back and making ambushes and machine-gunning the road, and there were lots of casualties on both sides. Every little way there were bodies of Japs and British soldiers and airmen, frightful things to look at. Some were torn and mutilated by the bullets, so that it nearly made me sick.

Eventually we made it into Palembang, where we found the streets packed with cars, lorries, and ambulances around the landing for the ferry on which they had to cross the river to travel south. It would have been a wonderful target for bombers, but fortunately the Dutch had fired their big oil storage tanks and the wind blew the smoke right over the city, hiding everything. I got my wound dressed, and the doc said there was a piece of shrapnel lodged inside my throat. I could only talk in a whisper. I stayed in Palembang overnight with some of the fellows, and we started south next morning.

Such was the adventure that Mickey was having while we were waiting at B Airdrome and wondering what was happening at Palembang!

A wing commander had another interesting little adventure that afternoon, in which he saved himself from capture by the greatest of coolness and quick thinking.

This wing commander was also at Palembang Airdrome when the parachutists arrived, and he didn't leave with the convoy which Mickey told about that fought its way down the road to Palembang. Instead, he stayed at the airdrome until quite late in the afternoon and then, accompanied by another officer, started out down the road in his car.

They had only travelled a couple of miles when they saw several Japs ahead in the road, and stopped. The Japs motioned them to get out of the car and approach, and they did so, covered by rifles and revolvers. One of the Japs was an officer, and when the two R.A.F. officers reached him he said, "You surrender. You my prisoners!"

Quick as a shot the wing commander came back at him. "Surrender, hell! *You* surrender! I've got two hundred men right back here on the airdrome. You haven't a chance!" (The truth was that there wasn't a man left on the airdrome, and the two officers were entirely alone.)

This took the Japanese officer a little aback, and he began to dicker, insisting that he had many more than two hundred men and it was useless for the British to fight. While this was going on the wing commander noticed out of the corner of his eye that some other Japs were stealing along through the jungle beside the road to *get* behind him.

"Here!" he admonished the Japanese officer sternly, pointing at the men in the jungle. "You call those men back!" The other meekly obeyed, calling out to the men in Japanese, and they came back.

The dickering continued. The Jap officer was anxious to get the wing commander to surrender his men without fighting. The wing commander appeared to be taken in and talked terms with him, cautiously leading up to his master-stroke.

Then, when he had got all the terms the Japs would offer him for surrender, he said: "All right. You wait here, and I'll go back and talk to my men, to see if they'll agree."

The Jap officer consented. The two R.A.F. officers walked back to their car, got in and turned around, and drove off towards the airdrome. Needless to say, they didn't stop there, not in fact until they were some fifty miles farther up in Central Sumatra, where they turned and made their way to the coast by roads that gave Palembang a wide berth!

As far as they are concerned, the trusting Japanese officer may still be there, waiting for them.

CHAPTER 12

A River Massacre and a Frightened Pilot

By that evening the situation looked definitely ominous. Reports from people coming from Palembang itself were not too bad on the whole, although conflicting. Some thought the battle was lost, others that our troops were getting the situation under control. All agreed that the city was still in our hands.

But another development had put a much more sinister aspect on it all. Throughout the afternoon a group of Blenheim and Lockheed bombers had been going out as often as they could return and load up, attacking an enormous troop convoy, escorted by warships, which was approaching from the direction of Singapore !

It was obvious that the parachute landing, which might be got under control, was only a prelude to invasion on a scale vastly larger than our small forces in Sumatra could hope to withstand. From now on our job was to give them everything we had, to gain time for preparations for the defence of Java, their big objective.

Our C.O. attended a conference in the Operations Room until late that evening. When he came back he told me I was to lead the six airplanes left in our squadron on a certain operation at dawn, and that on our way back we were to do a recco of Palembang and Palembang Airdrome to see what we could of the situation.

We pilots had crowded in on an already overfilled station and there were no beds for us, so we scrounged as many blankets as we could and slept in the mess—on the floors, on tables, and on chairs, each according to his preference.

I had a rather bad night of it, as I usually do when I have a particular operation planned for the morning, because I can't keep it out of the back of my mind, and so I go to sleep thinking about it. Then after I've been asleep a while, at the time when one's normal defences are way down and nerves and feelings all bared and sensitive, the dread sets in and all the dangers seem vivid and terrifying. After Singapore, my nerves weren't at their best anyway.

I'd arranged for Operations to ring the telephone in the mess at 5 a.m. to waken me, and through the dark night, in a sort of semi-slumber that I experienced between nightmares and wakeful moments thinking of the approaching invasion fleet and of our task at dawn, I seemed to see the telephone glowing in the darkness, menacingly, penetrating into my sleep.

Once when I awoke from a nightmare, shuddering from cold as well as from fright, I realised that it was storming and a cold wind with rain was blowing in on me through the open sides of the building; so I moved off the table I was sleeping on and spent the rest of the night on the floor in a more sheltered place.

It was still pitch-dark when the phone rang, and I stumbled to my feet to answer it dreamily. Five o'clock, time to get down to the field and get our airplanes ready. I roused the boys who were to go with me on the operation, and we stumbled sleepily out of the mess and trudged along the damp sticky roads to the drome. The rain was over, the sky just beginning to grey in the east, so that we could discern the ghostly outlines of our machines along the edge of the drome. An odd bird or two occasionally called back and forth in the jungle. I felt relieved at being in motion at last, with the knowledge that it would be over soon and then I could relax.

As soon as we reached the watch office I rang up Operations to see if they had any new instructions for me. They told me not to take off yet, but to wait until they phoned back; so after we got our airplanes ready and had our Mae Wests on we just killed time. Some of the boys found places to lie down and went to sleep.

It was broad daylight before Operations again called to say we could take off and get going. I roused the boys, and in the half-minute's final instructions I gave them I made a remark that was to recoil on me before the day was out. We were to make an attack during which we would have to fly through very heavy anti-aircraft fire, and I told the boys they shouldn't let it worry them—that I didn't think the Japanese anti-aircraft fire was very effective.

How little I knew!

As we taxied out I noticed little wisps of fog among the tree-tops just outside the airdrome, but I didn't think much about it. There were usually little isolated patches of fog around the countryside here on early mornings. The thick trees on each side of the runway made our position like that of being down in a little canyon, unable to see outside.

Turning at the far end of the runway I gave my engine the gun to take off without waiting for the others to get in formation with me, because I wanted them to take off one at a time. After I left the ground my attention was occupied for a moment by the mechanics of raising my wheels and changing my throttle and propeller pitch settings, so it was not until I was up perhaps a hundred feet that I looked around, and then realised that we were in a terrible jam!

A carpet of fast-forming fog lay all about the countryside and was quickly closing the hole which happened to open over the airdrome!

Hoping desperately that at least part of my formation might still be on the ground I switched on the transmitter and called out, "Don't take off! Do *not* take off!" But when I looked back I saw it was too late. There were all five Hurricanes in a long row trailing below and behind me, rising up from the grey blanket that covered the earth in all directions. The airdrome had disappeared completely. This was awful!

I switched on my transmitter again. "Hello, all Evitt aircraft. Wash-out! Wash-out! Land at once; land at once!"

At the same time I turned, dropped my wheels, and throttled back my engine, making for a slight depression in the fog which I hoped marked the airdrome. I was lucky, and when I broke through the bottom of the grey mist I was right over the runway, and I got down O.K.

Then began a nerve-racking half-hour, trying to get the others down. The fog was thin enough so that when they passed directly over they could see down through and spot the drome, but when they got away to make their approaches they, of course, lost sight of it immediately and had to guess where it was. I borrowed a Very pistol and all the available green cartridges from the watch office, and ran out to the middle of the runway. Then every time I heard an airplane approaching the field I'd shoot a cartridge straight up, the little ball of green fire rising and arcing over just at the top of the fog, to spot the field for him.

That helped, and soon one of the Hurricanes managed to break into sight more or less over the edge of the field, and by means of a hair-raising vertical turn close to the ground in order to get in line with the runway, and some violent fish-tailing to kill his speed, the pilot made it. He came taxi-ing back, and I saw it was Kelly. He grinned at me and made a motion as if wiping sweat from his forehead. I held up clasped hands in congratulation.

The other four were still droning around up there: first one, then another throttling down and gliding into the fog at a point where he hoped the airdrome was, the sound of his engine breaking out again at full throttle as he zoomed back up after finding he was wrong. Frequently one of them would come close enough for us to see him, but not lined up right to land.

Finally Bertie got down safely, and that made two safe, three to go.

As Bertie was shutting off his engine another Hurricane broke through into sight. It landed on the cross runway at the far side of the field, disappeared behind a slight rise in the ground; then its tail appeared above the rise, poised vertically for an instant, and went on over, and the next minute the fire-truck and ambulance went flying across the field in that direction. Two safe, one crashed. Another got down safely a couple of minutes later, but the last one spent a good fifteen minutes more milling around and making approaches that weren't quite right to bring him in, until finally he made it, too, and I sighed thankfully to see him roll to a stop, undamaged. We lost one machine in the whole affair. For a time I was afraid we were going to lose five.

The ambulance came back from the far side of the field, bringing the pilot of the wrecked airplane, Sergeant F——. He was sitting in front with the driver, bruised and dirtied, but uninjured. He said he had struck a bad soft spot in the field, which made his machine go over on its back.

Ever since the parachutists attacked Palembang the morning before and we landed here, other pilots of both squadrons who hadn't been flying that morning had been making their way down here from Palembang, by car and train, to rejoin us; now each of our two squadrons had enough pilots to man all the airplanes of both. It was decided therefore to pool all the airplanes of both squadrons until we got reinforcements, and change off using them, one squadron operating them half the time and the other the rest of the time.

The fog cleared away about nine o'clock, but it was too late now to carry out the operation I was going to lead, and it was cancelled. Then at about ten or eleven a bomber crew, back from a raid on an invasion convoy, reported that a large landing force of enemy troops in barges and small open boats were making their way inland from the Banka Straits, up the River Musi toward Palembang.

This news put everyone in a huddle. The force *must* be stopped before they reached Palembang, or the show would be over. It was decided to send our Hurricanes out at once. If the enemy were in open boats we should be able to wreak terrible havoc among them with our eight- and twelve-machine-gun Hurricanes.

175 Squadron were on duty at the time, so they were to make the first sortie, and took off at once. In the meantime we of 300 Squadron hiked back to the Mess to see what we could get to eat before they got back, when we would take over the airplanes to make the next raid.

They returned after an hour or so, all the pilots in great spirits, having had a wonderful show. There had been no enemy fighters to interfere and they had caught the unprotected boats and barges, each crammed tight full with enemy soldiers. It had been a massacre, and they estimated they had killed hundreds.

They recounted lurid details, like seeing some of their victims throw themselves into the air as they were hit, and boats full of dead soldiers sinking, with the water around them red from blood. It gave us some satisfaction to know that these fellows who dealt in horror had got some of their own!

There had been some light anti-aircraft fire from the boats, they said, apparently from machine-guns, but only one airplane was hit, and that had only a single bullet-hole.

Now it was to be our turn. We took over the airplanes and saw to getting them refuelled and rearmed while the 175 Squadron boys went off to lunch. In a short time we were all set, and we started up and taxied to the end of the runway, where we got into squadron formation before taking off. It was the first time we'd taken off in squadron formation since we came to the Far East, as normally the runways were too soft here, or narrow, or damaged by bombs. This runway was good and wide, and the hot sun had dried it. I felt we must be making a magnificent show as we roared up over the boundary of the field all together, and climbed away into the north-east.

Our objective was a hundred miles or so away, and we pulled up to three or four thousand feet, just under a gloomy overcast of heavy cloud. It was a dull murky sky that we flew in, with local rainstorms sitting around the countryside like great white pillars rising from the jungle up to the clouds, so that we appeared to cruise on and on through a great pillared hall—its floor the flat jungle-covered land below, and its ceiling the heavy flat clouds above. Nearing our objective we encountered enormous low cloud formations, detached from the ceiling and drifting independently through our hall; we passed over and through and between their great weird tumbled masses and the vast gloomy caverns in them.

Finally the dull blue-grey water of the Banka Straits appeared ahead, and as we neared the coast we swung northward, until the River Musi appeared ahead of us, winding snake-like inland through the dark carpet of jungle. Somewhere up its course we should find our enemies.

I already had my gun-sight turned on and my firing button off safety, for use if we should run into a patrol of Navy Zeros. We were in battle formation, well spread out to guard each other's tails, for it wouldn't be surprising if they had a patrol out guarding the boats this time, after 175 Squadron's devastating attack a couple of hours earlier.

We turned above the mouth of the river and started following upstream; after we'd gone a few miles our C.O. nosed down into a dive and then I saw a few boats parked close to one bank of the river, so tiny in the distance below us that I wondered how he noticed them. It was obviously too small a target for us all to attack at the same time, so I broke away with my number two and did a wide circle, coming around behind the rest. They were shooting the boats up pretty well, so when I got down to them I only put in a short burst from my guns, feeling sure there must be bigger and better game somewhere around.

We climbed up, re-formed, and followed on along the river; and when we'd gone perhaps fifteen or twenty miles farther we found them.

It was the first invasion force I'd ever seen. Boats, scores of them, in a long silent line perhaps two miles from end to end, were strung out parallel to the south bank of the river and a hundred yards or so away from it. From our height it looked like a great venomous snake crawling along the stream. This was one of *the* moments for which we had been sent halfway around the world!

When we were right above them the C.O. waggled his wings (the signal that we could break formation and go to it), and to each side of me I could see the grey fish-like bellies of Hurricanes turning away to diminish off downwards to the attack.

This seemed to be such a wonderful opportunity that I wanted to make the most of it, so I circled a moment, studying the line of boats and planning my approach. Soon I could see the other Hurricanes far below, like tiny moths floating over the jungle. Then one of them approached the line of boats from one side; as he drew near, his set of delicate white tracers appeared in front of him as if by magic, reaching out ahead and touching one of the boats like a wand, and a cloud of white spray almost completely enveloped it. I had seen twenty or thirty men killed in a twinkling!

I had never seen an opportunity like this. Often I had machine-gunned German soldiers, sailors, or airmen on the ground or in ships, but always where they either had a little shelter or concealment, or at least could scatter and throw themselves flat. These fellows had no shelter or concealment except the thin sides of their boats, no better than paper for stopping our bullets, and they were jammed in so tight that they couldn't scatter or throw themselves flat or do anything except just sit up and take it.

Other airplanes followed with their attacks, each in turn approaching one of the boats and raising a mountain of spray around it with his bullets. There were 160 or 240 bullets per second in each of these clouds of spray, depending on whether it was an eight- or twelve-gun Hurricane. What a massacre!

Now I could see light-blue smoke floating away from some of the boats, and I presumed it was from the light anti-aircraft fire which the boys of 175 had reported. Three or four boats were dropping out of line and appeared to be sinking.

My own plans made, I flew eastward until I was a mile or so east of the rearmost; I took a careful look all around for enemy fighters, and then turned downward into my dive, arcing around back towards them, tensing myself for the bath of anti-aircraft fire as one does when going under an icy shower. I was planning to attack lengthwise, down the line of them, and I levelled out perhaps a hundred feet above the water and about a mile behind them; I took a last glance all around for Navy Zeros, then concentrated on aiming. I was coming fast after my dive, the trees on my left streaking past in a blur.

I held my aim on the first boat as I neared it, waiting for it to grow large enough in my sights. Almost close enough now—aim a little high at first to allow for bullet drop—now!

There's nothing to it, really—you just press in with your thumb.

There was the abrupt shattering roar from the guns in my wings and then the eight ghostly white tracers snaking out ahead eagerly toward the boat and its helpless passengers. They would know nothing more.

Wanting to make the most of my ammunition I broke off after a short burst, not even waiting to see the first bullets strike, then turned and fired at another boat. Not so good; I was turning when I fired and the first bullets threw up their shower of spray to one side of it. I stopped turning and held the nose up in a side-slip to get the sights centred better, and the shower moved over to encompass the boat just as I broke off.

I snapped short bursts into two or three others at close range, just a second or so into each. They were looming in front of me faster than I could possibly shoot at them all. This was terrific !

I had got down too low now, so I nosed up and passed over a few to take good aim at one boatload farther on. I could see the Japs looking at me as I fired—twenty or thirty of them, riding backwards—and then my tracers smacking right into the middle of the close-packed bunch of faces, and for some reason I just held the sights on them, still firing, right up to point-blank.

I zoomed a little then, turning to aim at another boat, and then—
—*Wham!*

It's hard to recall all of what followed, and in what succession. I was conscious of having been hit, harder than I had ever been hit in my life—a quick, cruel blow in the calf of my left leg; I had a momentary glimpse through a big rent in my trousers of two holes in the side of my leg, one small and round, the other a gaping sort of thing an inch wide by a couple of inches long, with raw red and blue flesh and muscle laid open, before the blood welled up and started streaming out.

I was banking hard to the left to flee out over the jungle, more by instinct than plan probably, I was so stunned. Then my mind seemed to start working, and the first thing it told me was that I was in one of the worst jams of my life, for I was nearly a hundred miles from the airdrome, and a weakness of mine is that I tend to faint when I'm hurt and bleeding—and I had never been hurt like this before, and had never bled like this before!

Seemingly with the very thought I started feeling light and sick, the shock and heavy pain overwhelming. I'd grabbed my torn trouser-leg above the wound with my left hand, remembering what I'd heard about tourniquets, and twisted on it frantically, trying to stop the blood. Now I glanced down to see if it had done any good, but the blood was still running fast, down my trouser-leg, sock, and shoe, and dribbling off to form a sickening bright red puddle in the heel-rest—a sort of flat metal trough below the rudder pedal.

This was awful. At this low altitude it would be all over if I fainted for even a few seconds, and now the sight of the blood had made me worse. I looked straight ahead trying to keep my mind off it, but there were blood and bits of flesh spattered over my instrument panel and windshield. My ears were beginning to ring and bright specks floated around the cockpit. I was trying with dreadful urgency to clench my teeth and fight against it without having any strength to do so, saying to myself, "I mustn't faint, I mustn't faint!" Then it was worse and I was having trouble to see, and I thought, panic-stricken, "I *am* fainting—I mustn't faint—*I am* fainting! . . ."

Somehow it passed, after just a few seconds, I suppose. I'd had sense enough to lean back, relaxing what I could and drawing deep breaths. The noise of the engine, which had faded nearly away, was back, and the jungle still streaked past just beneath my wings. I still felt terrible, as if I couldn't hold out much longer, wondering wildly if I should shut off my engine and crash-land first. Then I thought of my oxygen supply and let go of the stick long enough to twist the regulator valve on my instrument panel, opening it until I was getting enough oxygen to fly at forty thousand feet. That should help.

I thought I must keep my mind off the wound, so I took time for a careful look around for enemy fighters, saw none, and then noticed that I still had my throttle at cruising setting. I let go of the stick again to reach over and shove it wide open—not daring to let go of my trouser-leg with the other hand. If I could just get that bleeding stopped . . .

I looked down again to check, and the blood was still running. Not good enough, I realised. I must do something better, and quick. I'm sure I could never do it now, but I was desperate then and it seemed easy. I let go the hold I had on my trouser-leg above the wound, grabbed up the torn cloth right over it, twisted it, and then jammed my gloved fist, knuckles first, as deep as I could into the large hole, and held it that way.

The effort, together with the sight of the blood and the thought of what I was doing, brought on my next fainting spell and for a long moment all I could do was sit back, taking deep breaths, controlling the airplane laxly, panic-stricken, trying to keep the awful sickness down and my eyes clear. If I never have another five minutes like those it will be quite soon enough for me !

Somehow that spell passed and things cleared up again. It gave me new confidence that I could make it, and for the first time I thought to check whether my machine was damaged. I glanced at the radiator temperature and oil pressure gauges. They were normal. Thank heavens! The radiator and engine hadn't been hit. Then I checked the fuel gauges. The main tanks were down a reasonable amount for the time I'd been flying, and my reserve was full. It was all comforting, for it meant that nothing important could have been hit except me. I kept looking around for enemy fighters, and scrooching as close down over the trees as I could to keep from being seen.

I don't think I had any more fainting spells, but, as I remember, the next minutes were just long and painful. At last the thick jungle beneath me began to give way to less wooded country, nearly all under water, divided up into rice-fields by earthen embankments, with houses here and there and an occasional roadway raised above the level of the water. I realised I must be nearing Palembang, for the only rice-farming land I had noticed was an area south and south-east of there. Then I saw a pall of smoke marking the city itself, a few miles ahead and on my right.

I'd been keeping my mind religiously away from thoughts of my wound since the last fainting spell, for fear that thoughts of it or the sight of it would bring on another, but now I took a chance and looked down, to find, almost incredulously, that the bleeding seemed to have stopped. The red rivulets down my leg and shoe seemed to be stationary, and the puddle of blood in the heel-rest was no longer bright red but dark, which meant that there couldn't be any fresh blood on it. The pain, which never had been agonizing, had settled to a heavy ache as from a badly bruised muscle. My hopes of making it really soared.

I passed about five miles south of Palembang, but couldn't see the city itself for the smoke and fires around and in it. Halfway there, I estimated. Now if I just didn't miss the railway and get lost . . .

My engine was bellowing away, wide open still, and I reached over and throttled it down a little. No use burning it up if I could help it. I kept talking to myself, trying to keep my mind off the wound, and kept looking around and above for signs of enemy planes as well as watching ahead for the railroad, which I should be crossing soon. The weather was worse here and I had to keep altering course to avoid passing through rainstorms, in which I might not notice the railroad when I passed over.

At last there it was, and my anxiety on that score was over. I swung left joyfully and scooted along over the tree-tops beside the tracks, feeling more confident than ever of success. I talked out loud, telling myself, "Only ten minutes more now, old boy, and you're all O.K. You'll sleep in bed tonight, too, and have breakfast in bed tomorrow morning!" That sort of chatter and lots of other silly things, anything to keep my mind away from the wound and how I felt. I thought of friends I'd write to in the hospital and what I'd tell them, and of all kinds of things like that, while the trees streaked by beneath my wings and the long curving miles of railway track unwound out of the distance ahead and spun past and reeled away behind, until all at once the jungle was broken ahead and there was the airdrome!

Getting down was somewhat of a problem, because there are lots of gadgets to work in landing a Hurricane, and I didn't dare to take my left hand out of the wound, for fear my glove should be stuck in it and cause a spasm of pain and bleeding. I decided to try to make it with one hand, cursing the unconventional type of control stick we have on R.A.F. fighters, which you can't handle with your knees like ordinary control sticks.

I flew low over the watch office on the edge of the field, slowly, rocking my wings as a warning that I was in trouble; then pulled up to two or three hundred feet and released the stick long enough to jerk the hydraulic control into "Wheels Down" position. A moment later there were a couple of thumps as the wheels locked in their lowered positions, and the two green lights came on in my instrument panel to show me they were down properly. I circled wide to make my approach on the runway, and when I was almost over the field I let go of the stick again to pull the throttle back and shove the hydraulic control into "Flaps Down" position, fish-tailed a little to get rid of the extra speed I had, and she settled down in a nice glide.

Then I had a little trouble because I hadn't pulled the throttle quite all the way back, so the engine was still idling too fast to allow me to land; I didn't notice it until I was too close to the ground to let go of the stick again and change it. However, I managed to get my left elbow hooked on the throttle while I was levelling off, and pulled it back that way. Then of course I had to go and mess up my landing, bouncing badly. Not being able to use my engine to help recover I had to just keep bouncing, for about one-third of the way across the field, until I didn't have enough speed to bounce any more.

I didn't mind though. The feeling of triumph at having made it safely made the bad landing seem inconsequential! I felt almost boisterous as I taxied up to the watch office.

Netherlands Indies Armed Services Communiqué:

Batavia, February 16. Early Sunday morning a large-scale bombardment was begun on the Japanese fleet in Banka Strait. American, British, and Netherland aircraft took part in these bombardments.

In the Musi Estuary the Japanese transferred their troops into all kinds of small craft, sloops, motor-boats, rowing boats and other local material. The invaders then sailed into various rivers and creeks, continuously harried by our very low-flying fighters and bombers, which played murderous havoc among the thousands of invaders.

Our losses in aircraft and men are not yet known, but it can be taken that they are considerably lower than the extent of the large action would make us expect.

Chapter 13

"We'll be Back"

There isn't much left to tell. Some of the boys lifted me out of my machine, and Flight-lieutenant S——, a good chap who was doing duty pilot there, put a field dressing on my leg. Then I was packed off in an ambulance to the dressing station, and I had a sinking feeling for a time as I realised they intended to put me in a hospital here, which meant that I'd be in grave danger of being captured by the rapidly advancing enemy.

My worries were short-lived, however, for a telephone call came to the dressing station shortly after I was brought in, saying I was to be sent back out to the drome, at once. I could think of only one reason for that, and I was right. When I arrived back at the drome I found that a Lockheed bomber bound for Java was held up waiting for me at Squadron Leader T——'s intercession.

Two hours later I was safely in bed, three hundred miles from the fighting zone, in the Dutch Military Hospital of Bandoeng, a beautiful city in the mountains of west central Java. I had all that I'd promised myself—a bed to sleep in, with clean sheets, and the prospect of breakfast in bed in the morning! In addition I had a very pretty nurse to look after me.

The nurses were swell, as was the Dutch army doctor who carefully examined my wound and then said, to my relief, "You are very lucky! "

I had been hit by a half-inch machine-gun bullet, he said—light anti-aircraft fire. And only that morning I had said I didn't think the Japanese anti-aircraft fire was very effective! The bullet must have struck some part of the airplane first, so that it was tumbling over and over when it hit me, with the result that it came out sideways, making the large hole that I had to plug with my fist. It hadn't touched the bone, however, so only flesh and muscle were damaged. The wound gave me surprisingly little pain, and I got along fine. I could hobble around a little at the end of four days.

The morning after I arrived there I overheard one of the nurses, in the hall outside my room, exclaim something in Dutch that sounded like "*Singapore iss ober-hagen!*" Anyway it was close enough so I knew what it meant, and later I learned that the surrender had taken place the day before.

Even though I had known when I left that only a miracle could ever save Singapore, the final news was overwhelming to me. Now the war would last much longer, and many, many more lives would have to be sacrificed to win it. The thought of thousands of those filthy little rats of humans swarming over the beautiful island and city was almost too much. One of them no doubt would be driving my Ford car now—too bad I hadn't set fire to it.

I thought too of the exotic dark-haired girl we'd watched on the lawn of the Sea View that last morning, and wondered what became of her and all the other civilians who were still there when I left.

The first two or three days I spent here at Bandoeng were marvellously peaceful, but things were happening fast and the change was rapid.

With the fall of Singapore and Palembang (which was taken by the enemy the day after I was wounded), the Japs began putting the pressure on Java, and within a few days they made their first air raid on Bandoeng. Some bombers attacked the airdrome on the outskirts of the town while a bunch of Navy Zeros fought a dog-fight with Brewster Buffaloes of the Duty Air Force within view of us a few miles away.

After that the raids were virtually a daily affair, and we knew that the invasion of Java would be only a matter of time. We British patients hoped we hadn't escaped from the enemy in Sumatra only to be trapped by them here.

That was how it stood when one morning Doc H——, an R.A.F. flight-lieutenant, came into our ward to tell us to hurry and get packed, as we were moving at once. He had fixed up our passage on a hospital ship, for which we will be for ever grateful to him.

Get packed! I had nothing to pack, as was true of most of the dozen or so others, for we had lost everything we had. I just put on my shirt and trousers and was ready.

I felt miserable as I went around shaking hands and saying goodbye to my friends among the doctors, nurses, and Dutch patients. They knew as well as I what they were being left to. It was betrayed in the harried looks on their faces, as I hope it was betrayed in shame on mine, but no one spoke of it. They only smiled, bravely, if wistfully, and wished me luck. I left my wings with Ann, the little nurse who first took care of me.

That afternoon we departed in a convoy of three ambulances on our trip of a hundred and twenty miles along winding, dusty, hilly country roads that passed through jungles, rubber plantations, irrigated rice farms, and native villages of woven palmetto huts with thatched roofs, all the way from the mountainous country where Bandoeng is located down to Batavia on the sea-coast, where we boarded our ship late that evening.

There I met Mickey, whose story of his experiences at Palembang I related in Chapter 11. He had his neck still bandaged and could only talk in a whisper because of the piece of shrapnel in his throat, and was in a very nervous state.

Later we were to pick up a couple of pilots of 175 Squadron, including Stewie, whose story I told in Chapter 9.

Our send-off from Batavia next morning was a thirty-minute air raid on the city and harbour. Dive-bombers plastered the docks and vicinity and Navy Zeros roared across low down, machine-gunning ships and patrol boats, chased by pom-pom shells that looked like little red sparks chasing each other across the bay.

At the same time a formation of large bombers made methodical attacks from high level on a cruiser anchored near us, missing it each time and sending up gigantic towers of water that subsided to leave great curtains of muddied mist. We patients who could get around were rushing from one side of the ship to the other, watching the various acts of the show, occasionally throwing ourselves flat when bombs or low-flying airplanes came near. The dive-bombers hit an oil storage tank close to the harbour and set it on fire, too.

The roar of engines, the mad chorus of anti-aircraft guns, the scream of falling bombs, and the crash of the explosions, all combined in a terrific din, while the black smoke and red flames from the blazing oil tank on shore completed the picture and made this the fifth time that I had evacuated a place to the noise of gunfire and bombs, and the sight of the flames and smoke of war.

We sailed about an hour later, and all afternoon the north-west coast of Java was an irregular green panorama bounding the warm blue sea on our left, as our little hospital ship sailed westward from Batavia; the pleasing sight of it, together with the feel of the soft tropical sea breeze, was soothing to the discouraged hearts and aching wounds of us patients as we lay on our mattresses on deck. About dusk we reached the western end of Java and swung southward, into the narrow Soenda Straits which separate it from Sumatra.

After supper I made my way up to the top deck, for a last look at these two countries.

It was nearly dark, and the ship's lights were on—the first time I had ever travelled on a lighted ship. Spotlights illuminated the red crosses on its deck, sides, and funnel.

I sat down on a hatch-cover to ease my leg. The sky was clear and most of the stars were already out. There are medium-sized mountains near this part of the coasts of both Java and Sumatra, and I could see both from where I sat—those of dark Sumatra on our right, already conquered and occupied by the enemy, and those of beautiful Java on our left, doomed to a similar fate in a few more days. They were great dark silhouettes against the stars, silent, and looked, I thought, sad and brooding.

I felt sad, too, and spiritually very tired. There's no need denying that I was terribly disillusioned by much of what I had seen and experienced out here—things that I have avoided or passed over in this story because it isn't in my province as a member of the forces to speak of them, and because I could only do harm by telling about them now. The enemy don't advertise their failings either, you know.

Doubtless you have seen references to this in the press, so there's no harm in admitting that I saw many things out here that were very bad. The humiliating memories of them, and the overwhelming realisation of the great defeat we had suffered, with the consequent imperilling of our entire cause, after all the bright hopes I'd had when I came out here less than a month before, combined to make me more discouraged and heartsick than I had ever been before.

Besides, my leg was aching again.

Of the forty-eight beautiful new Hurricanes we had flown to Singapore, scarcely a dozen were left the day I was wounded. No doubt they were all gone now. From Mickey I gathered that little more than half the pilots were alive, and we had little to show. We had stopped our enemies nowhere.

I reflected that in two and a half months these new enemies had overrun Malaya, Singapore, and Sumatra in rapid succession. They were winning in the Philippines and other places, and I thought to myself, "Where are we going to stop them?"

And then another thought came that made me shiver: "*Are* we going to stop them?"

Was it possible that we were really losing this war? Were these perhaps the last days of our civilization ?

Surely I had seen out here most of the things that had preceded the fall of other great civilizations—the softness and decadence that come from easy living—the lack of appreciation for the good things of life that comes from the too easy attainment of them—the failure to appreciate freedom that comes from taking it for granted too long.

It was only a mood, a discouraged, dismayed sort of mood, that came from the too recent, too vivid memories of all these "things that were bad," which tended to push older memories of bigger and better and much more important things out of my perspective and give me a distorted view, as an ant in a burning bush might think the world was on fire.

I began to realise this, as I sat there letting the cool night breeze and the soothing endless throb of the engines comfort and reassure me, and gradually my view of it all seemed to broaden.

After all, though we were beaten in this theatre of the war, it was only an outpost of the British Empire, garrisoned by a fraction of Britain's strength, which had been overwhelmed by almost the full strength of another great nation while Britain herself was engaged in a death-struggle with Germany and Italy, almost halfway around the world from here.

I, if anyone, should certainly know that the "things that were bad" out here were not typically British, for I had served more than a year in England, where the universal fighting spirit and loyalty had made me feel very inferior. The people there were anything but decadent, and the miserable creatures who had let down their king and country so woefully out here were no more true British than the fifth-columnists and saboteurs in my own country were true Americans.

I thought of the tremendous fighting forces being built up in England, readying themselves for the time when they could strike and let all the Axis know what the real British people will do when aroused.

And I remembered, too, the quotation the prime minister used in one of his speeches:

"Westward look—the land is bright!"

Yes, it was tragic that America had entered the war, but now that my people were in it they would brook nothing. We Americans aren't decadent either, although with a few more years of coddling we might have been.

I began seeing things in a better light, a light which seemed to show the Rising Sun very near its zenith.

Darkness had set about our ship now, but in a few hours it would begin to get light again. Another kind of darkness was settling over all the Far East, but in a few months, or a few years . . . ?

I stood up and started for the stairway, and at the top took a last long look at each of the two coastlines, very dark now against the sky.

I thought to myself, "We'll be back."

The story of the fighting career of Flight-Lieutenant Arthur Gerald Donahue, D.F.C., the first American pilot to take part in combat with the R.A.F., can, unhappily, be completed in a few sentences. In April 1942 he was travelling across India, fully recovered from his wound. In the same month he returned to duty, this time in Ceylon, and there heard that he had been awarded the Distinguished Flying Cross. The citation runs as follows:

> *'This officer carried out low level reconnaissance sorties and successfully attacked enemy shipping and ground objectives. On one occasion while attacking enemy troops who were attempting a landing in the Singapore area, he silenced the enemy's fire and enabled the rest of the squadron to press home attacks with impunity. He has destroyed several enemy planes.'*

In June he was in Bombay, and by August was back at an R.A.F. station on the English Channel, where for a few weeks he was acting Commanding Officer of the squadron, enjoying the novelty of administrative work though it did not allow him as much flying as he liked. He was looking forward to being home on leave in Minnesota for Christmas, but failed to return from a patrol, during which he is known to have badly damaged and possibly destroyed an enemy bomber. His death is officially presumed to have occurred on September 11, 1942. He left behind him the manuscript of Last Flight from Singapore *and the photographs with which it is illustrated.*

ALSO FROM LEONAUR
AVAILABLE IN SOFTCOVER OR HARDCOVER WITH DUST JACKET

THE ART OF WAR by Antoine Henri Jomini—Strategy & Tactics From the Age of Horse & Musket.

THE ART OF WAR by Sun Tzu and Pierre G. T. Beauregard—*The Art of War* by Sun Tzu and *Principles and Maxims of the Art of War* by Pierre G. T. Beauregard.

THE MILITARY RELIGIOUS ORDERS OF THE MIDDLE AGES by F. C. Woodhouse—The Knights Templar, Hospitaller and Others.

THE BENGAL NATIVE ARMY by F. G. Cardew—An Invaluable Reference Resource.

ARTILLERY THROUGH THE AGES—by Albert Manucy—A History of the DEvelopment and Use of Cannons, Mortars, Rockets & Projectiles from Earliest Times to the Nineteenth Century.

THE SWORD OF THE CROWN by Eric W. Sheppard—A History of the British Army to 1914.

THE 7TH (QUEEN'S OWN) HUSSARS: Volume 3—1818-1914 by C. R. B. Barrett—On Campaign During the Canadian Rebellion, the Indian Mutiny, the Sudan, Matabeleland, Mashonaland and the Boer War Volume 3: 1818-1914.

THE CAMPAIGN OF WATERLOO by Antoine Henri Jomini—A Political & Military History from the French perspective.

RIFLE & DRILL by S. Bertram Browne—The Enfield Rifle Musket, 1853 and the Drill of the British Soldier of the Mid-Victorian Period *A Companion to the New Rifle Musket* and *A Practical Guide to Squad and Setting-up Dtill*.

NAPOLEON'S MEN AND METHODS by Alexander L. Kielland—The Rise and Fall of the Emperor and His Men Who Fought by His Side.

THE WOMAN IN BATTLE by Loreta Janeta Velazquez—Soldier, Spy and Secret Service Agent for the Confederancy During the American Civil War.

THE BATTLE OF ORISKANY 1777 by Ellis H. Roberts—The Conflict for the Mowhawk Valley During the American War of Independenc.

PERSONAL RECOLLECTIONS OF JOAN OF ARC by Mark Twain.

CAESAR'S ARMY by Harry Pratt Judson—The Evolution, Composition, Tactics, Equipment & Battles of the Roman Army.

FREDERICK THE GREAT & THE SEVEN YEARS' WAR by F. W. Longman.

AVAILABLE ONLINE AT **www.leonaur.com**
AND FROM ALL GOOD BOOK STORES

ALSO FROM LEONAUR
AVAILABLE IN SOFTCOVER OR HARDCOVER WITH DUST JACKET

THE 9TH—THE KING'S (LIVERPOOL REGIMENT) IN THE GREAT WAR 1914 - 1918 *by Enos H. G. Roberts*—Mersey to mud—war and Liverpool men.

THE GAMBARDIER *by Mark Severn*—The experiences of a battery of Heavy artillery on the Western Front during the First World War.

FROM MESSINES TO THIRD YPRES *by Thomas Floyd*—A personal account of the First World War on the Western front by a 2/5th Lancashire Fusilier.

THE IRISH GUARDS IN THE GREAT WAR - VOLUME 1 *by Rudyard Kipling*—Edited and Compiled from Their Diaries and Papers—The First Battalion.

THE IRISH GUARDS IN THE GREAT WAR - VOLUME 1 *by Rudyard Kipling*—Edited and Compiled from Their Diaries and Papers—The Second Battalion.

ARMOURED CARS IN EDEN *by K. Roosevelt*—An American President's son serving in Rolls Royce armoured cars with the British in Mesopatamia & with the American Artillery in France during the First World War.

CHASSEUR OF 1914 *by Marcel Dupont*—Experiences of the twilight of the French Light Cavalry by a young officer during the early battles of the great war in Europe.

TROOP HORSE & TRENCH *by R.A. Lloyd*—The experiences of a British Lifeguardsman of the household cavalry fighting on the western front during the First World War 1914-18.

THE EAST AFRICAN MOUNTED RIFLES *by C.J. Wilson*—Experiences of the campaign in the East African bush during the First World War.

THE LONG PATROL *by George Berrie*—A Novel of Light Horsemen from Gallipoli to the Palestine campaign of the First World War.

THE FIGHTING CAMELIERS *by Frank Reid*—The exploits of the Imperial Camel Corps in the desert and Palestine campaigns of the First World War.

STEEL CHARIOTS IN THE DESERT *by S. C. Rolls*—The first world war experiences of a Rolls Royce armoured car driver with the Duke of Westminster in Libya and in Arabia with T.E. Lawrence.

WITH THE IMPERIAL CAMEL CORPS IN THE GREAT WAR *by Geoffrey Inchbald*—The story of a serving officer with the British 2nd battalion against the Senussi and during the Palestine campaign.

AVAILABLE ONLINE AT **www.leonaur.com**
AND FROM ALL GOOD BOOK STORES

ALSO FROM LEONAUR
AVAILABLE IN SOFTCOVER OR HARDCOVER WITH DUST JACKET

ESCAPE FROM THE FRENCH *by Edward Boys*—A Young Royal Navy Midshipman's Adventures During the Napoleonic War.

THE VOYAGE OF H.M.S. PANDORA *by Edward Edwards R. N. & George Hamilton, edited by Basil Thomson*—In Pursuit of the Mutineers of the Bounty in the South Seas—1790-1791.

MEDUSA *by J. B. Henry Savigny and Alexander Correard and Charlotte-Adélaïde Dard* —Narrative of a Voyage to Senegal in 1816 & The Sufferings of the Picard Family After the Shipwreck of the Medusa.

THE SEA WAR OF 1812 VOLUME 1 *by A. T. Mahan*—A History of the Maritime Conflict.

THE SEA WAR OF 1812 VOLUME 2 *by A. T. Mahan*—A History of the Maritime Conflict.

WETHERELL OF H. M. S. HUSSAR *by John Wetherell*—The Recollections of an Ordinary Seaman of the Royal Navy During the Napoleonic Wars.

THE NAVAL BRIGADE IN NATAL *by C. R. N. Burne*—With the Guns of H. M. S. Terrible & H. M. S. Tartar during the Boer War 1899-1900.

THE VOYAGE OF H. M. S. BOUNTY *by William Bligh*—The True Story of an 18th Century Voyage of Exploration and Mutiny.

SHIPWRECK! *by William Gilly*—The Royal Navy's Disasters at Sea 1793-1849.

KING'S CUTTERS AND SMUGGLERS: 1700-1855 *by E. Keble Chatterton*—A unique period of maritime history-from the beginning of the eighteenth to the middle of the nineteenth century when British seamen risked all to smuggle valuable goods from wool to tea and spirits from and to the Continent.

CONFEDERATE BLOCKADE RUNNER *by John Wilkinson*—The Personal Recollections of an Officer of the Confederate Navy.

NAVAL BATTLES OF THE NAPOLEONIC WARS *by W. H. Fitchett*—Cape St.Vincent, the Nile, Cadiz, Copenhagen, Trafalgar & Others.

PRISONERS OF THE RED DESERT *by R. S. Gwatkin-Williams*—The Adventures of the Crew of the Tara During the First World War.

U-BOAT WAR 1914-1918 *by James B. Connolly/Karl von Schenk*—Two Contrasting Accounts from Both Sides of the Conflict at Sea During the Great War.

AVAILABLE ONLINE AT **www.leonaur.com**
AND FROM ALL GOOD BOOK STORES

www.ingramcontent.com/pod-product-compliance
Lightning Source LLC
Chambersburg PA
CBHW031620160426
43196CB00006B/219